Complying with the Global Investment Performance Standards (GIPS®)

The Frank J. Fabozzi Series

Complying with the Global Investment Performance Standards (GIPS®)

BRUCE J. FEIBEL
KARYN D. VINCENT

WILEY

John Wiley & Sons, Inc.

For general information on our other products and services or for technical support, please
contact our Customer Care Department within the United States at (800) 762-2974, outside
the United States at (317) 572-3993 or fax (317) 572-4002.

Wiley also publishes its books in a variety of electronic formats. Some content that appears in
print may not be available in electronic books. For more information about Wiley products,
visit our web site at www.wiley.com.

ISBN 978-0-470-40092-0 (hardback);   978-1-11-09300-9 (ebk);
978-1-118-09301-6 (ebk);   978-1-118-09302-3 (ebk)

Printed in the United States of America.

10 9 8 7 6 5 4 3 2 1

To Eli and Sam
—BJF

To Erin
—KDV

Contents

Contents

About the Authors

Bruce J. Feibel, CFA is Managing Director of Products for Investment Manager Services at BNY Mellon. Formerly, Mr. Feibel was Chief Strategy Officer for Eagle Investment Systems, a BNY Mellon company. He also has been Director of Global Products for BNY Mellon Analytical Solutions and Product Manager of Performance Measurement Technology at Eagle Investment Systems. Prior to joining Eagle, Feibel was a principal at State Street Global Advisors. He is a past member of the CFA Institute Investment Performance Council and the GIPS Risk Standards Working Group. He is also the author of the book *Investment Performance Measurement* published by John Wiley & Sons. He earned his B.S. in Accounting from the University of Florida.

Karyn D. Vincent, CFA, CIPM is the founder of Vincent Performance Services LLC, which provides GIPS consulting and verification services. Previously, she served as the global practice leader for investment performance services at PricewaterhouseCoopers. Ms. Vincent is an active volunteer with CFA Institute and serves on the GIPS Executive Committee, which is responsible for overseeing the GIPS standards globally. She chairs the GIPS Interpretations Subcommittee and previously was a member of the CIPM Advisory Council. From 2002–2006 she chaired the AIMR-PPS® Implementation Committee and the GIPS Verification Subcommittee. She earned a B.S in Accounting from the University of Massachusetts Dartmouth.

Preface

Performance measurement is an important concept for anyone managing or investing institutional assets. *Complying with the Global Investment Performance Standards (GIPS®)* provides individuals and firms with two things: (1) guidance for the investment firm in achieving compliance with the Global Investment Performance Standards—the GIPS standards—and (2) detailed explanations of the rationale and methodology behind the numbers.

Expanding upon the information on the GIPS standards published by CFA Institute, this book is intended to be a comprehensive overview, but also detailed enough to provide the practical hands-on guidance required by investment professionals. Our intent is to explain not just what the GIPS standards are, but also how to comply with them. Our opinions on achieving and maintaining compliance with the GIPS standards are represented in the following chapters and when writing this book, we referred to the 2010 edition of the GIPS standards, which is officially titled, *Global Investment Performance Standards (GIPS®): As Adopted by the GIPS Executive Committee on 29 January 2010* (Charlottesville, VA: CFA Institute 2010). We also refer to other applicable interpretive guidance issued by CFA Institute and available on the GIPS standards web site as of March 19, 2011. As this book is not official guidance, individuals and firms should check the resources provided by CFA Institute if questions arise and consult with their GIPS advisors. Official CFA Institute resources for the GIPS standards, including any updates to the GIPS standards and any interpretive guidance, are located at www.gipsstandards.org.

This book covers the requirements and recommendations of the 2010 edition of the GIPS standards, which went into effect on January 1, 2011.

Acknowledgments

This book has benefited from countless conversations with clients and colleagues, and we thank all of them. Although we received advice and input from many people, any errors or omissions are our own. Our sincere hope is that this book helps firms achieve compliance with the GIPS standards, and simplifies the process of maintaining compliance. We welcome your feedback at feibels@yahoo.com and kvincent@vincentperformance.com.

BRUCE J. FEIBEL
Brookline, Massachusetts
KARYN D. VINCENT
Portland, Oregon

Introduction

The investment management industry has global standards for the calculation and presentation of investment performance to prospective investors. These are the Global Investment Performance Standards (GIPS®), which were created and are administered by CFA Institute. The topic of this book is how to calculate returns and present investment performance results in accordance with the GIPS standards. The GIPS standards are applicable to all investment firms globally that have discretion to manage assets.

CFA Institute is a nonprofit association of portfolio managers, analysts, and other participants in the investment management process. CFA Institute runs the Chartered Financial Analyst, or CFA program. An important goal of CFA Institute is to maintain and enhance the reputation of the investment management profession and its practitioners. In this role, CFA Institute has developed a Code of Ethics and Standards of Professional Conduct (together, the Code and Standards) outlining member responsibilities to the profession, employers, clients, prospects, and the general public. All CFA charterholders agree to uphold the Code and Standards, which include a requirement to make reasonable efforts to provide performance information that is fair, accurate, and complete. Complying with the GIPS standards helps CFA charterholders, and thus their firms, meet this requirement. The GIPS standards are widely used by firms who wish to adopt this same ethical approach to the fair presentation of performance results.

While past performance cannot guarantee future results, the reality of asset management is that the investment firm's historical performance record is a primary consideration for the investor looking to hire a new manager. Performance records are not just used to identify top-performing managers, but also to determine if the manager's track record reflects the firm's stated style and strategy. The main goals of the GIPS standards are that the performance presented to prospective investors is comparable across managers, has been prepared in such a way that it represents a complete and accurate record of performance for the strategy of interest to the prospect, and is accompanied with the disclosures necessary to ensure an accurate interpretation of the manager's record.

The competition between money managers today to attract assets from investors is intense. Thousands of organizations offer products with a myriad of strategies intended to align the opportunities presented by the capital markets with investor goals and objectives. The GIPS standards, and their predecessor standards, have been extremely successful in ensuring that investors are able to understand past performance in the process of choosing among different managers.

The GIPS standards are important to society as a whole. We all have a stake in the success of the institutions we depend on being able to make informed choices among asset management firms. After all, these managers are selected to implement investment programs that provide the funds to achieve vital goals such as the funding of retiree pensions, educating future generations of students, and performing charitable activities.

PERFORMANCE COMPOSITES

Assuming that an investment advisory firm manages more than one portfolio and periodically offers new strategies, what performance data is available to prospective clients? There are several types of returns that *could* be presented as part of the marketing process:

- For a manager who is currently managing money for multiple clients, a *representative* client account could be selected that demonstrates the performance experienced by the average client or client similar to the prospect.
- The manager may maintain a *model* portfolio that tracks the manager's intended strategy. Individual client funds are traded and rebalanced according to the model account strategy.
- Backtesting the manager's strategy or models could generate *hypothetical* performance numbers. A new manager or a manager with a new strategy will test how the strategy would have theoretically performed in the past.
- The performance of each of the firm's strategies can be presented using the aggregated or *composite* performance of all of the accounts following the same strategy.

For each of these alternatives, the manager could also choose to present the account or composite performance over particular time periods.

Given these options, prospective investors need to know exactly what the performance record represents. What would stop a manager from offering up as a representative account the best-performing account instead of the average account? Government regulations attempt to guard against the unscrupulous money manager or advisor. But institutional investors want not only honest, but also comparable and independently tested performance returns for use when evaluating the suitability of a manager.

To this end, the GIPS standards outline the process for creating performance composites. Each *composite* represents the aggregate performance history of all accounts managed in a particular strategy, and is used to support the marketing of the strategy to prospective investors. The GIPS standards provide guidance for:

- Accounting data inputs to the performance calculations.
- Methodology used to calculate the returns.
- Construction methodology for composites of portfolios.
- Disclosures of information about the strategy, the composite, and the firm.
- Presentation and advertising of performance information to prospects.

The GIPS standards are typically used when performance information is communicated between an investment firm and prospective institutional investors, such as a corporate pension fund, university endowment, or charitable foundation. But the GIPS standards' sphere of influence is broader than this. All aspects of performance measurement, including return calculation, performance attribution, and client reporting of performance to both individual and institutional investors, are influenced by the GIPS standards. The GIPS standards are a form of industry self-regulation. While there is no law that an investment firm must create its marketing materials according to the GIPS standards, compliance with the GIPS standards has become a de facto requirement in many parts of the world.

ABOUT THE BOOK

This book contains nine chapters grouped into the following three parts:

- *Part One.* Explanation of the GIPS standards and how to comply with them by creating composites representing the performance of the firm's strategies.
- *Part Two.* The methodology for calculating returns used to quantify the manager's historical performance and statistics gauging the risks taken to achieve these returns.
- *Part Three.* Guidance for reporting performance and maintaining compliance with the GIPS standards. The section on how to prepare

GIPS-compliant presentations and other marketing materials describes best practices for maintaining compliance, special requirements applicable to firms managing nontraditional portfolios, as well as the independent verification process.

Understanding how to report performance in compliance with the GIPS standards is only one component of the performance measurement body of knowledge. The scope of the book is limited to the performance measurement and presentation techniques required for GIPS compliance. For example, portfolio and composite performance calculations are explained but we do not delve into security-level performance calculations.

Although this book provides worked examples illustrating particular techniques for analyzing performance, there is an important qualification accompanying these examples: *We do not mean to imply that the methodology presented here is the only way to calculate returns.* The GIPS standards provide some flexibility for tailoring return calculations to the needs of the situation. Many of the other statistics documented in this book can also be calculated in different ways. The book is not intended as an encyclopedic listing of all the ways returns can be calculated. Instead, we describe the most commonly used methodologies for deriving the returns used for marketing purposes.

PART One

Explanation of the GIPS Standards

Fundamentals of Compliance

The institutional investor searching for a new investment manager will consider many factors before making a choice. The manager's reputation, the breadth of the firm's offerings, and the manager's fee schedule all play a role in this decision. While past performance cannot guarantee future results, this information provides valuable insight about an investment manager. One factor that is almost always considered in a search is the investment manager's historical track record. With only a few exceptions, investment managers have historically had minimal, if any, regulations or guidance that instructs the firm on how to calculate and report investment performance to prospective investors. The Global Investment Performance Standards (GIPS®), administered by CFA Institute, fill that void.

SCOPE OF THE GIPS STANDARDS

The Global Investment Performance Standards are a set of voluntary standards for calculating and reporting investment performance to a prospective investor. Institutional investors, such as pension plans and endowments, will often consider hiring only managers who have calculated and presented their performance in compliance with the GIPS standards. The GIPS standards provide investors with assurance that performance records are comparable and that they are prepared based on the ethical principles of fair representation and full disclosure.

The GIPS standards do not attempt to address every performance measurement issue that a money manager may face. For example, the GIPS standards are not intended to govern performance presented as part of internal reporting within the investment management firm or for client reporting to existing clients. The GIPS standards are primarily concerned with marketing performance history to prospective clients.

There is no global law that requires a firm to comply with the GIPS standards. (But if an investment manager claims compliance, the local regulator can and often does test that claim.) The GIPS standards are a form of industry self-regulation. An investment manager that chooses to comply with the GIPS standards must comply with all of the applicable *requirements* of the GIPS standards on a firmwide basis. The GIPS standards also include a series of *recommendations* that are considered industry best practices. A firm that complies with the GIPS standards may select which, if any, of these recommendations the firm will adopt and follow.

HISTORY OF THE GIPS STANDARDS

Several decades ago, the Association for Investment Management and Research (AIMR®, now known as CFA Institute) recognized the need for performance standards. In 1987, the AIMR Performance Presentation Standards (AIMR-PPS®) were issued and over the next decade became widely adopted in the United States, primarily by managers of institutional assets. At the same time, other countries were beginning to take notice of these standards. Recognizing that the AIMR-PPS standards were directed mainly at the U.S. and Canadian markets, several countries used the AIMR-PPS standards as a starting point and tailored them for local use. To facilitate the ability of money managers to do business across borders and address the proliferation of country-specific standards, in 1995 AIMR undertook the process of creating a set of performance standards that could be used by all firms globally. The end result of this effort was the issuance of the first edition of the GIPS standards in February 1999.

Several countries adopted the GIPS standards as their local standard as issued, making no changes. However, other countries that already had their own standards were hesitant to replace their current standards with the GIPS standards, particularly if the local standards had been widely adopted and extensively interpreted, as was the case in the United States and Canada. To take the first step toward unifying the different standards used globally, a concept of *Country Versions of GIPS* (CVG) was created. Each CVG would have as its core the GIPS standards themselves, but would allow for additional requirements and recommendations over and above those included in the GIPS standards. In 2000, the AIMR-PPS standards became a CVG. The process to become a CVG was quite simple for the AIMR-PPS standards, since the GIPS standards were primarily based on the concepts in the AIMR-PPS standards.

When the GIPS standards were originally created, it was agreed that they would be reviewed and updated every five years. This first five-year review resulted in the issuance of the 2005 edition of the GIPS standards in February of that year. This edition began the process of eliminating all CVGs as a key step toward meeting the stated goal of having one standard for performance calculation and presentation used globally. Firms that complied with a CVG could continue to do so until they reported performance for any period after December 31, 2005. Once a firm reported performance for subsequent periods, the firm was required to transition from CVG-based reporting to reporting in compliance with the GIPS standards.

To facilitate convergence to one global standard, the GIPS standards provided full reciprocity for historical periods. For example, a firm that previously complied with the AIMR-PPS standards and transitioned to the GIPS standards in 2006 could state that the firm complied with the GIPS standards for all periods and make no reference to prior compliance with the AIMR-PPS standards. Reciprocity allowed firms throughout the world to remove references to local standards from their presentations and to speak only about the GIPS standards.

The next five-year update was completed in January 2010 when the 2010 edition of the GIPS standards was issued. The 2010 edition has an effective date of January 1, 2011. Compliant presentations that include any performance results for periods beginning on or after January 1, 2011 must comply with the presentation and disclosure requirements of the 2010 edition. All input and calculation data requirements must be followed beginning on that date. (Unless explicitly stated otherwise, this book references and provides guidance for the 2010 edition of the GIPS standards.)

To facilitate global acceptance and adoption of the GIPS standards, local sponsoring organizations serve as "Country Sponsors" of the GIPS standards. Country Sponsors, such as The Securities Analysts Association of Japan, promote the GIPS standards in their local market, and provide feedback and input on country-specific concerns. As of December 2010, over 30 Country Sponsors have adopted the GIPS standards as their local standard. A current list of Country Sponsors is available on the GIPS standards web site (www.gipsstandards.org). In accordance with standard CFA Institute practice, for governance purposes Country Sponsors are pooled into three geographic areas: Americas; EMEA (Europe, Middle East, and Africa); and Asia Pacific.

GOVERNANCE OF THE GIPS STANDARDS

CFA Institute is an investments industry association that is best known as the administrator of the CFA and CIPM exams. The Chartered Financial Analyst® (CFA®) designation is a key credential for anyone in the investment management industry. The Certificate in Investment Performance Measurement (CIPM) program has a narrower focus on the investment performance

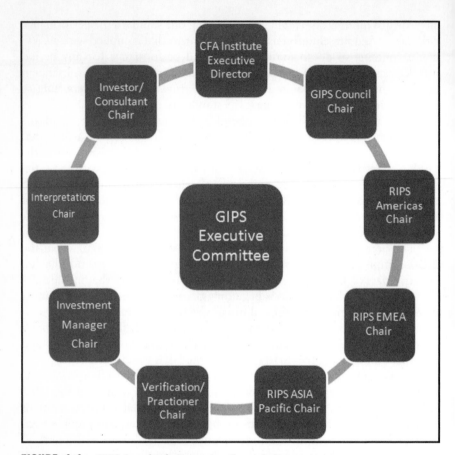

FIGURE 1.1   GIPS Standards Executive Committee

field. CFA Institute has ultimate responsibility for the GIPS standards and funds a permanent staff to promote and enhance the GIPS standards. CFA Institute recruits volunteers from a variety of constituents to guide and enhance the GIPS standards.

The *Executive Committee* (EC) serves as the decision-making authority for the GIPS standards. The EC, which functions as the equivalent to a company's Board of Directors, includes nine "seats" and is organized according to the structure illustrated in Figure 1.1.

Four of the nine seats (Investor/Consultant, Interpretations, Investment Manager, and Verification/Practitioner) are appointed by CFA Institute. Four seats represent Country Sponsors through the global *Regional Investment Performance Subcommittees* (RIPS) and the GIPS Council, and are elected by Country Sponsors. (The GIPS Council includes a representative from each Country Sponsor.) The ninth seat is held by the CFA Institute Executive Director of the GIPS standards.

With the exception of the CFA Institute Executive Director seat, which is a permanent position, all seats have term limits. The GIPS Council Chair seat rotates every two years, and rotates between the three geographical segments. All other seats are elected or appointed for four-year terms.

Each EC member chairs a subcommittee, and each subcommittee is supported by a CFA staff liaison. The subcommittees and CFA staff members do much of the detailed work required to maintain and improve the GIPS standards. Subcommittees and working groups are created as needed. For example, a working group of private equity specialists was created to oversee the update of the private equity guidance for the 2010 edition. The continued success of the GIPS standards globally is directly related to the active participation by committed and engaged volunteers and Country Sponsor organizations.

ORGANIZATION OF THE GIPS STANDARDS

Firms must comply with all requirements of the GIPS standards, as well as any interpretive guidance. This body of knowledge includes the GIPS standards, a series of Questions & Answers addressing narrow issues, and Guidance Statements, which are topical papers addressing issues more broadly. A firm must comply with the GIPS standards themselves as well as Q&As, Guidance Statements, and any other guidance issued by CFA Institute and the GIPS Executive Committee.

All guidance is available at the GIPS standards web site. Guidance is updated periodically, and CFA Institute notifies practitioners and other interested parties of changes via e-mail alerts.

The GIPS standards themselves are collected in a booklet that is organized into five chapters and three appendixes (see Table 1.1). Each provision, which represents either a requirement or a recommendation, has a number that references a section in Chapter I. (For example, Provision 0.A.4 states that the GIPS standards must be applied on a firmwide basis, and is included in Section 0.) The glossary in Chapter V defines the specific meaning of key words used in the GIPS standards. These terms are printed in the GIPS standards in SMALL CAPITAL LETTERS.

Each section of Chapter I contains both requirements and recommendations. All firms must comply with all of the applicable requirements within Sections 0 to 5 of Chapter I. A firm may choose, however, which recommendations it will follow. In the past, recommendations were viewed as

TABLE 1.1 Organization of the GIPS Standards

Chapter I, Section 0	Fundamentals of Compliance
Chapter I, Section 1	Input Data
Chapter I, Section 2	Calculation Methodology
Chapter I, Section 3	Composite Construction
Chapter I, Section 4	Disclosure
Chapter I, Section 5	Presentation and Reporting
Chapter I, Section 6	Real Estate
Chapter I, Section 7	Private Equity
Chapter I, Section 8	Wrap Fee/Separately Managed Account (SMA) Portfolios
Chapter II	GIPS Valuation Principles
Chapter III	GIPS Advertising Guidelines
Chapter IV	Verification
Chapter V	Glossary
Appendix A	Sample Compliant Presentations
Appendix B	Sample Advertisements
Appendix C	Sample List of Composite Descriptions

provisions that were likely to become requirements in future editions of the GIPS standards. This may have been true when the GIPS standards and their predecessor standards were new. However, given the maturity of the GIPS standards, this is no longer the case and we should view the recommendations as simply best practices.

FUNDAMENTALS OF COMPLIANCE

The Fundamentals of Compliance section (Section 0) was first included in the 2005 edition of the GIPS standards. Several of the provisions within this section were added to explicitly state what had been implicit and to remove any doubt about the responsibilities of a compliant firm. Other provisions within Section 0 speak to overarching principles of the GIPS standards. The following text explains the key provisions of Section 0.

Firmwide Compliance

An organization that chooses to comply with the GIPS standards must comply on a firmwide basis. *Firm* is used throughout this book to refer to an organization that has chosen to comply with the GIPS standards. Defining the firm is the first step in the GIPS compliance process. Chapter 2 of this book provides guidance on defining the firm.

Complete Compliance

An organization that does not claim compliance with the GIPS standards can make no reference to the GIPS standards. Investment managers cannot state that they are in "partial compliance" with the GIPS standards or are "in compliance with the GIPS standards except for...." There is no ability to partially comply with the GIPS standards. An organization either fully complies with the GIPS standards or does not comply at all.

Use of Composites

The GIPS standards are predicated on the use of composites. A composite is an entity representing a collection of all portfolios managed according to a particular style or strategy. We use composites to recognize that most investment firms manage multiple portfolios on behalf of multiple clients. However, portfolios managed according to the same strategy could still achieve a different return. One of the key notions underpinning the GIPS standards is that the requirement to use composites prevents a firm from "cherry picking" the best-performing portfolio for a strategy and using that portfolio's performance to represent the strategy's track record. A prospective client should be able to review the fairest possible representation of a firm's track record. This would take into account not just selected portfolios but all portfolios managed according to a specific strategy.

Composites must include only "actual" portfolios. The performance of *model* or *hypothetical* portfolios may be presented as supplemental information but may not be combined with the performance of actual portfolios. All actual, fee-paying, discretionary portfolios must be included in a composite. Chapter 2 provides a discussion on composite construction.

Policies and Procedures

A firm must document all policies and procedures that it has adopted for attaining and maintaining compliance with the GIPS standards. Firms combine these policies and procedures into a firm-specific document that is commonly named the *GIPS Manual*. GIPS Manual is the term that is used in this book to refer to these policies and procedures. A firm's GIPS Manual must address all requirements of the GIPS standards, as well as any recommendations of the GIPS standards that the firm has opted to follow. While many GIPS-related policies and procedures are included in the GIPS Manual, the firm may also choose to make reference to policies and procedures that are maintained elsewhere. For example, a firm may have pricing and other valuation policies already documented in a separate pricing manual. The firm could replicate this information in the GIPS Manual or simply refer to the pricing manual.

A common mistake is that firms document only policies, and not procedures. A firm must document not only policies that the firm has adopted but also the procedures by which those policies are applied. A policy can be thought of as a statement describing what the firm has selected to do with respect to a specific requirement. A sample policy is: "New portfolios are included in the respective composite after the first full month under management." Procedures are the steps the firm takes to ensure the firm follows the established policy. Some of the procedures to ensure new portfolios are included in composites at the correct time, in accordance with the firm's policy, could include:

- The Performance Measurement department is included on all notifications of new clients.
- For each new account, the assigned Relationship Manager completes a New Account Form, summarizing the account's mandate, benchmark, restrictions, expected funding amount and date, and so forth. The New Account Form is provided to all interested parties, including the Performance Measurement department.
- Upon receipt of the New Account Form, the Performance Measurement department determines which composite(s) the account should be assigned to.

Clearly articulated and detailed policies and procedures can be an invaluable tool for a firm to efficiently comply with the GIPS standards. A robust GIPS Manual can also serve as a powerful first line of defense when dealing with regulators. For example, in the United States, the Securities and Exchange Commission (SEC) oversees most managers of institutional assets. As part of its inspection program, the SEC may perform testing to determine whether a firm that claims compliance with the GIPS standards is actually in compliance with the GIPS standards. In 2007, the SEC issued the results of a series of examinations that were specifically focused on performance and advertising. A number of firms included in this "sweep" exam claimed compliance with the GIPS standards or the predecessor AIMR-PPS standards, but the SEC determined that a number of these firms had claimed compliance improperly. The top two deficiencies cited by the SEC were inadequate documentation of policies and procedures or a complete lack of policies and procedures. The regulatory risk alone should provide motivation for a firm to ensure the GIPS Manual is complete and as robust as possible.

Compliance with All Laws and Regulations

The 2010 edition of the GIPS standards includes a new Provision 0.A.2: "Firms must comply with all applicable laws and regulations regarding the calculation and presentation of performance." This makes explicit what has always been implicit in the GIPS standards. The GIPS standards have had a long-standing requirement for a firm to disclose any conflicts between the GIPS standards and applicable laws and/or regulations.

Firms claiming GIPS compliance cannot ignore regulatory requirements that go beyond the GIPS standards. Instead, a firm must consider both the GIPS standards and all applicable regulatory requirements. For example, the GIPS standards allow a firm to present a prospective client with gross-of-management fee returns only, net-of-management fee returns only, or both gross and net returns. If a firm that is registered with the SEC chooses to present only gross returns in materials provided to a prospective client in a one-on-one meeting, four additional disclosures, commonly referred to as the *ICI II disclosures* (see *Investment Company Institute*, SEC No-Action Letter (pub. avail. September 23, 1988)), must be included for SEC purposes. (No-action letters are issued by the SEC in response to questions asking if certain practices would be allowed.) Personnel responsible for GIPS compliance should work in tandem with the firm's legal and compliance personnel to ensure all regulatory requirements are met.

No False or Misleading Performance

Provision 0.A.3, new in the 2010 edition of the GIPS standards, states: "Firms must not present performance or performance-related information that is false or misleading." This new provision is a direct result of industry events over the time period when the GIPS standards were being updated. Several firms that were discovered to be Ponzi schemes or that were reporting fictitious assets under management had falsely claimed compliance with the GIPS standards. While adding this provision will not stop an unscrupulous firm from claiming compliance, it clearly articulates the high ethical standards that investment firms claiming GIPS compliance are expected to uphold.

Provide a Compliant Presentation

A firm that claims compliance with the GIPS standards must make every reasonable effort to provide a compliant presentation to all prospective clients. A compliant presentation is a composite-specific report that includes all statistical data and disclosures required by the GIPS standards. Chapter 6 describes the information that must be included in a compliant presentation. A prospective client is a person or entity that has expressed interest in one of the firm's composite strategies and qualifies to invest in the composite.

List of Composite Descriptions

One of the required disclosures that must be included in a compliant presentation is an offer to provide a list of composite descriptions. A composite description is general information about the composite's strategy (for example, "This composite represents the performance of all portfolios managed according to the firm's U.S. Active Equity Strategy and benchmarked to the S&P 500 Index"). This list must include all composites managed by the firm, whether a composite is marketed or not, as well as all composites that terminated within the past five years. Provision 0.A.10 requires a firm to provide the complete list of composite descriptions if requested to do so by a prospective client.

Once a firm provides the list of composite descriptions to a prospective client, the prospective client might wish to see a compliant presentation for another composite. Provision 0.A.11 requires a firm to provide a compliant presentation for any composite included on the firm's list of composite descriptions, if requested to do so by a prospective client. This includes any composite that terminated within the past five years.

While prospective clients rarely request to see the list of composite descriptions or ask for additional compliant presentations, the firm's verifier, and regulators, will ask for these items. In the United States, these items are standard requests made by the SEC when examining investment managers that claim compliance with the GIPS standards.

SUMMARY

This chapter described what the GIPS standards are and why they came to be, the basic tenets of GIPS compliance, and how the GIPS standards are governed by CFA Institute and volunteers representing the needs of institutional investors and the investment managers that serve them.

The GIPS standards are voluntary. If a firm chooses to claim compliance with the GIPS standards, the firm must comply with *all* of the required guidance. Failure to do so may subject the firm to regulatory scrutiny. The following chapters provide detailed guidance for complying with the GIPS standards.

CHAPTER 2

Defining the Firm and Composites

The GIPS standards facilitate the comparison of historical returns realized by money managers. Potential institutional investors, such as corporate pension plans or university endowments, narrow their search for a manager by first deciding on their asset class and strategy needs. For example, a pension plan may want to replace their current underperforming U.S. large capitalization equity money manager. To facilitate the evaluation of managers the pension plan is considering, the pension plan may ask each manager for a GIPS-compliant performance presentation that reflects their historical track record managing U.S. large capitalization stocks. Because firms that are not compliant with the GIPS standards will not be able to participate in the search, requests such as these often drive investment firms to attain compliance with the GIPS standards.

From the point of view of a money manager who wishes to attain compliance with the GIPS standards, the first key step is to formally define the firm that produced the historical performance. The next key step is to create composites that represent all of the strategies managed by the firm. These tasks can be surprisingly difficult challenges. For example, what if the firm is a product of several mergers over the past decade? Or what if many clients of the firm have highly customized asset allocations? These are the types of questions addressed in this chapter.

DEFINING THE FIRM

The first step toward GIPS compliance is to define the firm. Why? First, the GIPS standards must be applied, and complied with, on a firmwide basis. Second, the firm definition determines the universe of portfolios that must be included in firm assets and therefore considered for inclusion in a composite.

For a small, independent firm, defining the firm is typically a straightforward exercise. At the other extreme, defining the firm for a large multi-office, multi-product, multi-country investment manager is much more challenging. Large, complex organizations will often include multiple "GIPS-defined firms" as well as entities that do not claim compliance with the GIPS standards. This is allowed. While the *Guidance Statement on Definition of the Firm* describes a series of issues that should be considered when defining the firm, much of the guidance comes down to one key question: *How does the firm hold itself out to the public?* This is the primary consideration when defining the firm for GIPS compliance purposes. Each firm's history and structure create a unique case. The firm definition examples below are taken from actual firm literature (only the names have been changed) and demonstrate how firm definitions range from simple to complex:

Firm Example 1
[Firm A] is an independent investment advisor headquartered in Baton Rouge. [Firm A] manages a variety of fixed income, equity, and balanced strategies for its clients.

Firm Example 2
For the purpose of complying with the GIPS standards, the Firm is defined as [Firm B] and comprises all assets managed by the subsidiaries and divisions of [Firm B] in Switzerland (Geneva and Zurich), United Kingdom (London), and Japan (Tokyo).

Firm Example 3
[Firm C] is a registered investment adviser and a wholly owned subsidiary of [Ginormous Bank]. The firm was created in 1996 from an existing institutional business and investment management teams in place since 1981. During the fourth quarter of 1999, [Solong Investment Management] and [Firm C] were combined under the name [Firm C] following the merger of [Solong Corporation] and [Ginormous Bank]. In August 2001, [Super Special Advisors LLC] was created as a wholly owned subsidiary of [Firm C]. [Firm C] acquired three investment teams of [Cheatum Asset Management] in January 2003 and the firm [Buhba Associates] in November 2003. In January 2005, [Ginormous Bank] acquired assets of [Adios Financial] and several investment teams from [Adios Financial] joined [Firm C] as part of the transaction. In all cases, the investment teams involved in each acquisition and merger remain autonomous teams within [Firm C] and, since joining [Firm C], substantially all the decision makers and the investment processes of each team remain intact.

How does a firm go about creating the firm definition? A firm should adopt the broadest, most meaningful definition when defining itself, as opposed to narrowly defining the firm so as to encompass only a portion of assets managed by the firm. Consider firm example 2 previously, where Firm B is defined to include assets managed by four divisions in three countries. Firm B possibly could have made the argument that each country is a separate firm for GIPS compliance purposes. While it would be difficult to challenge a country-specific firm definition, given the subjectivity in making such a decision, the *spirit* of the GIPS standards encourages a firm to broadly define itself. To ensure a prospective client understands the universe of portfolios included in the defined firm, the firm definition is a required disclosure in compliant presentations.

Changes to Definition of the Firm

Firm definitions can, and do, change over time. A firm may be redefined, but only on a prospective basis. The most common reason for a firm redefinition is the acquisition of another firm or a portion of another firm by an existing money manager that claims compliance. As you can see in firm example 3, each acquisition required a modified definition of the firm.

A firm redefinition could also result from changes within the organization. For example, assume Firm D has two divisions: an institutional division and a high net worth division. The institutional division has long-claimed GIPS compliance and has been held out to the public and marketed as Firm D Institutional Asset Management. The high net worth division was marketed separately, and it did not claim compliance with the GIPS standards. For many years, claiming GIPS compliance for the high net worth division was not an important factor in marketing. However, at some point the marketing department decided that the lack of GIPS compliance was becoming a factor in the high net worth market and it was increasingly difficult to differentiate the two divisions in the marketplace. As of a certain date, Firm D redefines the firm to include both institutional and high net worth divisions, on a prospective basis. Subsequently, Firm D will bring all high net worth division portfolios into compliance as well.

To make the firm's history transparent to prospective investors, all firm redefinitions must be disclosed in compliant presentations.

Total Firm Assets

Related to the firm definition, the GIPS standards require the disclosure of the firm's total assets under management. This helps the prospective investor understand the size of the firm, as well as the growth of the firm over the period for which performance is reported. GIPS *firm assets* includes all assets managed within the defined firm. This encompasses both discretionary and nondiscretionary (for GIPS purposes) assets, as well as both fee-paying and non-fee-paying portfolios. If the firm has hired a subadvisor to manage a portion of the firm's assets, and the firm has the authority to hire and fire the subadvisor, those subadvised assets are also included in firm assets.

Excluded from firm assets are assets that are either advisory-only or model-only. *Advisory-only portfolios* are those for which the firm does not have the authority to make trades, but for which the manager is paid to make recommendations. Most brokerage relationship portfolios would be considered advisory-only portfolios. *Model-only portfolios* typically result when the firm agrees to sell its model portfolio to a third party, and the third party takes the model and implements the trades. The firm that provides the model has no control over the third party and whether or not the third party actually makes any trades to implement the model. Even if the manager's compensation is based on the market value of the portfolios a third party manages using the firm's model, those portfolios are not included in GIPS firm assets.

For periods beginning on or after January 1, 2011, firm assets are determined based on the fair value of assets managed by the firm. For GIPS purposes, *fair value* is the current value at which an asset could be exchanged between willing counterparties. The fair value concept differs from market value in that it considers the best information available at the time of the valuation. The best information available may be more recent than the latest market transaction. For example, the most recent portfolio valuation using market quotes may have occurred before a significant move in exchange rates. The price-moving event leads to a discontinuity between market quotes and current values. This would lead to the preparation of a fair value estimate.

Previously, firm assets were based on the market value of assets managed by the firm. Using market value as a basis for inclusion in firm assets, any assets for which a market value could not be obtained were excluded from firm assets. With the shift to fair value, some assets that were previously excluded from firm assets, such as *guaranteed investment contracts* (GICs) carried at book value, are now required to be included in firm assets using fair value techniques. Such assets must be included in firm assets on a prospective basis only.

Minimum Periods of GIPS Compliance

Once the firm has been defined, the next critical decision is determining the period for which the firm will claim compliance.

A main goal of the GIPS standards is to allow for comparability between investment managers. The GIPS standards allow a prospective client to compare performance information between firms by standardizing the reporting time frame going backward in time, and the periodicity of returns within this time period that must be presented.

A firm newly coming into compliance with the GIPS standards must attain compliance on a firmwide basis for a minimum of five years. If the firm has not been in existence for at least five years, then it must comply from the time of its inception. However, if the firm has more than five years of history but chooses to initially comply for only the most recent five-year period, the firm may not combine compliant and noncompliant data. There is one exception: A firm may show noncompliant performance linked to the compliant performance only if the noncompliant performance is prior to January 1, 2000. (This exception is allowed because the initial edition of the GIPS standards was issued in 1999 and a minimum effective date was set soon after in order to enable readers of compliant presentations to have one date by which all performance would be compliant and comparable.) Consider the following two examples:

1. Firm E was founded in June 2008. In January 2011, Firm E decides to comply with the GIPS standards. Firm E must comply with the GIPS standards for a minimum of five years, or since the firm's inception. Since the firm's inception was less than five years ago, the firm must attain compliance from the firm's inception in June 2008.
2. Firm F was founded in June 1998. In January 2011, Firm F decides to comply with the GIPS standards. Because the firm has more than five years of history, Firm F must comply for at least five years, resulting in a minimum compliance date of January 1, 2006. If Firm F attains compliance for the minimum required period, Firm F would be able to present a minimum five-year track record for the five-year period ended December 31, 2010.

If Firm F wishes to show more than five years of history, Firm F must attain compliance for the years for which Firm F wishes to present performance. If Firm F wishes to show 10 years of history, Firm F would need to attain compliance beginning January 1, 2001. If Firm F wishes to show history from the firm's inception, the firm must attain compliance as of January 1, 2000, at a minimum, as this is the minimum effective compliance date for historical periods. If the firm attained compliance as of January 1, 2000, the firm could present returns for periods prior to January 1, 2000 even if the returns are not compliant, as long as the firm discloses the period of noncompliance. (Previously a firm was required to disclose the reason for noncompliance. As of January 1, 2011, disclosure of the reason[s] for non-compliance is no longer required.) Of course Firm F could attain compliance for the entire history if it wishes, and then no disclosure about periods of noncompliance would be necessary.

What if a firm that wishes to comply with the GIPS standards is not able to attain compliance with the GIPS standards historically, or for the required minimum of five years? The firm would have to wait until it has a minimum five-year compliant track record before claiming compliance. Assume Firm G was founded in August 2004. In January 2011, Firm G decides that the firm will comply with the GIPS standards. During the efforts to attain compliance, the firm determines that it will not be able to comply with the GIPS standards for periods prior to 2008, but will be able to attain compliance beginning January 1, 2008. Firm G needs to wait until it has a five-year compliant track record, from January 1, 2008 through December 31, 2012. Firm G could then claim compliance beginning in 2013.

If a firm manages private equity, real estate, and wrap-fee/separately managed account (SMA) portfolios, the minimum compliance date for these three asset classes is January 1, 2006. These asset classes were not included in the original GIPS standards, so they have a special exception for the compliance time frame. Chapter 7 provides guidance for these types of investments.

If a firm previously complied with the AIMR-PPS standards, or another country version of GIPS ("CVG") that was based on the AIMR-PPS standards, the minimum effective compliance dates are different. If a firm previously complied with the AIMR-PPS standards, it may present only compliant returns for periods after January 1, 1993 for most assets. Minimum compliance dates for asset classes were as follows in the AIMR-PPS standards:

- January 1, 1993: nontaxable portfolios solely invested in U.S. or Canadian securities, including private equity and real estate.
- January 1, 1994: international and taxable portfolios.
- July 1, 1995: wrap-fee portfolios.

Given the time that has passed since these effective dates, firms that find themselves in this situation should assume a January 1, 1993 minimum compliance date if possible.

Composite Construction

Once the firm has been defined, and the time frame for which the firm will comply with the GIPS standards has been established, the next step is to identify which portfolios make up firm assets for each and every period within the entire time span for which the firm will claim compliance. From this list of portfolios, each one must be reviewed and considered for inclusion in a composite.

A composite is an aggregation of one or more portfolios managed according to a similar investment mandate, objective, or strategy. While there is a widely held belief that all portfolios must be included in a composite at all times, this is not true. Only actual, fee-paying, discretionary portfolios must be included in a composite. Nondiscretionary portfolios, of all types, as well as non-fee-paying portfolios, do not need to be included in a composite. The treatment of these portfolios is discussed later in the section "Portfolios Excluded from All Composites."

Actual Portfolios

Only actual portfolios managed by the firm are included in composites. A portfolio is considered *actual* if it has real money committed to it. A firm may not include model or hypothetical portfolios in a composite. Even if a firm runs a model portfolio as if it were an actual, live portfolio, such a portfolio may not be included in a composite. The performance of a model or hypothetical portfolio may be disclosed, but it must be identified as supplemental to the composite itself. Performance of a model or hypothetical portfolio may not be linked to, or combined with, the composite performance of the actual portfolios managed by the firm.

Fee-paying and Non-fee-paying Portfolios

Only fee-paying portfolios must be considered for inclusion in a composite. Non-fee-paying portfolios may be excluded from composites based simply on the fact that they do not pay a management fee. However, a firm may choose to consider non-fee-paying portfolios for inclusion in composites, and this decision may be made on a composite-specific basis. If a firm decides to include a non-fee-paying portfolio in the Core Equity Composite, then all non-fee-paying portfolios managed in the Core Equity style must be included in the Core Equity Composite. If a composite includes any non-fee-paying portfolios, the firm must disclose, in the composite's compliant presentation, the percentage of the composite that is composed of non-fee-paying portfolios, as of the end of each annual period.

Why would a firm be willing to manage a portfolio that doesn't pay a management fee? Typical non-fee-paying portfolios are portfolios managed on behalf of charitable organizations, or portfolios that are managed on behalf of the firm or the firm's management.

What should a firm do if it manages the personal portfolios for firm executives, charging a nominal management fee, such as $500 per quarter? While technically paying a fee, if the fee that is charged does not represent the management fee schedule that a client would pay, the portfolio should be considered non-fee-paying for purposes of disclosing the non-fee-paying composite percentage.

Non-fee-paying assets are often portfolios that are considered proprietary assets. *Proprietary assets* are defined in the GIPS Glossary as investments managed by the firm that are under the control of the firm, and are typically owned by the firm or the firm's management. Seed capital is considered a proprietary asset. *Seed capital* is money that the firm provides to establish a new strategy. Seed capital portfolios often do not pay a management fee. It could be quite helpful to a prospective client to know that an entire composite track record was based on internal money only, and has not been tested using live client assets yet. If a composite includes only a seed capital portfolio that is not fee-paying, the firm would be required to disclose that 100% of the composite is composed of non-fee-paying portfolios. However, a prospective investor would not know that the non-fee-paying portfolio is a seed capital portfolio. Also, there is nothing to stop a firm from charging a fee to a seed capital portfolio. While some might argue that the source of the funds that are included in a composite does not matter, others think it is meaningful information. Therefore, firms are recommended to disclose when a composite includes any proprietary assets.

Discretionary Portfolios

A portfolio is considered discretionary if the firm has the ability to manage the portfolio in its intended strategy. The next step in determining which portfolios must be included in composites is to review each portfolio and determine if it is truly discretionary. Firms often find this more challenging than it appears. (Note that discretion for GIPS purposes is not the same as legal discretion.)

Discretion must first be defined at the firm level. A typical policy is: "At the firm level, a portfolio is considered discretionary if we are allowed to manage the portfolio as we would wish, in accordance with the stated objectives, without undue restrictions." This level of definition acts as a filter, enabling the firm to eliminate obviously nondiscretionary portfolios from the population of portfolios that must be included in a composite. The next step is to define discretion relative to each strategy managed by the firm.

What makes a portfolio nondiscretionary for GIPS purposes? The first consideration is whether the portfolio is legally discretionary or not. If a portfolio is legally nondiscretionary, for example where the client has an advisory-only contract with the firm, the portfolio would not be a candidate for inclusion in a composite. However, there are instances where a legally nondiscretionary portfolio could be considered discretionary for GIPS purposes. For example, certain types of trust portfolios may be legally nondiscretionary, but they may be managed as if they were discretionary. A firm would need to prove that such a portfolio is effectively discretionary for GIPS purposes. One way this could be accomplished is by comparing trading activity for the portfolio to the strategy's representative account.

Portfolios that are legally discretionary are not automatically considered discretionary for GIPS purposes. A portfolio could be legally discretionary, but it could have a mandate that differs from the firm's stated strategy. Consider a client who hires a firm to manage an equity portfolio, gives the firm legal discretion in the contract to manage the portfolio, but specifies a mandate to make investments only in companies that manufacture toys. What if another client's mandate is to invest only in companies that are in the alcohol or tobacco industries? These very specific mandates may be acceptable to some firms, but other firms might consider these mandates nondiscretionary for GIPS purposes.

A firm must also consider investment restrictions. Most institutional portfolios have at least one restriction. The restrictions are sometimes no different from those the manager would impose, such as the requirement that no more than 5% of the portfolio be invested in any individual security. Some portfolios have restrictions that could have an impact on the portfolio, but the impact is nonexistent given the strategy the client has selected and the way the firm manages the strategy. A common restriction that often has no impact is a restriction against using options and futures. If the manager does not utilize derivatives in the strategy, then a restriction prohibiting the use of options or futures would not affect the portfolio's discretionary status.

The impact of restrictions is not always obvious. For example, assume Firm H is hired to manage a Core Equity strategy and the portfolio is benchmarked to the S&P 500 Index. The portfolio is legally discretionary but the client has a sin stock restriction (*sin stocks* normally refers to companies involved in alcohol, tobacco, gambling, etc.). Firm H's Core Equity strategy is an active equity strategy, and Firm H decides it can work around the sin stock restriction and identify substitutes for any sin stocks it would normally buy. Firm H considers this portfolio discretionary and will treat it just like any other Core Equity portfolio and include it in the Core Equity Composite. Firm I, on the other hand, is a quantitative equity manager where stocks are selected by a model. Firm I will have a trading restriction on any sin stocks and will not allow those stocks to be purchased for this portfolio. Firm I decides that the sin stock restriction does not allow the portfolio to be managed as it would wish, so Firm I considers this portfolio nondiscretionary. A third manager, Firm J, views sin stock restrictions as a variation on the core equity strategy and offers both Core Equity and a sin stock–free version of the strategy. Firm J considers this portfolio discretionary and includes it in the Core Equity Sin Stock Free Composite. Finally, Firm K does not invest in any sin stocks as it does not think they are good investments; therefore, all strategies automatically exclude sin stocks. The sin stock restriction is an immaterial restriction for Firm K, as Firm K would manage the portfolio on a sin stock–free basis whether the portfolio had a sin stock restriction or not. Firm K includes the portfolio in its only Core Equity strategy, the Core Equity Sin Stock Free Composite.

As Table 2.1 shows, portfolios with the same mandate and restrictions are handled differently by different firms. Each firm must consider the mandate and restrictions placed on each portfolio, and determine how these mandates and restrictions fit within their style of management.

Some clients may impose restrictions impacting only a portion of the portfolio. Assume Firm L has a new client with a large cap equity mandate who funds the portfolio with assets transferred in from a prior manager. The portfolio is discretionary and Firm L may trade the portfolio as it sees fit, with the exception that Firm L may not sell 500 shares of Caterpillar stock in the transferred portfolio, as the client wishes to retain this investment. Given this restriction, the portfolio is substantially discretionary, but is not 100% discretionary. However, a restriction such as this does not automatically require the portfolio to be classified as nondiscretionary. Firm L might approach this situation in a variety of ways:

- Firm L segregates the Caterpillar shares as "unmanaged" or "unsupervised" and includes the remaining portfolio in the Large Cap Equity Composite.
- Firm L considers Caterpillar an appropriate holding for this client and is happy to include the Caterpillar shares in the portfolio. The entire portfolio is included in the Large Cap Equity Composite.

TABLE 2.1 Impact of Sin Stock Restriction on Composite Assignment

Firm	View of Sin Stock Restriction	Discretion Status	Composite Assignment
Firm H	Immaterial	Discretionary	Core Equity
Firm I	Material	Nondiscretionary	None
Firm J	Material	Discretionary	Core Equity Sin Stock Free
Firm K	Immaterial	Discretionary	Core Equity Sin Stock Free

- Firm L has no view as to whether Caterpillar is or is not appropriate for this client. However, the value of the Caterpillar shares is less than 0.5% of the total portfolio's value, so Firm L views this restriction as immaterial. Firm L includes the entire portfolio in the Large Cap Equity Composite.
- Firm L has a strict model-based strategy, and does not have the ability to segregate portions of a portfolio. Firm L considers any portfolio that has a restriction as nondiscretionary; therefore the portfolio is not included in any composite.

The firm's view of discretion, at both the firm and composite levels, must be documented. This documentation is typically included in the GIPS Manual. Clear documentation of discretionary considerations and decisions will allow a firm to ensure that it treats portfolios sharing common mandates and restrictions consistently.

DEFINING COMPOSITES

After defining the firm, determining the period for which the firm aims to comply with the GIPS standards, and identifying the list of portfolios managed over that time period that must be included in a composite, the next step is to organize these portfolios into composites. The GIPS standards do not dictate exactly how composites should be defined. Each firm decides how to define composites that group its portfolios, and must document each of the rules for determining which portfolios are included in which composites.

Determining which portfolios are managed similarly and should be grouped together is a subjective process. A firm must determine how broadly or narrowly composites will be defined. Some firms take the approach that a composite must include only those portfolios that have the exact same mandate. Any variation on the mandate, such as a restriction, would disqualify the portfolio from the composite. Taking this approach may lead to a low dispersion in portfolio-level returns, but it will also result in the firm having a larger number of composites to manage. Alternatively, if the composites are more broadly defined, composites will likely have a greater dispersion of portfolio-level returns, and prospective clients may find it challenging to analyze composite returns. On the other hand, a broadly defined composite may be larger and perhaps more marketable than a narrowly defined composite. This is because manager searches sometimes include a minimum composite size requirement. A firm that broadly defines composites will also have fewer composites to maintain. Firms should attempt to strike the right balance between having composites so narrowly defined that each portfolio ends up as its own composite and composites that are so broadly defined that the composite returns are not meaningful.

When defining composites, the first consideration should be how the firm actually manages money. The second should be how the firm is currently marketing itself. Consider Firm M, which is a boutique value manager. All portfolios in the firm are managed following one model, and the firm has been marketing itself for the past 10 years using its representative account (the oldest portfolio that has followed the model strategy since firm inception). Firm M does not accept portfolios with restrictions that would impact the management of the portfolio. Firm M would probably create one value composite that would include all value portfolios. Now consider Firm N, which is also a boutique value manager. Like Firm M, all portfolios are managed following one model. However, Firm N does accept portfolios with restrictions and will manage around the restrictions. Firm N could either create one value composite that includes all portfolios (those with restrictions and those without), or create two or more separate value composites: one "unconstrained" value composite, which includes all value portfolios without restrictions, and one or more value composites that include portfolios managed around similar restrictions.

Pooled Funds

Firms that manage mutual funds or other pooled vehicles in addition to segregated (separate account) portfolios must consider whether or not pooled funds should be included in composites with non–pooled fund portfolios. Even if segregated portfolios and pooled funds are managed in the exact same strategy, a pooled fund will often be managed differently due to liquidity requirements. Mutual funds marketed to individuals, for example, typically hold themselves open for daily cash flows, whereas cash flows in and out of many segregated portfolios are infrequent. The impact of managing the daily cash flow activity may be enough of a reason to warrant placing the mutual fund in a different composite than segregated portfolios.

The decision to include or exclude pooled funds should be made on a composite-specific basis, and will depend primarily on the strategy. For example, for pooled funds that are invested in highly liquid securities, cash could be equitized using futures; therefore dealing with daily cash flows may not be a significant factor. Maintaining liquidity could be an important factor for a mutual fund invested in less liquid securities, or for a fund whose segregated portfolio counterparts are normally fully invested. Cash maintenance requirements could be a justifiable reason for including a mutual fund in a separate composite. If a firm also manages subadvised mutual funds, it should consider whether cash maintenance considerations apply equally to subadvised funds as well.

Also requiring special consideration are other types of pooled funds such as institutional commingled funds and limited partnerships, including hedge funds. The legal structure of the pooled fund could create some other differences to consider. Commingled funds could require special handling for cash flow activity so that transaction costs related to one participant's cash flow are not absorbed by other fund participants. Limited partnerships could have unique features, such as side pockets. A *side pocket* is typically used to segregate illiquid investments from the rest of the portfolio. Such differences in the management and structure of a portfolio do not automatically disqualify a pooled fund from being included in a composite together with segregated portfolios. The firm needs to define which unique portfolio characteristics have enough of an impact on strategy implementation to justify including a pooled fund in a different composite from separate account portfolios.

Client Types and Composites

Composites can be created based on client type if the client type impacts the way portfolios are managed. A good example is the tax status of the client. Assume Firm O manages mid cap strategies for both taxable and tax-exempt clients. The firm is an active trader, and taxable portfolios are managed differently from tax-exempt portfolios. The firm also seeks to minimize capital gains for taxable portfolios. Firm O should create a taxable composite and a nontaxable composite. Contrast this with Firm P, which manages both taxable and tax-exempt portfolios in its dividend yield strategy. Firm P rarely trades, and once a security is purchased it is normally held for several years. When Firm P does trade, it attempts to minimize the tax impact of trades, but feels as if this does not significantly impact its management of taxable portfolios. Firm P decides to include both taxable and tax-exempt portfolios in its Dividend Yield Composite.

New Portfolios

Once a composite is defined, a policy must be established for deciding when to include new portfolios in the composite. A firm is allowed time to invest a new portfolio's assets according to the stated strategy before the portfolio must be included in the relevant composite. How long this takes depends on several factors, including the firm's portfolio construction process and the liquidity of the underlying instrument types.

Once this policy is established, all new portfolios must be included in accordance with the respective composite's *new portfolio inclusion policy*. Typical policies include:

- New portfolios are included the first full month under management.
- New portfolios are included after the first full month under management.
- New portfolios are included the first full quarter under management.

The composite return calculation periodicity also influences this decision. While the GIPS standards allowed quarterly composite return calculations through December 31, 2009, and at the other extreme some firms calculate daily composite returns, most of the industry computes composite returns monthly. Because of this, most portfolios are included in composites using a monthly inclusion rule. A simple policy to administer is to include new portfolios in composites the first full month under management. For example, any new portfolio funded in January would be included in the appropriate composite in February.

However, a simple policy may not be the best approach. What happens if a portfolio is funded on the last day of the month? Unless the underlying instruments are highly liquid, the portfolio may not end up fully invested at the end of the day. In this case, it may not be proper to include the portfolio in the composite the very next day because the portfolio's performance for the month of February may not reflect a full month of performance as invested in the strategy. What if it took several days to fully invest new portfolios? Assume Firm Q manages a small cap strategy and it normally takes five to seven days to invest a new portfolio. Firm Q created this policy for its Small Cap Composite:

> *New portfolios that fund prior to the 16th of a given month are included in the composite the first full month under management. New portfolios that fund on or after the 16th of a given month are included in the composite after the first full month under management.*

Using this policy, if a portfolio funds between January 1 and January 15, the portfolio is included in the composite beginning February 1. If a portfolio funds between January 16 and January 31, then the portfolio is included in the composite beginning March 1.

While straightforward, this policy requires additional effort to capture exactly when a portfolio funds. An easier to administer policy is to include portfolios in a composite *after* the first full month under management.

Any portfolio that funds in January is included in the composite as of March 1. Any portfolio that funds in February is included in the composite as of April 1. This policy allows the firm to have a minimum of four weeks, and up to almost eight weeks, to get new portfolios invested. This policy would work for a vast majority of composites, except some highly illiquid strategies. This is a simple policy that can be objectively administered.

Quarterly composite inclusion rules are uncommon, but they can be quite useful for illiquid strategies. However, the same considerations apply when portfolios fund close to quarter end. As with monthly inclusion, the policy can be adapted to differentiate inclusion based on the exact day of funding within the quarter, or to include new portfolios after the first full quarter under management.

Some firms also include a test for "fully invested in the strategy." A sample policy where investment level is considered is:

Portfolios are included the first full month under management, as long as the portfolio is fully invested in the strategy.

A policy such as this can be subjective and thus quite difficult to administer. It would be particularly challenging to implement such a policy if the firm is attempting to retroactively attain compliance. "Fully invested" is a concept that can mean different things at different times.

Consider Firm R's aggressive equity strategy. Portfolios managed in this strategy normally have an equity allocation of at least 90%. For new portfolios, once the cash balance is 10% or less, the portfolio is considered fully invested and the portfolio is included in the composite. This policy may work well in normal markets, but not when a manager alters its asset allocation targets, for example to be more conservative in volatile markets. In periods such as this, Firm R might have changed their aggressive equity allocation from 90% equity/10% cash to 70% equity/30% cash. If the same cash percentage test was applied consistently, then a new aggressive equity portfolio could fail to qualify for inclusion for months if not years. Portfolios should be included in composites based on mandates and strategic decisions, not based on tactical decisions. For all new (discretionary) portfolios, for all strategies, at some point a firm should include the new (discretionary) portfolios in their proper composite, regardless of the allocation to cash. For a new portfolio, at some point the decision to not be fully invested in a strategy is a tactical management decision, and the portfolio should not be held out from the composite. An objective test for composite inclusion based on a time period is a much easier policy to manage, and removes subjectivity from the composite assignment decision-making process.

There can be valid reasons for making an exception to the composite's stated new account policy. An example is a portfolio funded with illiquid securities that the manager intends to sell and the proceeds will be used to create a portfolio aligned to the manager's stated strategy. Because it could take several months to sell the securities, this is an example where the new portfolio can be excluded from the composite for a longer period.

Another valid exception is the case where *transition managers* are used. Transition managers specialize in managing changes in institutional asset allocations. Assume New Client terminates their portfolio with Prior Firm and hires Firm S. New Client uses a transition manager to take the portfolio from Prior Firm and transform it into the correct portfolio for Firm S. The transition manager will work with Firm S to determine which securities in New Client's existing portfolio will be sold, which securities will be purchased, and which securities will be retained. Once the portfolio is traded into Firm S's selected holdings, the portfolio will arrive at Firm S looking just like a fully invested portfolio of Firm S. Firm S does not need to trade the portfolio, so the portfolio is ready to go into the composite as soon as it arrives.

The transition manager exception, and others, should be included in the firm's GIPS Manual. When a situation is handled differently from the composite's new portfolio inclusion policy, documentation of and support for the exception should be captured.

Terminated Portfolios

When a portfolio terminates, its history stays in the composite. One of the key concepts of the GIPS standards is that there is no "survivor bias." A composite's history must reflect all assets managed in that strategy for each respective period of time, regardless of whether the portfolio exists in subsequent periods.

To accomplish this, firms must establish a timing policy for removing closed or terminated portfolios from the composite. Provision 3.A.6 states, "Terminated portfolios must be included in the historical performance of the composite up to the last full measurement period that each portfolio was under management." Because a composite includes only actual, discretionary portfolios, a portfolio that is terminated must remain in the composite not through the last period under management, but through the last full period for which the portfolio is under *discretionary management*. By far the most common policy is to remove closed portfolios after the last full month for which the firm has discretion.

To ensure portfolios are removed from composites at the proper time, a firm must determine when discretion ends for each terminated portfolio. Because the focus is on the end of discretion, a firm cannot rely simply on the liquidation or termination date to determine when a closed portfolio is to be removed from a composite. Assume a client instructs the firm to halt trading on July 25, in anticipation of a redemption in-kind on August 2, and the firm includes terminated portfolios in the composite through the last full month of discretionary management. If the firm relies on the date the portfolio closed (August 2) the firm would assume that the portfolio should be removed from the composite after July. However, the firm did not have discretion for the entire month of July, so the portfolio should not be included in the composite for July and should be removed from the composite after June.

Client-Directed Strategy Changes

Periodically clients will change the strategy guiding the firm's management of the portfolio. When such a change is made, the portfolio will be considered a closed portfolio for the old strategy and a new portfolio for the new strategy. For example, on February 15 Client A informs Firm T that he wishes to change from the Growth Equity strategy to the Value Equity strategy. Firm T immediately places trades to migrate the portfolio from a growth portfolio to a value portfolio, and expects the portfolio to be fully transitioned to the Value strategy by February 20. Client A's portfolio is removed from the Growth Equity Composite after January. Client A's history stays in the Growth Equity Composite. For the month of February the portfolio is in transition, therefore it is not included in any composite. Because Firm T's new portfolio inclusion policy is to include new portfolios the first full month under management, Client A is included in the Value Equity Composite beginning March 1.

At times it may be appropriate to override the new portfolio inclusion policy for a changed portfolio's new strategy. Assume Firm U is a domestic equity manager. Firm U includes new portfolios in composites after the first full month under management; therefore a portfolio that funds in June would normally be included in a composite as of August 1. Firm U has a variety of equity strategies, but they are quite similar. When a portfolio changes from one strategy to another, it can normally be done in a day or two. Client B informs Firm U on June 10 that it wishes to change from the Core Equity strategy to the Core Equity with a Growth Tilt strategy. The difference between these two strategies is minor, and the portfolio can be adjusted within a few days. Because Client B's portfolio is not being established from a cash contribution, including the changed portfolio in the new composite as of July 1 would be reasonable, as opposed to waiting until August 1. This is another policy that should be documented in the firm's GIPS Manual.

In the examples above, we started with the assumption that the clients informed the manager that they wished to change their portfolio's strategy. This is the foundation for GIPS Provision 3.A.7, which states: "Portfolios must not be switched from one composite to another unless documented changes to a portfolio's investment mandate, objective, or strategy or the re-definition of the composite makes it appropriate. The historical performance of the portfolio must remain with the original composite." But what does "documented changes to a portfolio's investment mandate, objective, or strategy" mean? The change must be made at or under the client's direction. The firm must also maintain documentation of the client-directed change. Documentation can take many forms, such as a letter or e-mail. Institutional clients typically provide the manager with updated guidelines to support the new strategy. In other cases change requests may be received during a phone conversation or at a meeting with the client. Documentation of the phone call or meeting will suffice. However, best practice is for the firm to write the client a letter confirming the details of the change. In all cases, a firm should maintain a written record of the effective date of the change.

Some firms manage portfolios that have delegated authority to the firm to determine the appropriate strategy for the portfolio. This is quite common for banks, where the bank acts as the trustee over the assets. In such a situation, the firm faces the extra burden of proving that the strategy has in fact been changed, including proof of the timing of the change. The best practice is to document any planned changes in strategy, as well as the timing of the changes.

The only valid reason for a portfolio to be moved between composites when there is no client-directed change in investment mandate, objective, or strategy is if the composite has been "redefined." As described earlier, a composite definition is the set of rules that determines which portfolios are included in a specific composite. A firm may change one of these rules, which could result in a change in composite membership. For example, assume Firm V maintains a Core Fixed Income Composite, and included in this composite are all portfolios managed by the firm in the Core Fixed Income strategy, including institutional portfolios and a mutual fund. This strategy is normally close to fully invested, and maintains a very small cash balance. The mutual fund has done very well, and is ranked as the top-performing mutual fund in its peer group for the past five years. Based on positive publicity, money comes pouring into the mutual fund, and the fund's assets grow enormously. Because of the continual cash infusions, the portfolio manager can no longer manage the mutual fund in the same manner as the institutional portfolios, as she is now maintaining a much higher cash balance. Firm V could redefine the Core Fixed Income Composite to include only institutional portfolios as of a certain date. The mutual fund would be

TABLE 2.2 Balanced Asset Allocation Ranges

Composite	Description
Aggressive Balanced	Core balanced portfolios that normally have at least a 95% equity allocation
Moderate Balanced	Core balanced portfolios that normally have a 70 to 75% equity allocation
Conservative Balanced	Core balanced portfolios that normally have a 50 to 55% equity allocation

removed from the composite prospectively, but its history would remain in the Core Fixed Income Composite.

Portfolios must not be moved from one composite to another based only on tactical changes. A firm cannot move portfolios between composites at will, for example, based on asset allocation changes that are controlled by the firm. As stated above, portfolios should be included in composites based on strategic decisions, not tactical decisions. Consider Firm W, which manages three balanced strategies. The strategies are differentiated based on asset allocation, as shown in Table 2.2.

Portfolios should be assigned to their respective composite based on the strategy the client has selected. Once a portfolio is assigned to a composite, it should not be removed from the composite unless the mandate changes or the composite is redefined. If Firm W modifies the asset allocation of all portfolios in a composite on a tactical basis, the portfolios should continue in their assigned composite. Consider what happens when the manager takes a more conservative stance on asset allocation. Firm W decided to lower the equity allocation in aggressive strategy portfolios from 90% to 70%. The portfolios would stay in the Aggressive Balanced Composite, even if the manager also had a Moderate Balanced Composite with a target 70% strategic allocation to equities.

Composite Minimums

Firms may establish a minimum asset size for inclusion in a composite. The minimum is supposed to represent the amount of money needed to manage a portfolio consistent with the composite's strategy, that is, to make the portfolio discretionary. Composite minimums are not required, but if a firm does adopt such a policy the policy must be established on a composite-specific basis. Portfolios that do not meet the composite minimum size must not be included in the composite as they are not considered discretionary.

There is a difference between a "marketing minimum" and the minimum portfolio size for GIPS composite assignment purposes. A firm may have established a minimum portfolio size for marketing purposes—for example, the firm only accepts portfolios above $10 million—but this minimum size may have nothing to do with how portfolios are managed. The two minimums may coincidentally be the same, but only the GIPS composite minimum is considered for the purpose of constructing composites.

Firms should carefully decide whether to establish composite minimums. First, it can be a challenge to determine the exact amount of money that is needed to allow for discretion. Assume Firm X has established a $1 million minimum for inclusion in the Core Equity Composite. Can the firm say, with certainty, that a portfolio that funds with $975,000 would be managed differently from a portfolio funded with $1,010,000? Second, maintaining a composite that has a minimum size for inclusion can lead to portfolios frequently moving in and out of a composite. In addition to the effort required to ensure portfolios properly enter and exit the composite, the composite market value and number of portfolios could be volatile. Third, establishing a composite minimum (particularly for a composite that has a small number of portfolios) puts the composite's continuous track record at risk. For example, Firm Y has an Emerging Bond Composite with a composite minimum of $2 million. The firm's policy is to exclude portfolios from the composite if the assets fall below $2 million at the end of the preceding month. The Emerging Bond Composite consists of a single portfolio with a June 30 market value of $2,100,000. During the month of July, the client requests a withdrawal of $80,000 and the portfolio loses another $50,000 in market value, so that at the end of July the market value of the portfolio is below the $2 million minimum. During August, the market recovers and the portfolio ends the month with a market value of $2,020,000 as of August 31. According to the firm's policy, the portfolio would be excluded from the composite for the month of August and would reenter the composite as of September 1. Because the composite consisted of only this one portfolio, the composite would have a break in performance since no portfolios were included in the composite for the month of August. The composite's continuous track record would stop, and the composite would not have an annual return for the year. In this case, the firm would present performance from January 1 to July 31 and then have a separate line for performance from September 1 to December 31. A firm cannot link across the gap in the track record. Table 2.3 illustrates how a firm might show the break in performance in a GIPS-compliant presentation.

If a firm determines that a composite minimum is appropriate, then the firm must establish policies for how the composite minimum will be applied. Consider Firm Z, which has a Diversified Value Composite with a

TABLE 2.3 Performance Presentation Excerpt for a Break in Composite History
This shows the Emerging Bond Composite for Firm Y from February 1, 2006 (inception) through December 31, 2010.

Year	Gross Return (%)	Net Return (%)	Index Return (%)	Internal Dispersion (%)	Number of Portfolios	As of December 31 Composite Assets ($ millions)	As of December 31 Total Firm Assets ($ millions)
2010	29.41	28.63	28.68	n/a	<5	290.0	5,022
2009	−18.65	−19.02	−22.10	n/a	<5	270.8	4,300
9/08–12/08[a]	−2.77	−3.55	−4.62	n/a	<5	260.9	4,685
1/08–7/08[a]	−10.78	−11.46	−11.86				
2007	2.45	1.87	−9.11	n/a	<5	240.1	6,004
2006	13.34	12.71	21.05	n/a	<5	170.0	5,909

[a]For the period from August 1, 2008, through August 31, 2008, no portfolios were managed that qualified for inclusion in the composite.

composite minimum of $5 million. Firm Z's policy is to exclude portfolios from the Diversified Value Composite if the assets fall below $5 million due to client withdrawals at the end of the preceding month. The Diversified Value Composite includes one portfolio with a March 31 market value of $5,100,000. In April the client requests a withdrawal of $80,000 and the portfolio loses another $50,000 in market value, so that at the end of July the market value of the portfolio is below the $5 million minimum. Although the portfolio is below the $5 million minimum, part of the reason for falling below the minimum was the market conditions. Had the market been flat during the month, the value of the portfolio would have been $5,020,000 and the portfolio would still be included in the composite. The problem with setting such a policy is that some will interpret this policy one way and others will interpret it another.

A firm may change a composite minimum, but any change must be applied on a prospective basis only. A composite may not be restated historically to reflect a new composite minimum that is applied retroactively. A composite minimum, as well as any changes in a composite minimum, must be disclosed in the composite's compliant presentation.

Significant Cash Flow Policy

Sizeable client cash flows into and out of the portfolio also impact the manager's ability to manage a portfolio according to its stated strategy. When this happens, it may be appropriate to remove a portfolio from a composite. A *significant cash flow* for GIPS purposes is the level at which the firm determines that a client-directed external cash flow may temporarily prevent the firm from implementing the composite strategy, making the portfolio temporarily nondiscretionary. A firm may choose to adopt a significant cash flow policy on a composite-specific basis, whereby portfolios that have a cash flow above a predetermined level of significance are temporarily removed from the composite. The threshold can be defined using either a specific monetary amount (e.g., $50 million) or a percentage of portfolio assets (based on the most recent valuation). Common practice is to establish the threshold as a percentage of portfolio assets.

Sizeable client cash flows lead to a related consideration: the frequency of portfolio valuation and return calculation. A *large cash flow* is defined as the level at which the firm determines that an external cash flow may distort the return calculation if the portfolio is not revalued. Firms that do not value portfolios daily must adopt a large cash flow policy for each composite no later than January 1, 2010. The return calculation formula to use in this situation is explained in Chapter 3.

TABLE 2.4 Significant Cash Flow versus Large Cash Flow

Term	Description	Discretion Status
Significant Cash Flow	Client contribution or withdrawal that causes the manager to alter the way that the portfolio is being managed.	Cash flow causes the portfolio to become nondiscretionary temporarily.
Large Cash Flow	Contribution or withdrawal that triggers a recalculation of portfolio-level returns.	Cash flow has no impact on the portfolio's discretionary status.

When a portfolio has a large cash flow, it stays in the composite. The large cash flow policy determines the methodology used to calculate the portfolio return for the month. It does not affect the portfolio's inclusion in a composite. A significant cash flow, on the other hand, represents the size of cash flow above which a portfolio is temporarily considered nondiscretionary, resulting in the removal of a portfolio from the composite. Table 2.4 differentiates the two concepts.

Assume Firm AA values all portfolios monthly. As of January 1, 2010, Firm AA adopted a large cash flow policy for the Capital Growth Composite whereby portfolios in the composite are valued monthly and on the date of any cash flow during the month that is equal to or greater than 5% of the portfolio's beginning of month market value. One of the portfolios in the composite has a contribution on September 18 that is equal to approximately 12% of the portfolio's beginning market value. Firm AA would need to revalue the portfolio on September 18 (or on September 17, depending on the assumption the firm is using as to whether cash flows occur at the beginning or end of the day). Firm AA would calculate the portfolio's performance from September 1 through September 17, and from September 18 through September 30, and would then geometrically link these two subperiod returns to calculate the monthly return.

The large cash flow level, which is determined on a composite-specific basis, must be defined in terms of the value of the cash flow as a percentage of the portfolio or composite assets. The cash flow does not need to be actual cash only, and could reflect the movement of securities, or a combination of cash and securities, into or out of a portfolio. A large cash flow does not need to be client-directed.

The significant cash flow policy is determined on a composite by composite basis. The firm must decide if it will adopt a significant cash flow policy, and the composite-specific threshold for significant cash flows. For a highly liquid strategy such as one invested in large cap equities, the threshold may be set quite high, such as 50%, as the manager would have a relatively easy time getting contributed cash invested. However, for a strategy like Emerging Market Debt, the firm may set the level much lower, say 10%, as it may take a much longer time to rebalance the portfolio to the manager's intended strategy after the significant cash flow.

When implementing a significant cash flow policy, a firm must define the policy solely with reference to the cash flow threshold. The policy may not include any consideration as to the impact of the cash flow on the portfolio's return. For example, a firm may not adopt a policy that excludes portfolios from the composite if the portfolio experiences a cash flow above the level of significance *and* the portfolio's return is more than two standard deviations from the composite's return. Once a level of significance is adopted for a composite, the exclusion policy must be applied to all portfolios experiencing a significant cash flow.

A significant cash flow must be applied only to external, client-directed cash flows. If the firm has the discretionary ability to allocate cash among several portfolios or subportfolios, it may not apply the significant cash flow policy to cash flows that were directed by the firm.

Also, there should be no distinction between external flows of cash and in-kind transfers. If a client contributes or withdraws securities in kind, these transactions are also considered cash flows for the purpose of applying the significant cash flow policy. There is an exception to this rule: If a transition manager is used to purchase securities so that an incoming contribution in kind is already invested in the strategy, this type of cash flow would not cause the portfolio to be nondiscretionary so it would not be removed from the composite.

A firm should also consider whether the significant cash flow policy will be applied to individual cash flows or aggregated cash flows. If a firm wishes to use aggregated cash flows, the firm must determine over what time period the cash flows will be aggregated.

A firm must determine a composite inclusion/exclusion policy for portfolios that experience a significant cash flow. A firm should use the same policies as followed for new and terminated portfolios.

A firm with a composite that includes only one or two portfolios runs the same risk of experiencing a break in the composite's track record as was described for a composite that has a minimum size for inclusion. A firm may not suspend the significant cash flow policy just to prevent a potential break in the track record due to a decrease in the number of portfolios in the composite. If a firm believes that a cash flow over a certain size makes a portfolio temporarily nondiscretionary, then any portfolio that experiences such a cash flow must be temporarily classified as nondiscretionary and removed from the composite. The number of portfolios in the composite has no impact on the discretionary status of a portfolio.

However, one way a firm may be able to prevent a break in performance and also deal with the impact of cash flows is by using temporary new accounts. The GIPS Glossary defines a *temporary new account* as an account for temporarily holding client-directed external cash flows until they are invested according to the composite strategy or disbursed. Firms can use a temporary new account to remove the effect of a significant cash flow on a portfolio. When a significant cash flow occurs in a portfolio, the firm may direct the external cash flow to a temporary new account according to the composite's significant cash flow policy.

If a firm uses a temporary new account to handle a significant cash flow, the portfolio is not removed from the composite. Instead, the portfolio remains in the composite and the transactions related to the significant cash flow are done outside the portfolio. Assume Client C's portfolio is valued at $20 million, and the portfolio is included in the Core Equity Composite. This composite has a significant cash flow level of 25%, and significant cash flows are handled through temporary new accounts. Client C informs the firm that it will be contributing an additional $10 million to its Core Equity portfolio. The firm would establish a temporary account into which the $10 million is contributed. The firm would invest the $10 million and record the transactions in the temporary new account. Once the $10 million is invested, the securities held in the temporary new account would be contributed in-kind to the existing $20 million portfolio. Assuming the firm properly invested the contributed dollars, the impact of the $10 million contribution to the portfolio's performance should be minimal. The existing portfolio would reflect the transfer as a contribution-in-kind and performance would be calculated to include the cash/securities inflow at the date of the transfer from the temporary account.

In the case of a significant withdrawal, the firm would transfer the cash or securities to a new temporary account for liquidation and/or distribution to the client. Assume the same facts as described above, except that Client C informs the firm that it wishes to withdraw $10 million from its Core Equity portfolio. The firm would establish a temporary account and would transfer securities that will be sold to fund the withdrawal from the existing portfolio to the temporary account. The existing portfolio would reflect the transfer as a withdrawal-in-kind and performance would be calculated to reflect the cash outflow at the date of the transfer to the temporary account.

Note that a firm does not have to assign temporary new accounts to a composite. Such portfolios would never qualify for inclusion in a composite and would only be used to track total firm assets.

Finally, a firm cannot adopt a significant cash flow policy retroactively. A firm may not retroactively apply a significant cash flow policy and restate performance. Once adopted, a significant cash flow policy can be applied only on a prospective basis. A firm may change an existing significant cash flow policy, for example, by increasing the threshold from 20% to 30% due to increased liquidity in the asset class, but any change must be made on a prospective basis.

Firms adopting a significant cash flow policy for a particular composite are required to disclose in that composite's compliant presentation how the firm defines a significant cash flow for that composite, and over which periods the definition applies. Note that prior versions of the *Guidance Statement on Treatment of Significant Cash Flows* required several additional disclosures relating to the composite-specific significant cash flow policies. These disclosures were not carried forward to the 2010 edition of the GIPS standards or the current version of this Guidance Statement. A firm may remove from compliant presentations any disclosures that were previously required by the prior Guidance Statements.

Carve-Outs

Firms often manage portfolios that are invested in more than one asset class or strategy. An example is a balanced portfolio that invests in both equity and fixed income securities. An All Cap equity portfolio could be invested in small cap, mid cap, and large cap stocks. A fixed income portfolio might be invested in both corporate bonds and government bonds. Money managers often wish to present performance for a portion of a total portfolio and include these components in composites. For example, the firm may wish to extract the equity performance from a balanced mandate and include it in an equity composite.

To do this on a fair basis, the firm must follow the requirements related to *carve-outs*. The GIPS standards define a carve-out as the portion of a portfolio that is by itself representative of a distinct investment strategy. It is used to extract a track record for a narrower mandate from a portfolio managed to a broader mandate. The philosophy driving the carve-out rules is that the performance of a carve-out must be representative of a stand-alone portfolio managed according to the carve-out strategy. Because a real stand-alone portfolio would have a portion of its assets invested in cash, a carve-out portfolio must also include cash.

The carve-out rules have been the subject of considerable debate and have evolved with each edition of the GIPS standards. For periods beginning on or after January 1, 2010, a carve-out must be managed separately with its own cash.

Assume Firm BB is the manager of the All Cap portfolios described previously. Firm BB's All Cap strategy includes an allocation to small cap, mid cap, and large cap investments. Firm BB wishes to isolate the mid cap portion of All Cap portfolios and include the performance of the mid cap portions in the Mid Cap Composite. As of January 1, 2010, Firm BB may create a carve-out for the mid cap portion of a portfolio only if:

1. The mid cap portion is managed as if it is a separate portfolio and not a portion of a larger portfolio.
2. The mid cap portion is representative of a stand-alone portfolio managed to the mid cap strategy.
3. The mid cap portion has its own cash balance.

If all three tests are met, the firm may create a mid cap carve-out and include the mid cap carve-out in the Mid Cap Composite.

Prior to January 1, 2010, the rules relating to carve-outs were more permissive. A carve-out was not required to be managed with its own cash balance. If a carve-out did not have its own cash, a firm could allocate cash from the total portfolio to the carve-out to synthetically derive a return that includes a cash component. A firm could determine the allocation method, and then was required to apply it consistently and disclose the method used to allocate cash. The most common method was to allocate cash to a carve-out segment based on beginning of period relative value. For example, if the carve-out represented 40% of the total portfolio's beginning-of-month value, 40% of the cash and the cash return was allocated to the carve-out. Effective January 1, 2010, a firm may no longer allocate cash to create a carve-out.

So, beginning January 1, 2010, a carve-out must have its own cash balance. What does this mean? The carve-out's cash balance may be a separate cash portfolio at the custodian or on the firm's accounting system. Depending on the firm's portfolio accounting capabilities, a firm could also create a subportfolio, or sleeve, of the mid cap portion of the total portfolio that includes cash.

If a firm chooses to create carve-outs for one segment of a portfolio it is not required to create carve-outs for the remaining segments of the portfolio. Continuing with Firm BB's All Cap portfolio example, Firm BB chose to create mid cap carve-outs from All Cap portfolios, and includes these mid cap carve-outs in the Mid Cap Composite. Firm BB is not required to also create carve-outs for the large cap or small cap portions of the All Cap portfolios.

Under the new requirements, Firm BB is also not required to create a mid cap carve-out for each All Cap portfolio that could potentially have a mid cap carve-out. Assume Firm BB manages 50 All Cap portfolios. Prior to January 1, 2010, Firm BB allocated cash to the mid cap segment synthetically based on relative assets. Beginning January 1, 2010, the firm may no longer allocate cash. For five selected All Cap portfolios, Firm BB decided to break out the total All Cap portfolios into two subportfolios: a mid cap subportfolio and a subportfolio that holds all remaining assets and cash. The firm includes the mid cap subportfolios for the five selected portfolios in the Mid Cap Composite. But what about the other All Cap portfolios that Firm BB could divide up in a similar fashion? Firm BB is not required to create mid cap subportfolios for the mid cap segment of every All Cap portfolio. Instead, Firm BB may select which All Cap portfolios will have a mid cap subportfolio created. Once Firm BB decides to include Mid Cap subportfolios in the Mid Cap Composite, all mid cap subportfolios created as carve-outs must be included in the Mid Cap Composite.

Firms that used carve-outs and allocated cash prior to January 1, 2010 must leave the performance record of the composite that included carve-outs unchanged, with the carve-out portfolios included. Firms are required to disclose the policy previously used to allocate cash to carve-outs. Also, for annual periods beginning on or after January 1, 2006 and ending prior to January 1, 2011, a firm must present the percentage of the composite that is composed of carve-outs.

A firm may decide to not create a separate cash portfolio for carve-outs that previously had cash allocated to them. If the composite that included carve-outs included only carve-outs with allocated cash prior to January 1, 2010, the composite would be terminated, but must remain on the firm's list of composites for five years after termination. If the composite included separately managed portfolios along with carve-outs with allocated cash, by no later than January 1, 2010 the firm would be required to redefine the composite to exclude carve-outs with allocated cash.

Portfolios Included in Multiple Composites

All actual, fee-paying, discretionary portfolios must be included in at least one composite. If a portfolio meets the requirements of more than one composite definition, it must be included in every composite for which the portfolio meets the composite requirements. For example, a large cap growth portfolio that meets the composite definition of a broadly defined large cap equity composite as well as the more narrowly defined large cap growth composite must be included in both composites.

Assets of an individual portfolio may also be included in more than one composite. If a firm manages a multi-asset class portfolio, and the firm has been hired for a multi-asset class strategy, the total multi-asset class portfolio must be included in the appropriate multi-asset class composite (assuming of course that the portfolio is fee-paying and discretionary). If the individual asset class segments qualify for inclusion in a composite (because they meet the carve-out tests previously described), the firm may choose to include the asset class segments in a composite, but it is not required to do so.

For example, Firm CC manages 500 portfolios in a balanced strategy, with a strategic asset allocation of 60% large cap equity and 40% intermediate fixed income. All 500 balanced portfolios are included in the 60/40 Balanced Composite. Fifty of the portfolios are set up with their own cash in each of the individual asset classes (large cap equity plus cash and intermediate fixed income plus cash), while the other 450 portfolios each have a single cash portfolio. Firm CC may, if it wishes to do so, include the large cap equity segments (with cash) in a large cap equity composite. Firm CC is not required to include the equity segments (with cash) in an equity composite, as the equity segments are already included in the multi-asset composite.

The same is true for the fixed income segments. Firm CC may include the intermediate fixed income segments (with cash) in a fixed income composite, but only if it wishes to do so. Firm CC is not required to include the fixed income portion of multi-asset portfolios in a fixed income composite. If Firm CC chooses to include any of the 50 intermediate fixed income segments (with cash) in a fixed income composite, then all 50 of these intermediate fixed income segments (with cash) must be included in that fixed income composite. The remaining 450 balanced portfolios that do not have separate cash portfolios for the asset class segments must only be included in the multi-asset composite.

Portfolios Excluded from All Composites

There are a number of reasons why a firm would exclude a portfolio from every one of its composites. Some of those reasons lead to permanent exclusion from composites; others will cause a portfolio to be temporarily excluded. Common reasons for permanently excluding a portfolio from all composites include:

- The portfolio is not legally discretionary.
- The portfolio is legally discretionary, but the mandate is not in line with the strategies offered by the firm.
- The client must approve all proposed trades.
- The portfolio has client-imposed restrictions that keep the manager from implementing the intended strategy.
- The portfolio does not pay management fees and the firm has elected to exclude non-fee-paying portfolios from composites.

A firm should document the reason for permanent exclusion so that a verifier or regulator can validate that the portfolio is properly excluded from all composites.

There are also reasons why a portfolio may be temporarily excluded from a composite. Some of these reasons include:

- The portfolio is new to the firm and does not yet qualify for inclusion in a composite.
- The portfolio has terminated and is in the process of liquidating or closing.
- The portfolio has changed strategy and the portfolio is in transition from the old strategy to the new strategy.
- The portfolio is below the respective composite's minimum size for inclusion.
- The portfolio had a significant cash flow.
- The client directed the manager to engage in tax loss harvesting.
- The portfolio contributed in-kind stock with a low cost basis that made up a large majority of the portfolio and has directed the manager not to generate any taxable gains over a specific period.
- The portfolio is not allowed to trade while the portfolio's assets are transitioned to a new custodian bank.

A firm must document its policies and procedures relating to composite inclusion and exclusion. Capturing the facts that justify temporary exclusion can be a challenge. Procedures should be established so that client instructions leading to the removal of a portfolio from a composite are documented. These instructions are often made in a phone call or during a client meeting so sometimes there is no written instruction from the client. A firm must still formally capture this information and maintain it. One way to do this is to assign responsibility to those that receive the instruction from the client to write a memo to the client file or to the performance department documenting the client's instruction and the potential impact on composite assignment.

What happens to portfolios that are not included in a composite? Just as a firm must maintain records to support why a portfolio is included in a specific composite, a firm must also maintain records to support why a portfolio is not a member of any of the firm's composites. Firms often find it helpful to create an *administrative composite* to keep track of these portfolios. Setting up an administrative composite, or more than one administrative composite, helps a firm reconcile the list of GIPS composites to total firm assets. A firm might create several administrative composites, for different types of excluded portfolios. One administrative composite could include portfolios that are permanently excluded. Other administrative composites could hold portfolios that are temporarily excluded, and could be based on the reason for exclusion. No matter how a firm uses administrative composites, they are not considered a composite for GIPS compliance purposes and must not be included on the firm's list of composite descriptions that must be provided to prospective clients if requested.

Firm-Directed Strategy Changes

As discussed in the previous section, a composite definition is the criteria for determining the assignment of portfolios to composites. A change to any criterion resulting in a change to the composite membership is considered a *composite redefinition*. For example, the change to no longer include pooled funds in a composite would be a composite redefinition. Such a change is easy to rationalize and disclose. More involved are situations when a composite strategy evolves.

When a composite strategy is modified, the firm needs to decide whether the strategy change results in a composite redefinition or the creation of a new composite. Consider an example where Firm DD manages a core fixed income strategy that is benchmarked to the Barclays U.S. Aggregate Index. The composite has been in existence for 10 years, and Firm DD has decided that in order to better manage the duration of the portfolios in the composite, it wishes to start using futures. Firm DD never used futures before, and most of its clients' investment management agreements had no specific instructions regarding the use of futures, although several clients specifically prohibited their use. Firm DD decides to begin using futures as of January 1, 2011. Does the change to use futures result in a new strategy, and thus a new composite?

Firm DD decides that this is not a new strategy but instead is an evolution of the way that it implements its Core Fixed Income strategy. Firm DD approaches existing clients that have not authorized the use of futures and asks them to change their contract to allow the use of futures. As of January 1, 2011, only those portfolios that allow the use of futures will be included in the composite, as the core bond strategy requires the use of futures as of that date. Portfolios that prohibit the use of futures, or do not agree to allow the use of futures, will be removed from the composite. This is a composite redefinition. Firm DD discloses this change, and continues the history of the Core Fixed Income Composite. The redefinition is done only on a prospective basis, leaving the history of the Core Fixed Income Composite as is.

Firm DD also decides that the core fixed income portfolios that do not allow the use of futures represent a new strategy of the firm. The new strategy is a new variation of the firm's Core Fixed Income strategy.

Firm DD creates a new composite, named the Core Fixed Income Excluding Futures Composite, and includes the client portfolios that do not authorize futures in this new composite and removes them from the Core Fixed Income Composite. This new composite has no history.

Other firms might take a different approach. Another firm might argue that the use of futures results in a new strategy/composite, and it is not a composite redefinition. In this instance the old composite would continue along with only the portfolios that do not allow the use of futures as of January 1, 2011. A new composite would be created as of January 1, 2011, and included in this composite would be the portfolios that do allow futures. This new composite would have a composite inception date of January 1, 2011.

Any time there is a composite redefinition, the firm must disclose the effective date of, description of, and reason for the redefinition.

Performance Record Portability

The transition of a single portfolio manager to a new firm is a common event. Also fairly common is the transition of an entire portfolio management team from one firm to another. What happens to the performance record of the transitioned managers? Do both the old and new firms get to market the historical performance?

Portability refers to the ability of a GIPS-compliant firm to present a track record that was earned at another firm. When a firm hires a portfolio manager from another firm, the firm usually wants to market the portfolio manager's track record while employed at the prior firm. The same is true when a firm acquires or lifts out a team from another firm. When a compliant firm acquires or merges with another firm, how should the track records from the different entities be presented? Please note that while this discussion focuses only on the GIPS requirements related to portability, the firm must also consider any applicable regulatory requirements relating to the portability of investment track records.

The GIPS standards set a high bar for the portability of returns and are intentionally more stringent than even some regulatory rules. The thinking behind setting such a high bar is an underlying philosophy that *performance belongs to a firm, not to a person.* When a portfolio manager leaves a firm, there should be no change to that firm's performance history. A firm may need to disclose the departure of a portfolio manager, if it qualifies as a significant event. But the firm does not stop reporting composites that were managed by the now departed portfolio manager. The performance is that of the firm. The same approach is taken when a portfolio manager joins a firm. That track record belongs to the prior firm, not the portfolio manager.

The bar is set high so that track records do not move as frequently as personnel change jobs.

The GIPS standards include three portability tests that must be considered for each composite that moves or ports from one firm to another. Each test is discussed below. If the three portability tests are met for a specific composite, the performance of the composite from the prior firm *must* be linked to the performance at the new firm. The tests are written as if an acquiring firm would *not* want to show the track record from a prior firm. If the portability tests are met, the acquiring firm must show the history from the prior firm and link to the track record at the new firm. The rationale behind this approach is that an acquiring firm should be prohibited from selectively dropping those historical records from the prior firm that the acquiring firm does not wish to present. For a firm that does wish to port a track record from a prior firm, the guidance should instead be read as the tests that must affirmatively be met before a firm is allowed to use a track record from a prior firm. An acquiring firm must assess each composite, and determine if the tests are met for each composite it wishes to port to the new firm. One composite's failure to meet the portability tests has no impact on other composites.

While not explicitly stated within the portability guidance, only a composite is portable. An acquiring firm may not recreate a historical record from the prior firm using the performance of only selected portfolios that were managed at the prior firm. The composite's entire history, which includes all portfolios that were managed at the prior firm, must be used. This guidance was initially issued in a Q&A in September 2001. Prior to this date the GIPS standards were silent on this topic, and many firms in the United States did in fact show history from a prior firm that included performance of only selected portfolios. For money managers located in the United States, this approach is consistent with SEC no-action guidance.[1]

The first portability test requires substantially all of the key investment decision makers that managed the composite at the prior firm to be employed at the new or acquiring firm. While the portfolio managers will probably be the most important people that must be considered, an acquiring firm must consider others that played a key role in the management of the composite's portfolios, such as traders and analysts. Was the strategy managed by a single portfolio manager or by multiple portfolio managers? Were portfolios managed by a team? How was the portfolio management function supported? The acquiring firm should understand how portfolios were managed at the prior firm so a proper assessment of who was a key

---

[1] See *Conway Asset Management, Inc.* SEC No-Action Letter (pub. avail. January 27, 1989).

player at the prior firm can be made. Where possible, the acquiring firm should review marketing materials from the prior firm to see how the prior firm described its portfolio management function. Once all of the key players are identified, the acquiring firm must then consider how many of the key players have joined the new firm. There is no magic number that determines whether the "substantially all" test is met. Each situation is unique and the acquiring firm must assess the facts and circumstances of the acquisition and determine whether the "substantially all" test is met.

The second portability test requires the decision-making process behind the composite's performance to remain substantially intact and independent within the new or acquiring firm. Any significant factors in managing portfolios at the prior firm should be replicated at the new or acquiring firm in order to create continuity in the portfolio management function. For example, if a strategy was based on a proprietary research model, that same proprietary research model must be replicated at the new firm. However, this test should not be read as requiring every person that joins the new firm, and is part of the decision-making process, to stay with the new firm forever. There will often be departures of key personnel shortly after a merger or acquisition closes. Departures of key personnel are facts of life in investment management firms. If the departure qualifies as a significant event, the firm must disclose information about the departure in the compliant presentation, but would not be required to reconsider portability tests that were previously met.

The third portability test requires the new or acquiring firm to have records to support the performance of the composite from the prior firm. There is no specific guidance as to recordkeeping for portability matters, so the general recordkeeping guidance must be considered. As will be discussed in Chapter 8, a firm must have records that enable the firm to recreate the returns of both the portfolios in the composite and the composite itself. The same would be true for a composite that has ported from a prior firm. Simply having summary information from the prior firm would not suffice.

Although not listed as a portability test, there is a fourth test that an acquiring firm must consider. If the acquiring firm wishes to link the history from the prior firm to the record at the new firm, there must not be a break in performance between the prior firm and the new or acquiring firm. Just like any other composite, if there is a period of time when there are no portfolios included in a composite, the composite's track record stops. It may be restarted subsequently when portfolios are once again included in the composite, but performance cannot be linked across the break. If such a break exists, performance from the prior firm may be presented but may not be linked to the track record at the new firm.

In most cases, a new or acquiring firm will be able to meet all of the portability tests only if the acquisition or lift-out is "friendly." Many lift-outs are done without the approval or knowledge of the prior firm. In a typical unfriendly lift-out, where the portfolio manager or management team departs unexpectedly, the departing team will not have records supporting the historical performance. If clients from the prior firm follow the departing team to the new firm, the new firm may be able to obtain supporting records of the prior track record from the clients. However, the new firm must obtain records to support all of the portfolios that had been in the composite at the prior firm, and not just those portfolios that follow the departing team from the prior firm to the new firm. An unfriendly lift-out will also normally encounter a break of at least a few days in the continuity of the track record between the final date portfolios were managed at the prior firm and when at least one portfolio is up and running at the new firm.

If a specific composite does not pass all of the portability tests, the new firm may be able to present the performance from the prior firm as supplemental information to the new composite at the new firm. However, if the new firm cannot meet the GIPS recordkeeping requirements, the prior history may not be presented, even as supplemental information. A firm's recordkeeping requirements extend to any information, including supplemental information, that is included in a compliant presentation.

The recordkeeping issue is typically not a problem with a friendly acquisition or merger. The acquiring firm must ensure it has adequate supporting records for any acquired composite, so they are readily available in the future. In a friendly acquisition the new or acquiring firm can also ensure there is no break in the composite history by establishing a new portfolio at the new firm that is up and running on the first day the departing team joins the new firm.

What if a firm acquires another firm, both firms manage a similar strategy, and the strategies will be combined prospectively? Which historical track record must be presented? Assuming the portability tests are met, the acquiring firm determines which of the two composites will survive as the ongoing strategy. If the surviving composite is the acquired composite, and the portability rules are met, then the acquired history would be presented as the history of the composite. Portfolios in the acquiring firm's composites would be moved into the acquired composite on a prospective basis. The acquiring firm's composite would be terminated.

If the ongoing, surviving composite is the acquiring firm's composite, then the acquiring firm's history would be presented as the history of the composite. Portfolios in the acquired firm's composites that move to the new firm would be transferred into the acquiring firm's composite on a prospective basis. The acquired composite would be terminated.

If the acquiring firm determines that neither composite will survive, and that the two teams will be combined prospectively, a new composite, which does not have any history, will be created. The two similar composites would be terminated. The history from the two composites could be shown as supplemental information, but must not be linked to the new composite. The history from the two composites may not be combined.

As will be discussed in Chapter 6, all compliant presentations must disclose total firm assets (or composite assets as a percentage of total firm assets) as of the end of each annual period presented. What should be presented as total firm assets for a ported composite? For example, assume Firm EE, in a friendly acquisition, acquires the domestic equity team from Firm FF. The domestic equity team from Firm FF manages three composites, and the acquisition is arranged so that all of the portability tests are met and the history of each composite will be linked to the composite managed at Firm EE. When Firm EE prepares the compliant presentation for the acquired composites, what should be presented for firm assets for the period that the composites were managed at the old firm? If only a team is acquired from a prior firm, it would not be likely that the acquiring firm, in this case Firm EE, would have records to support historical firm assets from Firm FF. Common practice is to not report firm assets for any period prior to the acquisition date, and to simply disclose that firm assets are only applicable since the date of acquisition. Table 2.5 shows a part of a sample compliant presentation for an acquired composite.

After an acquisition of an entire firm, which firm assets total should the firm report for historical periods? This question can be difficult to answer. In this case the acquiring firm would likely have access to the records supporting total firm assets of the acquired firm. Assume Firm GG acquires 100% of Firm HH during 2010, and that both firms claim compliance with the GIPS standards. When acquiring Firm GG prepares the compliant presentation for a composite that was ported from acquired Firm HH, what should be presented for firm assets for the period that the composite was managed at Firm GG? While Firm GG could present firm assets from the prior Firm HH until the date of acquisition, this could cause some confusion in Firm GG's marketing efforts. As of a given date prior to the acquisition, Firm GG would be presenting different firm asset amounts for the same date. Although Firm GG would be required to disclose that the track record came from a prior firm, this could be terribly confusing to the market. Think of how much more complicated this would be if Firm GG acquired two different firms during the year. Theoretically there could be three different amounts representing firm assets for a particular date.

This shows the Small Cap Core Composite for Firm EE from January 1, 2001 through December 31, 2010.

Year	Gross Annual Return (%)	Net Annual Return (%)	ABC 2000 Index (%)	Composite Dispersion (%)	No. of Portfolios	Percentage of Firm Assets (%)	As of December 31 Total Composite Assets ($ millions)	Total Firm Assets ($ millions)
2001	5.0	4.0	21.3	0.3	14	n/a	689	n/a
2002	33.1	31.8	(3.0)	0.8	14	n/a	873	n/a
2003	4.3	3.2	2.5	0.8	13	n/a	892	n/a
2004	(19.6)	(20.4)	(20.5)	0.3	14	n/a	658	n/a
2005	35.2	33.8	47.3	0.6	13	n/a	647	n/a
2006	31.0	29.7	18.3	0.9	13	14.3	595	4,165
2007	13.8	12.6	4.6	1.1	14	21.9	592	2,698
2008	17.9	16.7	18.4	0.5	8	13.1	270	2,069
2009	(5.7)	(6.6)	(1.6)	0.8	11	8.7	227	2,612
2010	(29.3)	(30.0)	(33.8)	0.3	10	10.2	122	1,194

Firm EE is a registered investment adviser under the Investment Advisers Act of 1940. In August 2005, Firm EE acquired the domestic equity team and portfolios from Firm FF, a registered investment adviser and wholly owned indirect subsidiary of FF plc. The performance of this composite includes performance from Firm FF. In January 2007, one of the senior portfolio managers for the strategy resigned from the firm; the remaining Small Cap Core team members remain intact. A complete list of composites and additional information regarding policies for valuing portfolios, calculating performance, and preparing compliant presentations are available upon request. All returns are expressed in U.S. dollars.

The Small Cap Core Composite includes portfolios utilizing a fully invested equity allocation with an emphasis on the small cap core segment of the U.S. equity market. Portfolios within the composite are managed to a client-directed broad market index, typically the ABC 2000 Index. The composite was created in September 1998. Returns prior to August 2005 were achieved from accounts managed by the portfolio managers while employed at Firm FF, therefore total firm assets and the percentage of firm assets for such periods are not applicable (n/a).

To prevent confusion, common practice is to not report firm assets for any period prior to the acquisition date, and to simply disclose that firm assets are only applicable since the date of acquisition. A firm could always choose to present firm assets from the acquired firm in addition to the acquiring firm's assets, if the firm believed it was helpful to do so. However, it would not be correct to combine historical firm assets of the acquired firm and the acquiring firm.

The GIPS standards allow a firm that acquires another firm, or team, one year to bring any noncompliant assets into compliance. Assume Firm II, which claims compliance with the GIPS standards, acquires Firm JJ in its entirety, and that Firm JJ does not claim compliance with the GIPS standards. (Firm JJ chose to not claim compliance as its composites were created only for marketed strategies; no composites were created for nonmarketed strategies.) On the day that Firm II acquires Firm JJ, Firm II will now include in firm assets portfolios that should be included in a composite but are not. Although this violates the requirement that a firm must be in compliance on a firmwide basis, expecting a firm to bring all acquired assets into compliance on the date of acquisition is unreasonable. Therefore a special allowance is provided so that Firm II can take one year to bring the noncompliant assets into compliance while still continuing to claim compliance.

If your firm is contemplating a merger, acquisition, or lift-out, you should seek both legal and GIPS-related advice on portability prior to completing the transaction. This is true whether you are the acquiring or acquired firm.

SUMMARY

Defining the firm, identifying the list of portfolios that are eligible for inclusion in a composite, and grouping these portfolios in composites are at the heart of the GIPS compliance process. In this chapter we outlined the procedures for accomplishing these tasks. The next step is to calculate the actual portfolio and composite returns and associated statistics that will be presented to the firm's prospective clients. Guidance for the quantitative aspects of the GIPS compliance process is the subject of Chapters 3 to 5.

PART TWO

The Methodology for Calculating Returns

CHAPTER 3

Portfolio Return Measurement

The measurement of performance starts with the calculation of return. The periodic change in the value of a portfolio and the resultant growth of assets over time are the most basic concepts of performance. Particular return calculation techniques are required to both recognize and isolate the effects of investor and manager decisions on performance, and measure performance over single and multiple time periods.

The calculation of portfolio returns is the first step in creating the composite performance record. A *return* is the income and profit earned on the capital that the investor places at risk in the investment. Suppose $100 is invested in a portfolio and the portfolio subsequently increases in value such that the investor receives $130 back. What was the return on this investment? The investor gained $30. Taking this *dollar return* and dividing it by the $100 invested, and converting the result to a percentage gives us a return of 30%.

A *rate of return* is the gain or loss received from an investment over a period of time expressed as a percentage. Returns are a ratio relating how much was gained or lost given how much was risked. We interpret a 30% return over the period as a gain equal to almost one-third of the original $100 invested.

Although it appears that no special knowledge of investments is required to calculate and interpret rates of return, several issues complicate return calculations and make the subject worthy of further investigation:

- Selection of the proper inputs to the return calculation.
- Treatment of additional client contributions and withdrawals to and from the investment account.
- Adjusting the return to reflect the timing of these contributions and withdrawals.
- Differentiating between the return produced by the manager and the return experienced by the investor.

- Computing returns spanning multiple valuation periods.
- Averaging periodic rates of return.

This chapter summarizes the single period *portfolio* return calculations required as inputs to the *composite* returns used in a GIPS-compliant presentation. The chapter first explains the basics of return calculation. Then, these techniques are linked to the requirements of the GIPS standards for portfolio return calculation. Chapter 4 shows you how to aggregate the portfolio returns into composite returns.

SINGLE PERIOD RATE OF RETURN

Why do we compute rates of return to describe the performance of an investment when we could simply judge our performance by the absolute dollars earned over time? After all, there is no better gauge of investment success than money in the bank! There are several reasons that returns are the preferred statistic for summarizing investment performance:

- *The rate of return concentrates a lot of information into a single statistic.* Individual data points about the beginning and ending market values, income earned, cash contributions and withdrawals, and trades for all of the individual security positions held by the portfolio are compressed into a single statistic.
- *This single statistic, the return, is a ratio.* Analyzing proportions rather than absolute numbers is faster for an investor. For example, if an investor is told she earned an 8 percent rate of return, she can instantly begin to judge whether she is happy with this result, compared to the need to pore over valuation and transaction statements first.
- *Returns are comparable even if the underlying figures are not.* An investor can compare returns even when the portfolios are valued using different base currencies or have different sizes. For example, if an investor puts $100 at work and gains $10, she has earned the same return as the investor who put $1 million to work and ended up with $1.1 million.
- *Returns calculated for different periods are comparable.* That is, an investor can compare this year's return to last year's.
- *The interpretation of the rate of return is intuitive.* Return is the value reconciling the beginning investment value to the ending value over the time period we are measuring. An investor can take a reported return and use it to determine the amount of money he

would have at the end of the period given the amount invested, as follows:

$$EMV = BMV * (1 + \text{Decimal return})$$

where EMV is the ending market value at the end of the period and BMV is the beginning market value at the start of the period.

For example, if we were to invest \$100 at a return of 40%, we would have \$140 at the end of the period: \$100 * (1 + .40) = \$140. Adding one to the decimal return before multiplying gives a result equal to the beginning value plus the gain/loss over the period. Multiplying the beginning value by the decimal return of 0.4 will give the gain/loss over the period (\$40).

Let's look closer at the calculation of return. In our introductory example we earned a \$30 gain on an investment of \$100. By dividing the gain by the amount invested we derive the 30% return using:

$$\text{Return in percent} = \left(\frac{\text{Gain or loss}}{\text{Investment made}}\right) * 100$$

Suppose that instead of investing and then getting our money back within a single period, we held an investment worth \$100 at the beginning of the period, and we continued to hold it at the end of the period when it was valued at \$130. Multiplying the gain or loss to investment made ratio by 100 transforms the decimal fraction into a percentage gain: 30% in our example (0.3 * \$100 = 30%).

When we measure the return on an investment that we buy and hold across periods, we treat the beginning market value as if it were a new investment made at the beginning of the period, and the ending market value as if it were the proceeds from the sale of the investment at the end of the period.

We have used two forms of the return calculation so far. It does not matter which one we use. The two methods are equivalent:

$$\left(\frac{\text{Gain or loss}}{\text{Investment made}}\right) * 100 = \left[\left(\frac{\text{Current value}}{\text{Investment made}}\right) - 1\right] * 100$$

We can demonstrate that the two forms are the same by deriving the second form of the calculation from the first:

$$\left(\frac{EMV - BMV}{BMV}\right) * 100 \rightarrow \left(\frac{EMV}{BMV} - \frac{BMV}{BMV}\right) * 100 \rightarrow \left(\frac{EMV}{BMV} - 1\right) * 100$$

◢	A	B	C	D
1	**Month Ending**	**Market Value**	**Dollar Return**	**Percent Return**
2	December	100		
3	January	110	10	10.00
4	February	120	10	9.09
5				↑
6			=B4-B3	=((C4/B3)*100)

FIGURE 3.1   Percentage Return versus Dollar Return

Using the first form, the numerator of the rate of return calculation is the *unrealized gain or loss*: the difference between the starting and ending market value. If income was earned during the period—for example, via the accrual of periodic coupon income due to the holder of a bond held by the portfolio—we also add it into the numerator, making the numerator properly reflect the market value plus accrued income. In either form of the calculation the denominator is the *investment made*. The number we select for the denominator represents the *money at risk* or the *capital at work* during the period. For the first measurement period, the investment made is equal to the amount originally invested in the portfolio. In subsequent periods, assuming the money is left in the investment, it is equal to the ending market value of the previous period. Let's consider the calculation of a return where we invested $100 at the end of December and it rises to $110 in January and then $120 in February, as shown in Figure 3.1.

Notice that even though we earned the same $10 dollar return in January and February, the percent return is higher in January (10/100 = 10.00%) than it was in February (10/110 = 9.09%). The reason for the lower February return is that the money at risk in the portfolio for February equals not only the original investment of $100 but also the $10 gained in January. With more money put at risk, the same dollar gain results in a lower return for the investment.

By using the *market value* of the investment to calculate returns, we recognize a gain on the investment even though it is not actually *realized* by selling the investment at the end of the period. To calculate returns that include unrealized gains or losses, we value the portfolio at the end of each measurement period. These dates are the periodic *valuation dates*. A return calculated between two valuation dates is called a *single period, holding period*, or *periodic* return. The periodicity of single period returns is related to the frequency of portfolio valuation. For example, single period returns can be calculated on a daily basis for mutual funds that are valued at the close of the market each night, but may be calculated only monthly for institutional separate accounts if they are valued only monthly.

Components of Single Period Returns

When there are no transactions into or out of an investment account and no income earned, to calculate a single period return we need to know only the beginning and ending market values for the period. Total portfolio market values are derived by summing up the values of the underlying investments within the portfolio. If we are calculating the return earned on our share of a commingled fund, such as a mutual fund, the market value equals the sum of the shares we own multiplied by the value of each share on the valuation date. Portfolio holdings are typically determined on a trade date basis. With *trade date accounting*, we include securities in the portfolio valuation on the day the manager agrees to buy the securities, as opposed to waiting for the day that the shares are settled (exchanged for cash) with the broker.

The *market value* of each security is the amount we would expect to receive if the investment were sold on the valuation date. It is calculated using observed market prices and exchange rates wherever possible. Determining market value is easy for instruments like exchange-traded equities, but we need to estimate the current value of other investment types. For example, bonds that do not trade often are marked to market by reference to the price of similar bonds that did trade that day. Although it is possible, say for liquidity reasons, that we could not actually realize the observed market closing price used in the valuation if we were to actually sell the investment, this method avoids introducing subjective estimates of trading impact into return calculations. Short-term instruments are valued at their amortized cost. If the portfolio holds cash and cash equivalents, they too are included in the valuation of the portfolio.

The individual security market values include a measure of income earned or *accrued* on the investment. Accrued income is income earned but not yet received. For example, if an investor sells a bond between coupon dates, the investor sells the interest accrued from the last coupon payment date through settlement date to the buyer of the bond. Because the interest accrued would be part of the proceeds if the security were sold on the valuation date, we also include it in the calculation of market value. In a similar manner, the total portfolio market value can be adjusted for accrued receivables and payables to and from the portfolio. For example, the accrued management fee payable to the investment manager is subtracted from the total market value. Returns that reflect both the change in market value and the income earned during the period are called *total returns*. Total returns must be used in a GIPS-compliant presentation.

While itemizing the finer points of valuing every type of instrument the portfolio could invest in is outside the scope of this book, the principles of market quote–driven, trade date–based valuation are used to judge the worth of each security in the portfolio, which are then summed to the portfolio level and result in the single period return calculation formula, as follows:

Percent rate of return

$$= \left[\left(\frac{\text{Ending market value} + \text{Ending accrued income}}{\text{Beginning market value} + \text{Beginning accrued income}} \right) - 1 \right] * 100$$

Taking note of which factors we do not explicitly include in the return calculation is also worthwhile. The *cost of investments* is *not* considered in performance measurement after the first period's return calculation (except for securities that are valued at their amortized cost). For each subsequent period, the ending market value for the previous period is used as the beginning market value for the next period. The justification for this practice is that we assume the investment cycle begins afresh with each valuation period, and that the current market value, and not the original cost, is invested, or put at risk again, in the next period.

The return calculation makes no reference to gains or losses *realized* in the course of security sales during the period. In fact the portfolio beginning and ending market values include both *unrealized capital appreciation/ depreciation* and *realized gains/losses* generated by trading within the portfolio during the period. Consider a portfolio with this sequence of activity:

December 31
- Holds 100 shares of Stock A priced at $1 per share = $100 BMV.

January 31
- Stock A is worth $110 for a 10% ($10/$100 = 10%) return in January.

February 28
- Stock A is valued at $115 for a 4.55% ($5/$110 = 4.55%) return in February.

March 1
- Fifty shares of Stock A are sold for $1.15 per share, netting $57.50.
- The realized gain on the sale is $7.50 ($57.50 − $50 = $7.50).
- Ten shares of Stock B at $5.75 a share are purchased with the proceeds.

	A	B	C	D	E	F
1	Date	MV Stock A	MV Stock B	Total MV	Gain/Loss	% Return
2	December 31	100.00	0.00	100.00		
3	January 31	110.00	0.00	110.00	10.00	10.00
4	February 28	115.00	0.00	115.00	5.00	4.55
5	March 1	57.50	57.50	115.00		
6	March 31	50.00	50.00	100.00	-15.00	-13.04
7						
8					=D6-D5	=((E6/D5)*100)

FIGURE 3.2 Reinvestment of Gain Impact on Returns

March 31

- Stock A is valued at $1 per share (50 shares * $1 = $50).
- Stock B is valued at $5 per share (10 shares * $5 = $50).
- The total portfolio is worth $100, for a –13.04% (–$15/$115 = –13.04%) return in March.

Figure 3.2 shows that we do not explicitly use the realized gain of $7.50 in the return calculation for March.

The realized gain on the sale of Stock A was committed to the purchase of Stock B, which was then marked to market at the end of March. We explicitly calculate the unrealized market value change during the period (–$15.00), and this market value change implicitly includes any realized gains/losses on securities sold during the period.

It is possible that the manager might not reinvest the sale proceeds via the purchase of another security. In this case, we still do not explicitly include the realized gain in the calculation of return. Instead, we include the cash received on the sale in the total portfolio market value. Figure 3.3 illustrates

	A	B	C	D	E	F
1	Date	MV Stock A	Cash	Total MV	Gain/Loss	% Return
2	December 31	100.00	0.00	100.00		
3	January 31	110.00	0.00	110.00	10.00	10.00
4	February 28	115.00	0.00	115.00	5.00	4.55
5	March 1	57.50	57.50	115.00		
6	March 31	50.00	57.90	107.90	-7.10	-6.17
7						
8					=D6-D5	=((E6/D5)*100)

FIGURE 3.3 Holding Gains in Cash

the fact that we do not need to know about the transactions *within* the portfolio during the valuation period in order to calculate portfolio-level returns.

Transactions within the portfolio during the period do not affect the total portfolio-level return calculation because they have an equal and opposite impact on performance—a purchase of one security is a sale of another (cash). This is also true of income received during the period if income is accrued. Income received on a security is an outflow from that security's income accrual but an inflow of cash. To calculate portfolio-level performance when there are no additional contributions and withdrawals, we only need to sum up the market value and accrued income of all of the securities in the portfolio plus cash balances at the beginning and end of the holding period.

Return on Investment

So far we have looked at the calculation of a return for periods where there are no client cash flows into or out of the portfolio. Individual and institutional investors also make periodic *contributions* to and *withdrawals* from investment accounts. Any contributions to the portfolio are *not* included as a component of investment return; they represent an increase of money or capital at risk but not a gain on our investment. For this reason, when a portfolio receives new money, measuring performance by simply observing the change in market value is not possible.

These asset transfers into and out of the portfolio are sometimes called *external cash flows*. Cash flow is a generic term for different transaction types. For a defined benefit pension plan, the cash flows include periodic corporate contributions to fund the plan and withdrawals to pay benefits to retirees. For a mutual fund, cash flows include purchases or redemptions of fund shares. Figure 3.4 shows the generic transactional relationships between the investor, the manager, and the portfolio.

This figure also illustrates the difference between an *internal cash flow* and an external cash flow. An exchange of cash for a security within the portfolio is an example of an internal cash flow. We do not need to consider internal cash flows in order to calculate a portfolio-level return.

The value of the external cash flow is the amount of money deposited or withdrawn. A positive cash flow is a flow into the portfolio. A negative cash flow is a flow out of the portfolio. Sometimes contributions are made in securities and not cash; for example, when a portfolio is transitioned from an existing manager to a new investment manager. The monetary value of these "in-kind" contributions is measured by the current value of the assets transferred at the time of the contribution. In these situations using the current

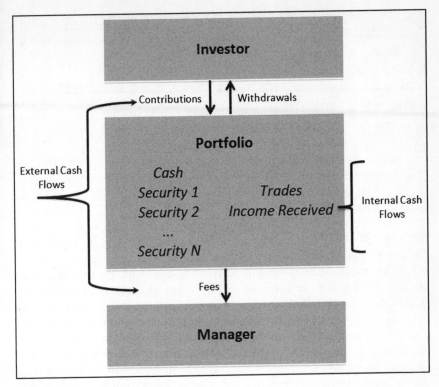

FIGURE 3.4 Portfolio Cash Flows

market value rather than the original cost is important. If the original cost were used, the first return calculation after the contribution would incorrectly credit the new manager with the unrealized appreciation/depreciation that existed in the securities that were contributed in-kind on the date of the transfer.

When there are cash flows, we need to adjust the calculation of gain/loss in the numerator of the return calculation to account for the fact that the increase or decrease in market value was not entirely due to investment earnings. For example, suppose we have a portfolio with a BMV of $100 and an EMV of $130. What is the gain if we invested an additional $10 during the period? We started off with $100 and ended up with $130. We subtract out the additional investment to calculate the gain or loss:

$$\text{Gain or loss} = (EMV - BMV - \text{Inflows} + \text{Outflows})$$

	A	B	C	D	E
1	BMV	InFlows	OutFlows	EMV	Return on Investment %
2	100.00	10.00	0.00	130.00	18.18
3			=(((D2+C2)/(A2+B2))-1)*100		
4					

FIGURE 3.5   Return on Investment

In this case the gain equals $20 ($130 − $100 − $10 + $0). The $20 gain during the period combines two amounts: the gain/loss on the original $100 and any gain/loss on the additional $10 invested. If, instead of a net inflow, we had a net outflow because we took money out of the portfolio during the period, the two components would be the gain/loss earned on the amount withdrawn up until the money was withdrawn, and the gain/loss on the capital that remains in the portfolio for the entire period.

When there are cash flows, in addition to modifying the numerator, we need to modify the denominator of the return calculation to account for additional capital invested or withdrawn during the measurement period. We can modify the rate of return calculation to account for additional investment or withdrawals; the result is the *return on investment* (ROI) formula (see Figure 3.5 for an illustration of the ROI calculation). ROI is the gain or loss generated by an investment expressed as a percentage of the amount invested, adjusted for inflows (contributions) and outflows (withdrawals), as follows:

$$ROI \text{ in percent} = \left[\left(\frac{EMV + \text{Outflows}}{BMV + \text{Inflows}} \right) - 1 \right] * 100$$

Here we assumed contributions were made at the beginning of the period and withdrawals occurred at the end. The expression in the numerator (EMV + Outflows) replaces the EMV used in the calculation of return without reference to cash flows. We adjust the ending market value for any withdrawals from the portfolio. In the denominator, we are adding the additional amount invested to the beginning market value in order to determine the total invested amount over the period. By adding the contributions to the BMV, we reduce the return because we are dividing the same gain by a larger number, making the assumption that all of the assets were at work during the period. With this assumption, it is not $100 but $110 ($100 + $10) that generated a $20 profit during the period.

Is 18.18% a fair return to account for the case where BMV = $100, EMV = $130, and there was an inflow of $10? The answer is: It depends. Note that there is an implicit assumption that the $10 inflow was available for investing, or at risk, for the complete period. If the additional inflow was put into the portfolio at the beginning of the period, the investor did not have use of the money for other purposes over the whole period. He would expect a higher portfolio return to compensate for the loss of the availability of this money for the entire period as compared to his keeping the money and investing in the portfolio only at the end of the period. So, returns should take into account the timing of the additional cash flows. If the investment were made sometime during the period, the investor did have use of the capital for some part of the period. For example, if the measurement period was a month and the $10 contribution came midway through the month, the portfolio had $100 of invested capital for the first half of the month and $110 for the second half. The gain of $20 was made on a smaller invested balance, therefore the return credited to the portfolio and its manager should be higher than 18.18%.

Except when used to calculate a daily return, while ROI adjusts for portfolio contributions and withdrawals, it does not adjust for the *timing* of these cash flows. (Keep in mind that assumptions need to be made as to whether cash flows occur at the beginning or end of the day. Here we assumed contributions at the beginning of the period and withdrawals at the end.) Because of the assumption that contributions were available for the whole period, ROI will give the same return no matter when in the period the flows occur. Another drawback of the ROI as a measure of investment performance is that it does not adjust for the *length* of the holding period. The ROI calculation gives the same result whether the gain was earned over a day, a year, or 10 years. For these reasons, we need return measures reflecting both the timing of cash flows and the length of the period for which the assets were at risk. Both adjustments are derived from concepts related to the time value of money, which we review in the next section.

TIME VALUE OF MONEY

Returns can be equated to the interest rates used in the calculation of the future value of a fixed income investment. However, unlike returns, coupon interest rates are known ahead of time, so we can project the future value at the beginning of the period. The future value of an investment equals the present value plus the income/gains (net of any expenses/losses) earned over the period, as shown in the following equation:

$$EMV = BMV * (1 + R)^N$$

where EMV = value at end of period
         BMV = value at beginning of period
         R = rate of income earned per period
         N = number of valuation periods

In return calculations, it is the R that is unknown. We calculate this rate R using observations of the beginning and ending market values.

The difference between the beginning and ending market values is the sum of the net gains and income earned. *Compounding* is the reinvestment of income to earn more income in subsequent periods. In a *simple interest* scenario, the income earned is not reinvested in order for it to compound in the following periods. For example, if $1,000 were put to work for a period of four months at an interest rate of 5% per month, we calculate an ending value of $1,200, as shown:

$$EMV = BMV * \left[1 + \left(\left(\frac{\text{Rate in percent}}{100} \right) * \text{Number of time periods invested} \right) \right]$$

$$\$1,200 = \$1,000 * \left[1 + \left(\left(\frac{5}{100} \right) * 4 \right) \right]$$

We use the simple interest calculation if the investor withdraws the income earned at the end of each period. In this example, the total gain over the four months is $200. This equals the monthly periodic dollar return of $50 multiplied by four. Dividing the $200 gain by the $1,000 invested gives a 20% return for the four-month period.

If the income and gains are retained within the investment vehicle, or *reinvested,* they will accumulate and increase the starting balance for each subsequent period's income calculation. For example, in Figure 3.6 we show that $100 invested at 7% for 10 years, assuming yearly compounding, produces an ending value of $196.72, or $100 * (1 + 0.07)^{10} = \$196.72$.

Notice that our original principal of $100 invested at 7% doubled in 10 years *before* the addition of any more principal. This was possible because we reinvested all of the gains, also at 7%.

The reinvestment assumption is important because the power of investing lies in the *compound interest,* the interest on the interest earned in prior periods. When interest earnings are withdrawn after each period, the simple interest calculation is a better measure of the situation. If income is left to

	A	B	C	D	E	F	G	H
1	Year	BMV	Interest Rate	EMV	Principal	Interest	Interest on Interest	% of Value
2	0			100.00	100.00			
3	1	100.00	0.07	107.00	100.00	7.00	0.00	
4	2	107.00	0.07	114.49	100.00	14.00	0.49	0%
5	3	114.49	0.07	122.50	100.00	21.00	1.50	1%
6	4	122.50	0.07	131.08	100.00	28.00	3.08	2%
7	5	131.08	0.07	140.26	100.00	35.00	5.26	4%
8	6	140.26	0.07	150.07	100.00	42.00	8.07	5%
9	7	150.07	0.07	160.58	100.00	49.00	11.58	7%
10	8	160.58	0.07	171.82	100.00	56.00	15.82	9%
11	9	171.82	0.07	183.85	100.00	63.00	20.85	11%
12	10	183.85	0.07	196.72	100.00	70.00	26.72	14%
13								
14		=D11		=B12*(1+C12)		=C12*B3*A12	=D12-(E12+F12)	=G12/D12

FIGURE 3.6 Compound Interest

earn more income, then compound interest is the better measure. Compound interest is assumed in almost all investment applications. With interest rates, we usually assume that interest is reinvested at the same interest rate for subsequent periods. The difference between working with returns instead of interest rates is that in return calculations, while we also assume that the income is reinvested, we recognize that the periodic returns fluctuate over time.

While we understand that earning a higher return over the holding period will increase the ending investment value, the frequency of compounding also impacts the ending value. As shown in Figure 3.7, an investment that has the same return has a higher value if the income is compounded more frequently.

	A	B	C	D	E
1	Frequency	BMV	Periods	Return	EMV
2	Yearly	1000.00	1.00	0.07	1070.00
3	Monthly	1000.00	12.00	0.07	1072.29
4	Daily	1000.00	365.25	0.07	1072.50
5			=FV(D4/C4,C4,0,B4*-1)		
6					

FIGURE 3.7 Future Value and Compounding Frequency

Interest rates are usually quoted on a yearly or *annual* basis. We can adjust the future value formula to account for more frequent compounding as such:

$$EMV = BMV * \left(1 + \frac{r_{\text{period}} * m}{m}\right)^{m * \text{periods}}$$

where $r =$ the periodic interest rate
          $m =$ times per period that interest is paid, or compounds

For example, if a $100 investment yielded 3% for the first six months (i.e., BMV = $100 and EMV = $103) and then yielded 3% for the second six months, the value at the end of one year, assuming semiannual compounding and reinvestment of the interest, is $106.09:

$$106.09 = 100 * \left(1 + \frac{0.03 * 2}{2}\right)^{2 * 1(\text{year})}$$

Given the fact that money has a time value, let's return to a question that we considered earlier: What is the proper holding period return to attribute to a portfolio where the BMV equals $100, we invest an additional $10 during the period, and the EMV = $130?

No matter when in the period the investment was made, the dollar gain is $20 ($130 – $100 – $10) for the period. The return over the period depends on the timing of the additional investment. The return could be as low as 18.18% or as high as 20%. If the $10 was invested at the *beginning of the period,* capital employed equals the original investment of $100 plus the additional investment of $10, therefore $110 was available for investment for the entire period:

$$\left(\frac{130 - 100 - 10}{100 + 10}\right) * 100 \rightarrow \left(\frac{130 - 110}{110}\right) * 100 \rightarrow \left(\frac{20}{110}\right) * 100$$
$$= 18.18\%$$

If the additional investment was made precisely at the *end of the period* instead, the capital employed during the period is just $100, so the return is 20%:

$$\left(\frac{130 - 100 - 10}{100}\right) * 100 \rightarrow \left(\frac{130 - 110}{100}\right) * 100 \rightarrow \left(\frac{20}{100}\right) * 100$$
$$= 20.00\%$$

Given the same dollar gain, we should credit the overall investment with a higher return as the contribution is made closer to the end of the period and less capital was available for investment for the period. In this instance, because the investment is made at the very end of the period, the additional contribution is not included in the denominator. The same numerator divided by a smaller denominator leads to the higher return. The higher return is justified when the contribution is made at the end of the period because the capital at risk during the period was lower, yet we earned the same dollar gain.

This example shows that tracking the time when contributions or withdrawals are made into an investment account in order to accurately determine returns is important. We always adjust the numerator for the additional contributions or withdrawals during the period. We either include the full amount of the contribution in the denominator, none of it, or a partial amount, depending on the timing of the cash flow. When the denominator of a return calculation is adjusted for contributions or withdrawals we call the denominator the *average capital employed,* or the *average invested balance.*

PERFORMANCE OF THE INVESTOR: MONEY WEIGHTED RETURNS

In this section, we establish the need to recognize the effects of both investor and manager decisions when calculating the return earned by the investor, by isolating the effects of investor decisions when calculating the return to be attributed to the manager. The dollar or *money weighted return* (MWR) is the performance of the investment portfolio and incorporates the effects of both decisions.

Timing of Investor Decisions

In addition to the time value of money, the *market timing* of the investor contributions and withdrawals will affect realized returns. The capital markets provide us with positive long-term returns but volatile periodic returns. Market timing is a term that relates the time an investor makes his investment to the market cycle—that is, is the investor buying low and selling high or vice versa?

For example, suppose we are investing via a mutual fund and during the month the fund's net asset value per share (NAV) varies between $10 and $12 and there are no distributions, as shown here:

Date	NAV per share
5/31	$10.00
6/10	$12.00
6/20	$10.00
6/30	$11.00

The monthly return that will be published for this fund is 10%. Figure 3.8 shows the calculation of various holding period returns for the month.

The investor with perfect foresight (or good luck) invested on 5/31 and redeemed on 6/10 to earn a 20% return. The investor with poor timing, who bought at the high on 6/10 and sold at the bottom on 6/20 had a –16.67% return. This spread of 36.67% represents the return differential due to the timing of the investor cash flows. The important point for investment performance measurement is that these cash flows were at the *discretion of the investor,* not the manager. Actions of the investment manager would have had no impact on this differential return; he would have put the money to work according to his mandate. In a time when the market moved up, down, and back up again, the returns earned by different investors in the same fund can be quite different depending on the timing of their cash flows and the volatility of the returns over the period.

In the previous example, the fund's advertised return for the period would be the 10% return, which was measured from the start of the monthly period to the end. Even though different investors experienced different returns, the investment manager for the mutual fund had no control over these timing decisions, therefore 10% is an accurate representation of his performance. This is the appropriate return to use when comparing the manager's performance to a peer group average or a market index.

	A	B	C	D	E
1	Period	Return From	Calculated As	% Return	
2	1	5/31 – 6/10	((12 / 10) – 1) * 100	20.00	
3	2	5/31 – 6/20	((10 / 10) –1) * 100	0.00	Published Return
4	3	5/31 – 6/30	((11 / 10) – 1) * 100	10.00	
5	4	6/10 – 6/20	((10 / 12) –1) * 100	-16.67	
6	5	6/10 – 6/30	((11 / 12) – 1) *100	-8.33	
7	6	6/20 – 6/30	((11 / 10) – 1 * 100	10.00	

FIGURE 3.8   Cash Flow Timing and Returns

	A	B	C	D
1	**Segment**	**BMV**	**Percent Return**	**EMV**
2	Cash	10	1.00	10.10
3	Equity	100	-10.00	90.00
4	Total	110	-9.00	100.10
5			↑	
6			=((D4/B4)-1)*100	=SUM(D2:D3)

FIGURE 3.9   Manager 1 Timing Decision

Timing of Investment Manager Decisions

When we calculate returns, we can also consider the timing of decisions that are the responsibility of the manager. Consider two managers starting with the same $100 equity portfolio at the beginning of the month. Both receive $10 client contributions at the beginning of the month. Their strategies differ only in that Manager 1 attempts to time the market as shown in this example. Assume that the market moves down 10% during the month. Manager 1 leaves the contribution in cash. Figure 3.9 shows that Manager 1's return is –9%.

Figure 3.10 shows that Manager 2 invests the contribution in equities at the beginning of the month and receives a –10% return.

Despite the negative returns, Manager 1 earned 1% in *value added* over Manager 2 due to the beneficial decision to leave the contribution in the relatively higher yielding cash segment and to have less money invested in the lower performing equity segment during the month.

	A	B	C	D
1	**Segment**	**BMV**	**Percent Return**	**EMV**
2	Cash	0.00	1.00	0.00
3	Equity	110.00	-10.00	99.00
4	Total	110.00	-10.00	99.00
5			↑	
6			=((D4/B4)-1)*100	=SUM(D2:D3)

FIGURE 3.10   Manager 2 Timing Decision

Segregating Investor and Manager Timing Decisions

The preceding sections illustrate a performance measurement problem: Since the manager and investor are typically two different people, decisions made by the investor and the investment manager must be segregated in order to properly calculate returns that reflect their respective responsibilities.

The ideal statistic for measuring the return experienced by the investor would include the effects of both:

- The timing of investor decisions to make an investment into the portfolio.
- The decisions made by the manager to allocate assets and select securities within the portfolio.

The first effect is purely attributable to decisions made by the investor. The second also can be considered attributable to the investor because he made the decision to hire the manager. The actual returns experienced by the investor are affected by the combination of the two effects. The ideal statistic for measuring the return produced by the investment manager neutralizes the timing effect because he (in many situations) has no control over the timing of client-directed external cash flows. Because of this need to isolate the timing of investor decisions, we need two different measures of return.

The money weighted return is used when we need to measure the performance as experienced by the investor. MWR is a performance statistic reflecting how much money was earned during the measurement period. This amount is influenced by the timing of decisions to contribute to or withdraw money from a portfolio, as well as the decisions made by the manager of the portfolio. The MWR is contrasted with the statistic used to measure manager performance, a time weighted return (TWR), which is discussed later in this chapter. As we will see, money weighted returns are important even if we are interested only in evaluating manager performance because they are:

- Frequently used as an input into the estimation of the TWR.
- Used to measure performance in situations where the manager *does* influence the timing of cash flows. These cases include closed-end Real Estate funds and Private Equity, where the GIPS standards require that returns are calculated using an MWR.

MWR is the return an investor actually experiences after making an investment. It reconciles the beginning market value and additional cash

TABLE 3.1 Impact of Cash Flows on Performance

Transaction	Before the Market	Effect on Performance
Contribution	Goes up	Positive
Contribution	Goes down	Negative
Withdrawal	Goes up	Negative
Withdrawal	Goes down	Positive

flows into the portfolio to the ending market value. The timing and size of cash flows impact the ending market value, as shown in Table 3.1.

To accurately reflect these transactions, the MWR takes into account not only the amount of the flows but also the timing of the cash flows. Different investors into the same fund will invest different amounts and make their investment on different dates. Because of the differences in cash flow timing and magnitude, comparing the MWR calculated for two different investors is not appropriate.

When there are no cash flows, the return is calculated as the ending market value over the beginning market value. If there was a cash flow, we need to take into account the amount and the timing of the flow in order to calculate the proper capital invested for the period. To account for the timing of the flow, we calculate a weighting adjustment, which is used to adjust the cash flow for the portion of the period that the cash flow was invested. If we are calculating an MWR for a one-year period and there were two contributions, the first at the end of January and the second at the end of February, the flows will be weighted by 0.92 for the January month end flow (the flow will be available to be invested for 92% of the year) and 0.83 for the February month end flow (the flow will be available to be invested for 83% of the year).

INTERNAL RATE OF RETURN

Suppose we invest $100 at the beginning of the year and end up with $140 at the end of the year. We made cash flows of $10 each at the end of January and February. What is the MWR return for this situation? The MWR we are looking for will be the value that solves this equation:

$$100 * (1 + MWR) + 10 * (1 + MWR)^{.92} + 10 * (1 + MWR)^{.83} = 140$$

	A	B	C	D	E	F
1	Date	Months Invested	Period Weight	Value	Future Value of Flow	
2	December 31	12	1.00	100	117.05	=D2*((1+E8)^C2)
3	January 31	11	0.92	10	11.55	=D3*((1+E8)^C3)
4	February 28	10	0.83	10	11.40	=D4*((1+E8)^C4)
5	December 31			140	140.00	=SUM(E2:E4)
6						
7	IRR calculated using solver			Difference:	0.00	=D5-E5
8				IRR:	0.1705	
9				Percent Return:	17.05	=E8*100

FIGURE 3.11   Internal Rate of Return

The return that reconciles the beginning value and any cash flows to the ending value is the *internal rate of return* (IRR). The return is the value that solves for IRR in this equation:

$$EMV = BMV * (1 + IRR) + CF_1 * (1 + IRR)^N \ldots CF_2 * (1 + IRR)^N$$

where CF = amount of each cash flow in or out of the portfolio
           N = percentage of the period that each CF was available for investment

The IRR is the rate implied by the observed market values and cash flows. For all but the simplest case, we cannot solve for the IRR directly. Unfortunately, we cannot use algebra to rearrange the terms of the equation to derive the solution. The IRR is calculated using a trial and error process where we make an initial guess and then iteratively try successive values informed by how close we were to the solution in the last try, until we solve the problem. Techniques have been developed to perform the iteration efficiently and converge on a solution quickly. Figure 3.11 shows the calculation of the IRR using the Excel solver utility.

In this example, we set the difference between the ending market value in cell D5 equal to the sum of the future values in cell E5. We then solve for the IRR in cell E8. The IRR is 17.05% because, as demonstrated below, it is the return that resolves the flows to the ending market value:

$$100 * (1 + .1705) + 10 * (1 + .1705)^{.92} + 10 * (1 + .1705)^{.83} = 140$$

Notice that there is an assumption embedded in the IRR formula: The rate of return is assumed to be constant within the period. In this example,

	A	B	C	D	E	F
1	Date	Days Invested	Period Weight	Value	Future Value of Flow	
2	December 31	31	1.00	1000	919.85	=D2*((1+E8)^C2)
3	January 10	22	0.71	400	376.97	=D3*((1+E8)^C3)
4	January 20	12	0.39	-100	-96.82	=D4*((1+E8)^C4)
5	January 31			1200	1200.00	=SUM(E2:E4)
6						
7		IRR calculated using solver		Difference:	0.00	=D5-E5
8				IRR:	-0.0802	
9				Percent Return:	-8.02	=E8*100

FIGURE 3.12 IRR for Periods Less than a Year

each cash flow is compounded at 17.05% for the complete portion of the year invested.

We can calculate an IRR for periods that are less than a year. The period weight used for each of the cash flows is the percentage of the total period under consideration. For example, a cash flow on the 10th of a 31-day month would be weighted at $(31 - 10 + 1)/31 = 0.7097$ of the month (assuming that the contribution was made at the beginning of the day on the 10th; do not add a day in the numerator if we assume cash flows occur at the end of the day). The results of IRR calculations done for less than a year are interpreted as an IRR over the period measured.

Figure 3.12 shows the calculation of the monthly IRR where BMV = $1,000 on December 31, EMV = $1,200 on January 31, and we had two cash flows, $400 into the portfolio on January 10 and $100 out of the portfolio on January 20.

When we have withdrawals from the account, we make the cash flow adjustments used in the IRR negative. The one-month IRR for this pattern of cash flows is 8.02%.

Problems with the IRR

We classify the IRR as an MWR because it takes into account both the timing and size of cash flows into and out of the portfolio. It is an appropriate measure of the performance of the investment as experienced by the investor. The fact that the IRR needs to be calculated via iteration made the IRR an expensive calculation in the past because of the computer time used by the iteration algorithm. This is not a problem today. However, the historical problem led to the development of various creative methods to cheaply estimate the IRR. One of these methods, the Modified Dietz method, is still the most common method used by analysts to compute MWRs and, as we will see, estimate returns between valuation dates when we are calculating a TWR.

Modified Dietz Return

The Modified Dietz return is a simple interest (as opposed to compound interest) estimate of the MWR. The Modified Dietz calculation is the same as the ROI calculation, except the cash flows added to or taken from the beginning market value are adjusted according to the time they were invested in the portfolio. The monthly periodicity Modified Dietz return is arguably the most common return presented by money managers to institutional investors. So we will walk through several permutations of the calculation. Note that in all cases, when netting cash flows, inflows are positive and outflows are negative. First, here is the formula:

$$\text{Modified Dietz return} = \left(\frac{EMV - BMV - CF}{BMV + \text{Weighted cash flows}} \right) * 100$$

where EMV = portfolio ending market value + accrued income
BMV = portfolio beginning market value + accrued income
CF = sum of the net cash flows for the period

The weighted cash flows in the denominator are calculated by

$$\text{Weighted cash flows} = \sum \left[\left(\left(\frac{CD - C_i}{CD} \right) * CF_i \right) \right]$$

where, assuming end of day cash flows,

CD = total days in the period
C_i = day of the cash flow
CF_i = amount of the net cash flow on C_i

The calculation is named for the developer, Peter Dietz, who was associated with the Frank Russell pension consulting company. The original Dietz method, not currently used but discussed later in this chapter, makes the assumption that cash flows occurred midway through the period.

To illustrate the calculation of a Modified Dietz return, consider the following situation. We have a portfolio with a market value + accrued income of $100 at the beginning of the month. At the end of the month, the portfolio was worth $120. But not all of the $20 increase in value was due to the appreciation of the assets or income earned during the period. Instead, the client contributed an additional $10 during the month. What was the return that was attributable to the efforts of the manager? First let's look at the situation intuitively. The manager should be credited with $10 of gains (or income) during the period. Why? Subtracting the initial investment of $100 and the subsequent investment of $10 from the ending market value of $120 leaves a gain of $10. In other words,

$$EMV - BMV - CF = \text{Gain/Loss}$$

That is,

$$\$120 - \$100 - \$10 = \$10$$

Next, we know that we need to divide this $10 gain by some value representing the investment made by the client. If the whole investment, including both the initial investment and additional investment, was made as of the first day of the month, then that would be easy. We would divide the $10 by the total investment of $110 to derive a return of 9.09%. But what if the contribution was made at the end of the month? Assuming that the manager earned the same $10, he should be credited with a higher return. Why? Because he earned the same $10 on a smaller base of investable assets over the period. In fact, if the client contributed the extra $10 at the very end of the day at calendar month end, the return credited to the manager should be equal to the $10 gain divided by $100 (beginning market value), or 10 percent. These two extremes illustrate the rationale behind the Modified Dietz formula. It adjusts contributions and withdrawals according to the time they were at work during the period in order to derive a weighted average asset base that was at work over the whole period.

Let's return to our situation, where the client made an additional contribution of $10 and assume the contribution was made on the 20th of the month. The first step in calculating the asset base is to take the contribution and day weight it. *Day weighting* the cash flow will adjust the contribution for the percentage of the month that the manager was able to invest it. We know that the contribution occurred on the 20th, so the manager had access to the contribution for approximately a third of the month (the last 10 days of a 30-day month). But, to come up with a factor for day weighting the flow, we need to make an assumption as to whether the cash flow occurred on the 20th at the beginning of the day or the end of the day. If we assume that the cash flow occurred at the end of the day, the manager had access to the contribution for one-third of the month. In other words:

1. The flow occurred at the end of the day on the 20th.
2. We assume the manager had access to it for 10 days (the full day of the 21st through the 30th).

3. If we divide the 10 days by the 30 days in the month, we derive a cash weighting factor of 33% (10/30 = 0.33).

Next, to determine the appropriate amount of capital to add to the denominator, we adjust the cash flow by multiplying the amount by the adjustment factor:

$$.33 * \$10 = \$3.33$$

Then, to calculate the return, we add the adjusted flow to the beginning market value in the denominator and derive the Modified Dietz return equal to 9.68%:

$$9.68\% = \left(\frac{120 - 100 - 10}{100 + 3.33} \right) * 100$$

Let's review. We first determined that the return for this situation would be 9.09% if the manager had access to the cash contribution for the whole month. And, given the same gain over a smaller investment base, the return should be 10% if the manager did not have access to the contribution at all because it was given right at month end. So the 9.68% day weighted Modified Dietz return seems intuitive. Because the manager had access to the contribution for only one-third of the month, the Modified Dietz formula credits a return of less than but closer to the 10% return, which assumes that he did not have access to the contribution at all.

A special note on day weighting: We made the assumption that the cash flow was available only at the end of the day on the 20th. If we instead had assumed that the flow was available at the beginning of the day, the return credited to the manager would have been lower. How? First we would have determined the cash flow adjustment factor equaled 36.67% (11/30 = 0.3667). This is because we are assuming that the manager had access to the cash flow for one more day during the period (the full day of the 20th). So the adjusted cash flow would be $3.67. With that adjustment, the return assuming beginning of day cash flows would have been:

$$9.65\% = \left(\frac{120 - 100 - 10}{100 + 3.67} \right) * 100$$

What if there were several cash flows over the period? The formula is the same. Day weighted withdrawals are subtracted from the denominator. Each cash flow is adjusted by the appropriate day weighting factor given the beginning or end of day assumption being used. For both contributions and withdrawals, the goal is to determine the average invested balance over the monthly period.

Both the IRR and Modified Dietz formulas are money weighted returns. MWR results are affected by the timing and magnitude of the cash flows during the period. Both formulas are sometimes used to approximate the true time weighted return. Return statistics that completely eliminate the impact of investor cash flows are time weighted returns.

PERFORMANCE OF THE INVESTMENT MANAGER: TIME WEIGHTED RETURNS

A rate of return is the percentage change in the value of an asset over some period of time. Total returns are calculated by dividing the capital gain/loss and income earned by the value of the investment. As we saw earlier in this chapter, investors experience different returns investing in the same portfolio depending on the timing and magnitude of their cash flows into and out of the portfolio. Returns are used in evaluating the performance of an investment manager, but since he (usually) has no control over the timing and amount of investor flows, we need a performance measure that judges the manager by the return on money invested over the whole period and negates the effect of these cash flows.

Time Weighted Return

The *time weighted return* is a form of total return that measures the performance of a dollar invested over the complete measurement period. The TWR eliminates the timing effect that external portfolio cash flows have on performance, leaving only the effects of the market and manager decisions. Because the GIPS standards are concerned with the presentation of the *manager's* performance, we use a TWR for GIPS reporting purposes.

To calculate a time weighted return, we break the total performance period into subperiods, calculate the returns earned during each of the subperiods, and then compound these subperiod returns to derive the TWR for the whole period. The subperiod boundaries are the dates of each cash flow. Specifically, the steps to calculate a TWR, assuming a beginning of day cash flow assumption, are as follows:

1. Begin with the market value at the beginning of the period.
2. Move forward through time toward the end of the period.
3. Note the value of the portfolio immediately before a cash flow into or out of the portfolio.

4. Calculate a *subperiod return* for the period between the valuation dates.
5. Repeat steps 3 and 4 for each cash flow encountered.
6. When there are no more cash flows, calculate a subperiod return for the last period from the last cash flow to the end of period market value.
7. Compound the subperiod returns by taking the product of (1 + the subperiod returns).

The last step is called *geometric linking*, or *chain linking*, of the returns. Chain linking has the same function as compounding in the future value calculation. We employ chain linking instead of the future value formula because in portfolio performance measurement we assume that the periodic returns change from subperiod to subperiod, as shown in the following formula:

$$\text{Time weighted return} = [(1 + R_1) * (1 + R_2) * \ldots (1 + R_3) - 1] * 100$$

where R_N = the subperiod returns

The TWR assumes compounding and reinvestment of the gains earned in the previous subperiods. The expression [1 + the subperiod return] is called a *wealth relative* or *growth rate*, which represents the increase in capital over the subperiod. For example, if a portfolio is worth $100 at the beginning of the subperiod, and $105 at the end of the subperiod before the next cash flow, the subperiod return is 5% and the growth rate for the subperiod equals 1.05.

Below we illustrate the steps to calculate a TWR. We calculate the TWR for one month with one cash flow into and one cash flow out of the portfolio, as shown in Table 3.2.

TABLE 3.2 Valuations and Cash Flows

Date	End of Day Valuation	Cash Flow
5/31	1,000	
6/9	1,100	
6/10		200
6/19	1,200	
6/20		−100
6/30	1,200	

Divide the Period into Subperiods

The first step in the TWR calculation is to divide the period we are interested in into subperiods, where the subperiods are segregated by the cash flow dates, as shown in Table 3.3. The next step is to note the value of the portfolio before each cash flow. If we are working with a beginning of day cash flow assumption, we use the valuation performed on the night prior to the cash flow.

As shown in Table 3.2, we have two cash flows and three subperiods:

1. 5/31 to the end of day 6/9.
2. 6/10 to the end of day 6/19.
3. 6/20 to the end of day 6/30.

Note that there are (1 + the number of cash flow dates) subperiods.

Calculate Subperiod Returns

Next we calculate a single period return for each subperiod. The time of day assumption governs the treatment of the cash flows in the subperiod return formula. Here we assume that cash flows occur at the beginning of the day. With a beginning of day assumption, we add the net cash flow to the beginning of day market value to form the denominator of the return. Cash flows into the portfolio are added to the denominator, as we assume that the additional money contributed was available for investment at the beginning of the day. Cash flows out of the portfolio are subtracted as we assume that the money withdrawn was not available for investment on that

TABLE 3.3 Valuations and Subperiod Cash Flows

Date	Begin of Day Valuation	Cash Flow	End of Day Valuation
5/31			1,000
6/9			1,100
6/10	1,100	200	
6/19			1,200
6/20	1,200	−100	
6/30	1,200		1,200

	A	B	C	D	E	F	G
1	Sub Period	Return From	BMV	CF	EMV	Percent Return	Growth Rate
2	1	5/31 – 6/10	1000	0	1100	10.00	1.10
3	2	6/10 – 6/20	1100	200	1200	-7.69	0.92
4	3	6/20 – 6/30	1200	-100	1200	9.09	1.09
5				=((E4/(C4+D4))-1)*100		=1+(F4/100)	
6							

FIGURE 3.13   Subperiod Returns

day. If there is more than one cash flow during the day, we net the flows together:

$$\text{Subperiod return beginning of day cash flow assumption} =$$
$$EMV \text{ divided by the (BMV + Net cash flows)}$$

The calculation of the three subperiod returns (10.00%, –7.69%, and 9.09%) is shown in Figure 3.13.

Calculate Period Returns

The percentage return for the period, in this case one month, is calculated by geometrically linking the subperiod returns:

$$[(1.1000) * (.9231) * (1.0909) - 1] * 100 = 10.77\%$$

By calculating the return in this way, we have completely eliminated from the return the impact of the cash flows into and out of the portfolio. Figure 3.14 shows a way to visualize how the TWR eliminates cash flow effects from the return calculation.

As discussed previously, there are exceptions to the general rule that TWR is the appropriate measure of manager performance. In some situations, the portfolio manager does have discretion over the timing of cash flows. For example, in the management of private equity funds, the general partner draws down the capital committed when he wants to invest it. Therefore, returns calculated for private equity portfolios should reflect the impact of the timing of cash flows. However, in most performance measurement applications, the TWR is the appropriate measure of manager performance.

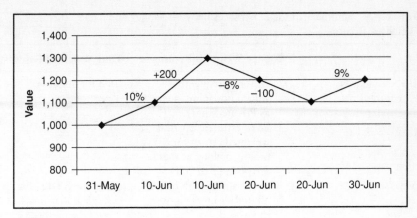

FIGURE 3.14 Time Weighted Return

Estimating the Time Weighted Return

There is a potential hurdle to implementing this methodology. TWR requires a valuation of the portfolio before each cash flow. Unfortunately, these periodic valuations are not always available. For example, many institutional separate accounts are valued on a monthly frequency, but the client may deposit or withdraw funds from the account at any time during the month. While the industry has been trending toward daily valuations (and the GIPS standards require a valuation on the date of any large cash flow as of January 1, 2010), until daily valuations are available for all portfolios, we need a way of estimating the true TWR when contributions and withdrawals are made between valuation dates.

We can approximate a TWR by calculating an MWR for each subperiod between valuation dates and compounding them over longer periods using the chain linking method to link subperiod returns into a TWR. This linked MWR estimate of TWR provides a reliable approximation of the TWR in situations where the cash flows are small relative to the portfolio size and there is low return volatility within the subperiod. If the cash flows are large and the market is volatile during the period, the MWR estimate of TWR will be inaccurate. So it is important to note that the linked MWR is an *estimate* of the TWR over the longer period. In an MWR, even though the cash flows are weighted within the subperiod, the cash flows are influencing the returns. The linking process does not remove the effect of the cash flows from the return calculation. A compromise solution to calculating a true TWR is to perform a special valuation whenever there are large cash flows

TABLE 3.4 Summary of the Differences between Money and Time Weighted Returns

	Money Weighted Returns	Time Weighted Returns
GIPS standards requirements	Used for infrequently valued portfolios, such as Private Equity. Used to estimate the time weighted return for a month, as long as there are no large cash flows.	Used for all other portfolios.
Measures	The average growth rate of all dollars invested over the period.	The growth rate of a single dollar invested over the period.
Usage in analyzing investment results	Appropriate measure of investor or portfolio performance.	Appropriate measure of pooled fund or manager performance. Appropriate for market comparison. Appropriate for comparing managers.
Effect of external cash flows	Reflects both the timing and amount of dollars at work over the period.	Eliminates the effect of both timing and amount of money at work.
What the statistic represents	The return that reconciles BMV, CF, and EMV.	The return of $1 invested in the portfolio from beginning to end.
Calculation drawbacks	Iteration required for IRR calculation.	A valuation is required before each flow.

and then link the subperiod MWR. Table 3.4 summarizes the differences between money and time weighted returns.

PORTFOLIO RETURN CALCULATIONS FOR THE GIPS STANDARDS

In this chapter thus far we reviewed the generic techniques required to calculate portfolio returns. But which calculations should be used for GIPS compliance purposes? There are several points to consider when selecting the appropriate portfolio return calculation. These include:

- Input data.
- Frequency of portfolio returns.
- Time versus money weighted returns.
- Cash flow weighting.
- Selecting a portfolio return methodology.

Let's begin with Input data.

Input Data

The GIPS standards have several requirements that specify the accounting data inputs to the portfolio return calculation, as detailed below:

1. *Market value.* Portfolio returns are calculated using accounting data representing the total market value of all of the assets in a portfolio, including cash balances.
2. *Valuation policy.* Market value for each security held is determined with reference to the security's fair value. The GIPS standards define *fair value* as "the amount at which an investment could be exchanged in a current arm's length transaction between willing parties in which the parties each act knowledgeably and prudently." For marketable instruments, fair value will equal the latest market quote for the security at the date of the valuation. For thinly traded issues or unique assets, fair value is equal to the best estimate of current market value.
3. *Interest income.* Income earned on fixed income securities must be recognized on an accrual, not cash, basis. For example, corporate bonds typically pay interest income once every six months. A portfolio that holds a corporate bond must recognize, or accrue, income on the bond throughout the period it holds the bond, even though the cash payment for the interest is not received until the end of the six-month period. The income *earned but not yet received* for fixed income securities in the portfolio is included in the portfolio market value.

   An exception to the requirement to accrue interest income is provided for short-term cash and cash equivalents (e.g., STIF and cash sweep vehicles). Because many short-term investments have no stated interest rate, a firm may not be able to accurately accrue income. Because of this difficulty, a firm may instead recognize short-term interest income on a cash basis. Any short-term interest income that is accrued is included in the portfolio market value.

4. *Dividend income.* The GIPS standards recommend that dividend in-come on stocks be accrued and recognized on the ex-dividend date. While accruing dividend income is common practice, a firm may choose to recognize dividends on either a cash or accrual basis. Any accrued dividends are included in the portfolio market value.

5. *Withholding taxes.* Portfolios that hold foreign securities may be subject to withholding taxes on income earned overseas. To eliminate double-taxation or reflect the fact that many investment portfolios are nontax-able, this tax or a portion of the tax can in many cases be reclaimed at a later date. The GIPS standards recommend that portfolios accrue as income any taxes that are reclaimable, and not recognize as income any taxes that cannot be reclaimed. Suppose that a portfolio holds a foreign bond subject to a 10% nonreclaimable withholding tax. In this situa-tion, the portfolio would accrue only 90% of the bond's stated coupon and this will be reflected in the return calculation via a lower portfolio market value.

6. *Management fees.* The GIPS standards recommend that management fees be subtracted from the portfolio market value on an accrual ac-counting basis when calculating net returns. For example, suppose that management fees are paid out of the portfolio quarterly. To reflect the fact that the manager has earned a portion of the fee during the quar-ter, a more accurate inter-quarter monthly valuation would subtract a portion of the management fee from the portfolio market value.

7. *Security Transactions.* As of January 1, 2005, all security purchases and sales must be accounted for on trade date. A firm can use either trade date or settlement date for prior periods. Transaction amounts are recorded net of all trading expenses, such as commissions.

Frequency of Portfolio Returns

After determining the inputs to the portfolio return calculation, the next question is determining how often portfolio returns must be calculated. While daily frequency return calculations create the most accurate time weighted returns, they require a firm to value the portfolio each day. In recognition that many firms do not either have the capability to do daily valuations or do not want to incur the cost of daily valuations, the GIPS standards do not require daily returns. Instead, there are requirements for portfolio returns to be calculated with a minimum specified frequency, de-pending on the ending date of the period for which the return is calculated. Over time the required frequency has increased, to allow for the calculation of more accurate time weighted portfolio returns. For the respective periods, portfolio returns must be calculated with the following frequency:

- Periods ended prior to January 1, 2001, at least quarterly.
- Periods ended from January 1, 2001 to December 31, 2009, at least monthly.
- Periods ended after December 31, 2009, at least monthly and on the date of any large cash flow.

What is a large cash flow? It is a cash flow that is so large that it would cause the monthly time weighted return to be distorted if the portfolio was not revalued during the month at the time of the cash flow. This raises the question: What size of cash flow is big enough to be considered a large cash flow? This is left to the judgment of the investment firm. The firm must define the appropriate threshold for a large cash flow, composite by composite. For example, a cash flow greater than 5% of the value of the portfolio may be considered to be a large cash flow by one firm, but not another firm. What is the appropriate threshold? While the threshold is subjective, it should be set as low as possible in order to avoid distortion of returns due to client-directed cash flows. In practice, the threshold can usually be set higher for lower-volatility strategies. Most fixed income strategies will be less volatile than a strategy implemented using equities.[1]

Beginning January 1, 2010, in addition to considering the frequency of the return calculation, a firm that does not calculate portfolio returns daily must also consider the end date of the monthly period. Common practice today is to calculate monthly returns using the monthly period as determined by business (nonweekend or holiday) days. For example, a return for the month of December would be calculated from the first business day in December through the last business day in December. However, there are some instances where customary practice is to calculate a monthly return through the last Friday of the month. There are also instances where weekly returns are calculated, as opposed to daily or monthly returns. Beginning January 1, 2010, a firm that follows these practices for calculating returns would not meet the requirements of the GIPS standards. Calendar month ends must be used after this date.

---

[1]Note that there is a closely related issue, discussed in Chapter 2, which is temporary exclusion of a portfolio from a composite for a period after a significant cash flow. This concept is different from the large cash flow valuation requirement. Temporary exclusion of portfolios that experience significant cash flows from composites accounts for the fact that it may take time for a manager to fully invest client cash flows or meet significant cash flow withdrawal requests, and the cash flow may be so big that the manager is not able to manage the portfolio according to the intended strategy.

How does a firm perform a valuation on calendar month end, if the calendar month end falls on a weekend? Common practice is to carry prices and exchange rates forward from the last trading day, but to accrue income through the month end.

After determining the frequency of the portfolio-level return calculation, the next step is to determine which method will be used to calculate the portfolio-level returns.

Time vs. Money Weighted Returns

The GIPS standards are concerned with disclosure of the manager's returns, unaffected by the timing of client contributions and withdrawals. So time weighted returns are required by the GIPS standards, with two exceptions:

1. Private Equity portfolio returns must use money weighted returns instead of time weighted returns in order to capture the fact that the manager retains discretion over the timing of cash flows into or out of the portfolio. Closed end real estate funds must use both money weighted and time weighted returns. Private equity and real estate are discussed further in Chapter 7.
2. The money weighted return can be used to estimate the time weighted return as long as the requirements related to the minimum frequency of portfolio-level return calculations are met.

Cash Flow Weighting

If portfolio-level returns are calculated using any method except a daily return method, the formula used to calculate returns will include a process to weight cash flows that occur between valuation dates. Beginning January 1, 2005, the method used to weight cash flows during the period must reflect the actual day of the cash flow. For periods prior to this date, there is no specific requirement as to the weighting of the cash flows. A firm could assume that all cash flows occurred in the middle of the month (the original Dietz method calculation assumed mid-month cash flows). Consider a portfolio that has the values and cash flows for the month of September shown in Table 3.5.

In all cases, the numerator is calculated as $150 ($1,250 − $1,000 − $200 + $100). However, the denominator, or assets at work, can differ depending on the cash flow assumption used. Assuming the calculation is for September 1999, and the original Dietz method is used, the cash flows would be weighted by half, as it is assumed that each cash flow happened on the 15th of the month (see Table 3.6).

TABLE 3.5 Market Values and Cash Flows

Date		Amount
8/31	BMV	1,000
9/3	CF	200
9/28	CF	–100
9/30	EMV	1,250

Note that the total weighted cash flow can be calculated as the sum of the individual cash flows that are each weighted by 50%, or can be calculated by summing all cash flows during the month and weighting the total cash flows by 50%. Using either of these methods to calculate weighted cash flows, the denominator is calculated as $1,050 ($1,000 + $50). This denominator assumes that an investment of $1,050 was used to generate a profit of $150 during the month, which generates a monthly return of 14.29%.

Now let's assume the month is September 2005. At this date a mid-month assumption for cash flows is no longer allowed, therefore a daily weighted cash flow assumption must be used. Weighted cash flows (using an end of day cash flow assumption) are calculated as shown in Table 3.7.

Using the Modified Dietz method, the denominator is calculated as $1,173.33 ($1,000 + $173.33). This denominator assumes that a beginning market value of $1,173.33 was used to generate a profit of $150 during the month, which generates a monthly return of 12.78%.

The daily weighted cash flow method calculates a more accurate return as it reflects the actual time of the cash flows into and out of the portfolio. In this case it more accurately reflects the fact that the $200 was invested in the portfolio for a longer period of time during the month than is assumed by the mid-month formula.

This simple example shows why a daily weighted cash flow assumption is required beginning in 2005, as it generates a more accurate return than would be calculated using a mid-month assumption.

TABLE 3.6 Market Values and Mid-Month Weighted Cash Flows

Date	CF	Weight	WCF
9/3	200	0.50	100
9/28	–100	0.50	–50
Total	100	0.50	50

TABLE 3.7 Market Values and Day Weighted Cash Flows

Date	CF	Weight	Weighting Factor	WCF
9/3	200	(30 − 3)/30	0.90	180
9/28	−100	(30 − 28)/30	0.0667	−6.67
Total	100			173.33

A daily weighted cash flow assumption is required not only for all monthly return calculations, but also for cash flows that occur during a subperiod. Remember that beginning January 1, 2010, portfolios must be valued monthly and at the time of any large cash flow. This requires a firm to calculate subperiod returns within a month when a large cash flow occurs. Any cash flows within the subperiod that are not large enough to cause the portfolio to be revalued must be weighted for the days within the subperiod. Consider the example illustrated in Table 3.8.

During the month of May, the portfolio experiences cash flows on 6/10 and 6/20 that are large enough to cause the portfolio to be revalued. The portfolio also has a cash flow on 6/5 that is not large enough to cause the portfolio to be revalued. When the first subperiod return is calculated for the period from 5/31 to 6/9, the cash flow on 6/5 must be day weighted based on the nine-day period. Assuming a beginning of day cash flow assumption, the first subperiod return is calculated as:

1. Numerator: $1,100 - 1,000 - 40 = 60$
2. WCF: $40 * [(9 - 5 + 1)/9] = 22.22$
3. Denominator: $1,000 + 22.22 = 1,022.22$
4. Subperiod return: $60/1,022.22 = 5.87\%$

TABLE 3.8 Valuations and Cash Flows

Date	Begin of Day Valuation	Large Cash Flows	Other Cash Flows	End of Day Valuation
5/31				1,000
6/5			40	
6/9				1,100
6/10	1,100	200		
6/19				1,200
6/20	1,200	−100		
6/30	1,200			1,200

TABLE 3.9 Portfolio Return Requirements and Allowable Methods under the GIPS Standards over Time

Date	Minimum Frequency	Weighted CF Assumption	Trade Date/ Settlement Date	Portfolio Valuation	Acceptable Methods
Prior to 1/01	Quarterly	None	Trade or settlement	Market value	Original Dietz Modified Dietz Modified Dietz with revaluation for large cash flows Daily
1/01–12/04	Monthly	None	Trade or settlement	Market value	Original Dietz Modified Dietz Modified Dietz with revaluation for large cash flows Daily
1/05–12/09	Monthly	Daily	Trade	Market value	Modified Dietz Modified Dietz with revaluation for large cash flows Daily
1/10 forward	Monthly and for large cash flows	Daily	Trade	Fair value	Modified Dietz with revaluation for large cash flows Daily

Selecting a Portfolio Return Methodology

We have described the various GIPS requirements a firm must consider when determining which method it will use to calculate portfolio-level returns. The return methodology selected must:

- Reflect the proper components (market value, accrued income, etc.).
- Be calculated at least as frequently as required for the respective period.
- Weight cash flows as required for the respective period, if not using a daily calculation.

Table 3.9 summarizes the requirements for portfolio-level input data and return calculations that have changed over time, including the applicable dates of each, and lists methods that would be acceptable for the given period.

We now know that investors need to analyze the performance of a money manager using a time weighted return. It may be hard to look back in time and understand why quarterly periodicity return calculations using a mid-quarter cash flow assumption were a perfectly acceptable method for calculating portfolio returns. Remember that not very long ago computing resources such as disk space were expensive resources that needed to be conserved. Today, most investment firms have the technology available to them to allow for daily returns. But even today the cost of valuation or data auditing sometimes makes quality daily performance calculations too expensive for some firms. And since some firms need to bring historical track records into compliance, knowing the allowable return calculation frequency for each period going back in time is important.

SUMMARY

In this chapter, we outlined the procedures for calculating and interpreting the meaning of single period returns. Periodic portfolio valuation and cash flow figures are transformed into single period returns. Time weighted returns measure the results attributable to the investment manager. Money weighted returns reflect both the performance of the manager and the timing of investor transactions. We then discussed how to calculate portfolio returns that meet the requirements of the GIPS standards.

Rates of return are a description of one facet of investment performance. Performance measurement is also concerned with measuring the risks taken to earn these returns. This topic is taken up in Chapter 5. But before doing that, in the next chapter, we explain how to take portfolio-level returns and aggregate them into composite-level returns.

CHAPTER 4

Composite Return Measurement

The GIPS standards are based on the ethical principles of fair representation and full disclosure. As discussed in Chapter 1, the use of model, hypothetical, or representative portfolio returns for the purposes of marketing performance to a prospect can be misleading. So the GIPS standards require that the performance of each of the firm's strategies be presented using the aggregated or *composite* performance of all of the portfolios managed to the same strategy. Chapter 2 provided detailed guidance on the process of deciding how to group portfolios to represent the firm's strategies. This chapter builds on Chapter 3's portfolio-level return calculation discussion to show how portfolio returns are used to calculate composite returns. Here we demonstrate the methodology for calculating the composite returns over both single and multiple periods.

COMPOSITE CONSTITUENTS

The first step in calculating composite returns is to determine the members of the composite. Composite membership is determined on a period-by-period (usually monthly) basis. As discussed in Chapter 2, a firm must establish a series of rules that determine which portfolios are included in which composites for which periods. A firm will apply these rules to all portfolios managed by the firm and will identify the portfolios that belong to each composite. These portfolios represent the composite's *constituent portfolios.* Because common practice is to calculate composite returns monthly, in this chapter we assume that the composite calculation period is monthly unless stated otherwise. For each composite, the constituent list could change from month to month. Most changes to the composite constituent list from period to period are made because a new portfolio has opened or an existing portfolio has closed. However, for purposes of calculating composite-level returns, the specific reason a portfolio is included in or excluded from a composite

	A	B	C	D	E	F
1	Portfolio	A	B	C	D	E
2	BMV	1,000	2,000	3,000	-	1,000
3	Inflow	-	100	-	400	-
4	Outflow	-	-	100	-	1,200
5	EMV	1,100	2,300	3,300	500	-

FIGURE 4.1   Possible Composite Members

does not matter. All that we need to know is the list of portfolios to be
included in the composite for that month. Once the firm has determined
which portfolios are included in a composite for a specific month, the firm
must then determine how to aggregate the individual portfolio returns into
a single composite-level return.

If the composite return is calculated monthly, only those portfolios that
exist for the entire month are included in the monthly composite calculation.
Any portfolio that opens or closes during the month is not included in the
composite calculation, regardless of the method that is used to calculate
the composite return. For example, Figure 4.1 shows five portfolios that
are managed in the firm's Equity strategy during the month of November.
Portfolios A, B, and C were managed for the full month; portfolios D and E
were not managed for the full month, therefore they are not included in the
composite calculation for this month.

After we determine the constituent portfolios, which in this example are
Portfolios A, B, and C, the next step in calculating a monthly composite return is to gather the required input information. For each portfolio included
in a composite, the firm must have previously determined the portfolio's
monthly time weighted return and beginning of month market value for
each period. (The beginning of month market value is equal to the prior
month's ending market value.) Figure 4.2 contains beginning market value
(BMV) and monthly returns that were calculated using the Modified Dietz
method for the portfolios that are included in the composite for the month.
We use these to demonstrate the composite return calculations.

	A	B	C	D
1	Portfolio	A	B	C
2	BMV	1,000	2,000	3,000
3	Modified Dietz Return	10.000%	9.677%	13.483%

FIGURE 4.2   Equity Composite Membership Data

COMPOSITE RETURNS

Once we determine the composite constituent list for each period, we can calculate the return for the composite. Consistent with the objective of creating performance presentations that are comparable between similar strategies offered by competing investment firms, the GIPS standards require a certain level of uniformity in the methods used to calculate composite returns. The composite return calculation must consider the size of each portfolio relative to the other portfolios in the composite—that is, larger portfolios should have a bigger impact on the composite return than smaller portfolios. The weighting must be done based on the beginning market value, not the ending market value. If the weighting were done based on ending market value then the composite returns would be skewed upward as, all other things held equal, better performing accounts would carry more weight in the return calculation than worse performing accounts.

There are three acceptable methods for determining the single period asset weighted composite return:

1. The beginning assets weighted method.
2. The beginning assets plus weighted cash flow method.
3. The aggregate method.

Beginning Assets Weighted Method

The most commonly used way to calculate single period (typically monthly) composite returns is the *beginning assets weighted method*. Using this method, we weight the individual portfolio returns by the beginning of period market values. One five-step approach to calculating the monthly composite return using this method is:

1. Take the beginning market value of each portfolio in the composite.
2. Sum the balances to compute the composite total beginning market value.
3. Calculate the portfolio weight within the composite by dividing each portfolio's beginning market value by the total composite beginning market value.
4. Multiply the portfolio weight by the portfolio return to calculate a contribution to composite return for each constituent portfolio.
5. Sum the contributions to obtain the composite return.

In Figure 4.3, we calculate the asset weighted return for our Equity Composite, weighting the returns by the beginning assets. The composite

	A	B	C	D	E
1	Portfolio	A	B	C	Composite
2	BMV	1,000	2,000	3,000	6,000
3	Modified Dietz Return	10.000%	9.677%	13.483%	
4	Weight	16.667%	33.333%	50.000%	100%
5	Contribution to Return	1.667%	3.226%	6.742%	11.634%
6		=B4*B3			=SUM(B5:D5)

FIGURE 4.3   Single Period Composite Beginning Assets Weighted Method

return is 11.63%. It was calculated using a weighted average of the three constituent portfolios included in the Equity Composite for the month.

The monthly portfolio returns in our example range from 10.00% to 13.48%, yet the composite return is 11.63%. Does this make sense? We can see that the composite return is impacted the most by Portfolio C, as this portfolio has the highest return and the highest beginning market value of all of the composite constituents. All portfolios contribute to the composite return based only on their beginning of month market value. But is it fair to make the assumption that a static value as of the beginning of the month should dictate how much each portfolio contributes to the composite return? What if a portfolio doubled in size during the month—should such a portfolio have a greater impact on the composite return? What if a portfolio experienced a large withdrawal during the month—should it have less of an impact on the composite return? If a firm wishes to refine the composite calculation to reflect changes in portfolio size during the month, it would use the beginning assets plus weighted cash flow method.

Beginning Assets plus Weighted Cash Flow Method

To better reflect changes in portfolio size during the month, we could use the *beginning assets plus weighted cash flow method*. Using this method, portfolio returns are weighted using the average invested balance instead of beginning market value. The *average invested balance* is the portfolio's beginning market value plus the weighted external cash flows for the period. This method results in a more accurate composite return because it includes the effect of cash flows within the month. For example, a portfolio with a large contribution on the second day of the month will have a larger weight in the composite using the average invested balance than if only the beginning market value was used. To perform this calculation, we must obtain the weighted cash flows for the month as well as the beginning market value and monthly returns. Using the same Equity Composite, we obtain the weighted cash flows for each portfolio and incorporate them into our input data set. To calculate the monthly composite return using this method, follow these six steps:

1. Take the beginning market value and weighted cash flows for each portfolio in the composite.
2. Sum these two amounts to calculate the average invested balance for each portfolio.
3. Sum the balances to compute the composite total average invested balance.
4. Calculate the portfolio weight within the composite by dividing each portfolio's average invested balance by the total composite average invested balance.
5. Multiply the portfolio weight by the portfolio return to calculate a contribution to composite return for each constituent portfolio.
6. Sum the contributions to obtain the composite return.

Figure 4.4 illustrates the calculation of the composite return using the beginning assets plus weighted cash flow method. The return computed using this method, 11.60%, is slightly lower than the return calculated using the previous method. The reason for this is that Portfolio B, which had the lowest return during the period, had an increased weighting after taking cash flows into account.

	A	B	C	D	E	F
1	Portfolio	A	B	C	Composite	
2	BMV	1,000	2,000	3,000	6,000	=SUM(B2:D2)
3	Cash Flow	-	100	(100)	-	
4	Weighted Cash Flow	-	66.67	(33.33)	33.34	=SUM(B4:D4)
5	EMV	1,100	2,300.00	3,300.00	6,700.00	=SUM(B5:D5)
6	Dollar Value Added	100	200	400	700.00	=SUM(B6:D6)
7	Average Invested Balance	1,000.00	2,066.67	2,966.67	6,033.34	=E2+E4
8	Modified Dietz Return	10.000%	9.677%	13.483%	11.602%	=E6/E7
9						
10	Weight	16.575%	34.254%	49.171%	100%	=SUM(B10:D10)
11	Contribution to Return	1.657%	3.315%	6.630%	11.602%	=SUM(B11:D11)

FIGURE 4.4 Single Period Composite Beginning Assets plus Weighted Cash Flow Method

Aggregate Method

Using the *aggregate method*, all of the market values and cash flows from the underlying portfolios are combined and treated as if they were the market value of and cash flows for a single portfolio. The return calculation is performed using a portfolio-level return methodology that meets the requirements of the GIPS standards, as discussed in Chapter 3. Once the market values and cash flows are aggregated, then the calculation procedure is the same as that for a single portfolio.

Cell E8 of Figure 4.4 illustrates the aggregate return method, which in this case also results in an 11.60% return. To calculate the return, we first aggregated all of the market values and cash flows for each of the portfolios in the composite. Then, because Modified Dietz is the method used to calculate the portfolio-level returns, we calculate a Modified Dietz return using the methodology described in Chapter 3.

Just like the beginning assets plus weighted cash flow method, the aggregate method creates a size weighted return because the market values (and cash flows) of the smaller portfolios will have a lesser impact on the total composite return than those of the larger portfolios. Although this is a perfectly acceptable composite return calculation methodology, the large amount of input data required makes the aggregate method impractical for many firms to use.

Equal Weighted Method

The GIPS standards require that the composite returns presented to investors are market value or *asset* weighted. We have reviewed three composite calculation methods meeting this requirement. Firms may also wish to calculate composite returns that *equally* weight portfolios. In an equal weighted composite return, the size of the individual portfolios is not considered. As shown in the calculation in Figure 4.5, the equal weighted return is 11.05%. This return is lower than all of the assets weighted method returns because Portfolio C, which is both the largest and the highest performing portfolio in the composite, contributes equally to the composite return using this method.

	A	B	C	D	E	F
1	Portfolio	A	B	C	Composite	
2	BMV	1,000	2,000	3,000	6,000	
3	Modified Dietz Return	10.000%	9.677%	13.483%	11.053%	=AVERAGE(B3:D3)

FIGURE 4.5   Equal Weighted Method

SINGLE PERIOD COMPOSITE RETURN CONSIDERATIONS

The previous section showed the acceptable methods for calculating the single period composite return. Here we discuss several concerns related to calculating the periodic (usually monthly) composite returns. After this discussion, we will turn to the last section, which discusses the methodology for taking the single period returns as inputs to calculating annual and other multi-period returns.

Composite Return Frequency

So far in this chapter, we have assumed that the composite return is calculated monthly using monthly portfolio-level returns. However, depending on the date for which the composite return is calculated, a firm may calculate composite-level returns with a different frequency. Until the 2005 edition of the GIPS standards, no composite calculation frequency was specified. Table 4.1 summarizes the required frequency for the respective periods.

Although no period was specified for periods prior to January 1, 2006, common practice was to calculate composite-level returns either monthly or quarterly.

To calculate a quarterly period composite return using monthly portfolio-level returns, we would first calculate quarterly portfolio-level returns by linking monthly portfolio-level returns. Then, we'd weight these quarterly portfolio-level returns using one of the methods described above. If either of the methods that utilize cash flows is used for determining each portfolio's contribution, then the length of the period for determining the portfolio average invested balance or day weighted cash flows would be a quarter, instead of a month. Figure 4.6 provides a quarterly composite return example, where the return is calculated using the beginning assets weighted method.

TABLE 4.1 GIPS Composite Return Frequency Rules

Period	Composite Calculation Frequency
Through December 31, 2005	None specified
January 1, 2006 through December 31, 2009	At least quarterly
After December 31, 2009	At least monthly

	A	B	C	D	E	F	
1	Portfolio	A	B	C	Composite		
2	12/31 Market Value	1,200	2,600	3,500	7,300	=SUM(B2:D2)	
3	January Return	2.24%	2.75%	2.69%			
4	February Return	1.64%	1.62%	1.58%			
5	March Return	0.89%	1.01%	0.94%	={PRODUCT(D3:D5+1)-1}		
6	Q1 Return	4.84%	5.47%	5.29%			
7	Weight (Quarterly BMV)	16.44%	35.62%	47.95%			
8	Contribution (Quarterly	0.80%	1.95%	2.54%	5.28%	=SUM(B8:D8)	
9		=B6*B7	=C6*C7	=D6*D7			

FIGURE 4.6 Quarterly Frequency Composite Return

The firm could also calculate a daily composite return, and then link these returns to form the monthly composite return. First, each daily composite return is calculated, and then the daily composite returns are linked together. Each day's beginning of day market value (or beginning of day market value plus weighted cash flows) is used to weight the daily portfolio returns. A firm could also use the aggregate method on a daily basis.

Gross- and Net-of-Fee Returns

The GIPS standards generally provide investment management firms with the flexibility to present composite returns that are either gross of or net of management fees. A firm may also choose to present both. The GIPS standards recommend that gross returns be presented, as gross returns are more comparable between firms than net returns. But because of regulatory requirements, common practice in the United States is to include both gross and net returns in a compliant presentation.

There are two ways to compute a net-of-fee composite return for GIPS purposes:

1. Use actual management fees paid by or accrued for the composite's constituent portfolios.
2. Apply a model fee to either the gross composite return or the constituent portfolio returns.

Using the first method, we simply replace the gross-of-fees portfolio-level returns with the net-of-fees portfolio-level returns in the composite calculation. Then, we calculate the composite returns using one of the three methods described previously in this chapter.

	A	B	C
1	Annual Fee Percentage	1.00000	
2	Annual Growth Rate	1.01000	=1+(B1/100)
3	Monthly Growth Rate	1.00083	=B2^(1/12)
4	Monthly Fee Percentage	0.08295	=(B3–1)*100

FIGURE 4.7 Converting an Annual Fee to a Monthly Equivalent

The second method is simpler and more commonly used. Instead of performing the composite calculation using portfolio-level net-of-fee returns, the starting point for a model fee composite calculation is the composite-level gross-of-fee return. Then a model fee, in percentage terms, is subtracted from the gross-of-fee composite return. When using a model fee, the GIPS standards permit firms to use the highest investment management fee that is incurred by any portfolio in the composite as the model fee. Common practice is for the model fee to be the top tier of the applicable fee schedule for the composite's strategy.

How is a net-of-fee composite return calculated using this method? Let's assume a composite's model fee, on an annual basis, is 1.00%. Let's also assume that the firm wishes to calculate composite net-of-fee returns monthly. The firm will deduct a monthly equivalent of the annual management fee, or 0.08295%, from the composite monthly gross return expressed in percentage terms. Figure 4.7 shows one method for converting a fee expressed as an annual percentage into a monthly equivalent that can be subtracted from the monthly gross-of-fees composite return to form the monthly composite net-of-fees return.

Note the implicit assumption in this calculation: that the monthly equivalent model fee percentage *should* compound to equal the annual model fee. In some cases, the annual fee will instead be divided by 12 (in this case, 0.08333%). If so, this monthly model fee would not compound to equal the annual fee. We can see that the difference between the two methods is quite small, and both methods are used in practice. Each firm must decide for itself which method will be used to calculate the model fee used in the composite calculation.

A firm could also choose to do the calculation quarterly. In this instance the firm would instead deduct 0.2491% (or 0.25% if a simple one-fourth of the annual fee is used) from the composite gross quarterly return. This would be appropriate if the fee is calculated and assessed quarterly. However, if the firm does the calculation quarterly, for two months in each quarter the monthly gross and net composite returns will be the same.

This same approach can be taken using portfolio-level returns instead. The model fee would be applied to each portfolio in the composite, and the net composite return would then be calculated using the model portfolio-level net returns for the period.

Investment management fees can and do change over time. If the firm determines that the model fee should change, the firm should reflect the new fee schedule in the composite-level net return calculation on a prospective basis. The firm should not recast historical net returns using the new model fee. In this case, a firm should consider disclosing the change in the model fee used to calculate composite-level net returns.

The calculation of the net-of-fee return is usually straightforward, but determining the fee percentage to apply can sometimes be difficult. Portfolios within the composite may pay a wide range of fees, including performance-based fees, and the fees may be calculated and assessed differently. A firm must determine, for each composite, the appropriate model fee for the composite.

MULTI-PERIOD COMPOSITE RETURNS

After computing periodic composite returns, a firm will then be able to calculate annual composite returns, as required by the GIPS standards. The GIPS standards require that the investment firm present annual returns to a prospective investor. Assuming composite returns are calculated monthly, the annual rates of return are computed by geometrically linking the twelve monthly returns. In a GIPS presentation, we can also present returns for other periods of interest to the prospect, for example three- and five-year returns. Compound returns for periods greater than a year are often restated to an annual average basis. The methodology for compounding and annualizing returns is covered in this section.

Cumulative Returns

We saw the compounding process at work in Chapter 3 when we employed subperiod returns in the chain linking process to create a multi-period time weighted return. To compound the returns, we multiply 1 + Decimal return for each period or subperiod as follows:

Cumulative return

$$= [(1 + \text{Decimal return}_1) * (1 + \text{Decimal return}_2) \ldots - 1] * 100$$

A GIPS-compliant presentation will show the prospect annual returns, each calculated by compounding the periodic composite returns. Again

	A	B	C	D	E	F
1	Month	Monthly		Quarterly		
2		Return	Growth Rate	Return	Growth Rate	
3	January	9.00%	1.0900	=1+B4		
4	February	6.00%	1.0600			
5	March	-2.00%	0.9800	13.23%	1.1323	
6	April	8.00%	1.0800			
7	May	-4.00%	0.9600			
8	June	8.00%	1.0800	11.97%	1.1197	
9	July	0.10%	1.0010			
10	August	1.00%	1.0100			
11	September	-5.00%	0.9500	-3.95%	0.9605	
12	October	2.00%	1.0200			
13	November	4.00%	1.0400			
14	December	7.00%	1.0700	13.51%	1.1351	
15						
16	Annual Return (using Monthly Returns)			38.22%	={PRODUCT(B3:B14+1)-1}	
17	Annual Return (using Monthly Growth Rates)			38.22%	=PRODUCT(C3:C14)-1	
18	Annual Return (using Quarterly Growth Rates)			38.22%	=PRODUCT(E3:E14)-1	

FIGURE 4.8 Cumulative Returns

assuming that composite returns are calculated monthly, we can calculate quarterly and annual composite returns by linking the monthly returns, as in Figure 4.8.

Notice that we can link both the monthly and quarterly growth rates to determine the annual returns. In this same way, we can derive cumulative returns for periods greater than a year, such as five-year and since-inception returns.

Also, notice that Excel provides a tool called *array formulas* that can be used to calculate a multi-period return in a single cell. Cell E16 in Figure 4.8 shows how to use array formulas. To enter the formula, select the range of returns in the normal way, add the +1)-1, and then press the CTRL, SHIFT, and ENTER keys at the same time. Excel will automatically add the braces.

Figure 4.9 shows the calculation of a cumulative five-year return given the series of yearly returns of 9%, 6%, –2%, 8%, and –4%.

By compounding the five yearly returns we find that the cumulative five-year return is 17.4%. In other words, if $1 was invested at the beginning of the five-year period and remained in the investment for the five years, that $1 investment would be worth $1.17 at the end of the five-year period.

Since we are often interested in the performance of an investment over time, we can use cumulative growth rates. Cumulative growth rates are

▲	A	B	C	D	E	F	G
1				**Growth Rates**			
2	Year	Return	Single Period	Compounded	Cumulative Return		
3	1	0.09	1.09	1.0900000	9.000	=(((1+0.06)*(1+0.09))-1)*100	
4	2	0.06	1.06	1.1554000	15.540		
5	3	-0.02	0.98	1.1322920	13.229		
6	4	0.08	1.08	1.2228754	22.288		
7	5	-0.04	0.96	1.1739603	17.396		
8				=PRODUCT(C3:C7)	=(D7-1)*100		

FIGURE 4.9   Cumulative Returns

useful for quickly calculating the cumulative return over multiple periods because we do not need to reference the intermediate returns or growth rates. Cumulative growth rates are calculated by taking the previous period-ending cumulative growth rate and multiplying by 1 + Current period return. We can use cumulative growth rates to calculate the expected value of an investment by multiplying it by the cumulative growth factor. For example, $100 invested into a portfolio with a compound five-year growth rate of 1.174 will result in an ending value of $117.40:

$$\$100 * 1.174 = \$117.40$$

We calculate cumulative returns when we are interested in the performance of investments over long-term time periods. Note that cumulative returns incorporate the assumption that investment gains are reinvested into the portfolio and compounded over time. The appreciation (or depreciation) at the end of each period, as measured by the return, is treated as if it is income that is reinvested into the portfolio in the next period.

Growth rates can also be used to derive the return between any two dates, as shown in this equation:

$$\text{Return} = \left[\left(\frac{\text{End period growth rate}}{\text{Begin period growth rate}} \right) - 1 \right] * 100$$

For example, the return from the end of year 3 to the end of year 5 = 3.68% [((1.1739/1.1323) − 1) * 100].

Cumulative Net Returns

While reviewing the cumulative returns, a firm may encounter situations where the difference between the annual gross and net returns does not *seem* to be correct. For example, in Figure 4.10, we calculate gross and

	A	B	C	D	E
1		Annual Fee	1.000%		
2		Annual Growth Rate	1.01000	=1+C1	
3		Monthly Growth Rate	1.0008295	=C2^(1/12)	
4		Monthly Fee	0.08295%	=(C3-1)	
5					
6	Month	Gross Return	Monthized Fee	Net Return	
7	1	2.0000%	0.08295%	1.91705%	
8	2	4.0000%	0.08295%	3.91705%	
9	3	3.0000%	0.08295%	2.91705%	
10	4	7.0000%	0.08295%	6.91705%	
11	5	0.0000%	0.08295%	-0.08295%	
12	6	3.0000%	0.08295%	2.91705%	
13	7	9.0000%	0.08295%	8.91705%	
14	8	8.0000%	0.08295%	7.91705%	
15	9	-6.0000%	0.08295%	-6.08295%	
16	10	9.0000%	0.08295%	8.91705%	
17	11	1.0000%	0.08295%	0.91705%	
18	12	1.0000%	0.08295%	0.91705%	
19					
20	Annual	48.1628%	1.0000%	46.74051%	1.422%
21		={PRODUCT(B7:B18+1)-1}	={PRODUCT(C7:C18+1)-1}	={PRODUCT(D7:D18+1)-1}	=B20-D20

FIGURE 4.10 Compounding Gross and Net Returns

net returns, where the monthly net returns are determined by subtracting a model fee from the composite gross return. The model fee was determined by "monthizing" a fee expressed as an annual percentage equal to 1%. The cumulative net return equals the compounded monthly net returns.

We might expect that doing this calculation in this manner would result in a 1% difference between the composite's annual gross and net returns. However, this is rarely the case. The annual impact of the model fee is affected by two forces: the volatility of returns over the period and the effect of compounding the monthly fee. While care needs to be taken to ensure the returns are calculated properly, the difference between the multi-period gross and net returns does not need to equal the fee expressed in annual terms. In Figure 4.10, we see that an annual fee of 1% results in an annual difference of 1.422%.

Averaging Returns over Time

Often, we are interested in calculating average, or mean, investment returns. Average returns can be used to compare the performance of investment managers or portfolios over time. There are two methods for calculating the average of a series of returns: the arithmetic and geometric methods. As a measure of the average return, a mean return can be calculated by adding the periodic returns together and dividing by the number of returns. This *arithmetic mean return* cannot be used in all applications. For example, we may want to use an average yearly return to project the future value of an investment. One problem with using arithmetic mean returns is that they do not take into account the compounding of returns over time. For example, suppose we have two yearly returns, 9% and 6%. The arithmetic mean return is 7.5% [(9 + 6)/2]. The compound 2-year return is 15.54%:

$$[(1.09) * (1.06) - 1] * 100 = 15.54\%$$

If we take the arithmetic mean return and plug it into the compounding formula we will get a higher result than we did using the actual periodic returns:

$$[(1.075) * (1.075) - 1] * 100 = 15.56\%$$

Use of the arithmetic mean return to reconcile the beginning to ending investment value overstates the ending value. The average return we use when using returns to reconcile market values should be lower than the arithmetic mean return in order to account for the compounding process.

When we multiply the average yearly return by the total number of years, it does not equal the compounded return because it does not take into account the income earned by reinvesting the prior period earnings. In the previous example, the 6% return in Year 2 was earned, in part, by reinvesting the 9% Year 1 return, but that is not accounted for in the arithmetic average. To fix this, instead of taking the arithmetic mean return we calculate the geometric mean return. The *geometric mean return* is the *n*th root of the cumulative return, where n = the number of periods used to calculate the cumulative return. Finding the root is the inverse of multiplying the growth rates.

$$\text{Geometric mean return} = \left[\left(\sqrt[N]{(1 + \text{Cumulative return})} \right) - 1 \right] * 100$$

Figure 4.11 shows that the geometric average yearly return derived from a two-year compound return of 15.54% equals 7.4895%.

	A	B	C	D
1	Year	1	2	
2	Return	9.000%	6.000%	
3	Single Period Growth Rate	1.090	1.060	=1+C2
4	Compound Growth Rate	1.090	1.155	=PRODUCT(B3:C3)
5	Cumulative Return	9.000%	15.540%	=C4-1
6				
7	Arithmetic Yearly Average Return		7.500%	=AVERAGE(B2:C2)
8	Geometric Yearly Average Return		7.4895	=((C4^(1/2))-1)*100

FIGURE 4.11   Geometric Mean Return

Plugging the geometric mean return into the compound growth formula yields the compound return for the period:

$$\text{Compound return} = \left[(1 + (\text{Geometric mean return}/100))^N - 1\right] * 100$$

We can back into the 15.54% compound return for two years using the geometric average return of 7.4895%:

$$[(1.074895 * 1.074895) - 1] * 100 = 15.54\%$$

Column C in Figure 4.11 shows that one advantage of using geometric average returns is that we do not need to know the actual periodic returns in order to calculate a future value.

Annualizing Returns

Returns are typically presented on a yearly or *annual basis*. We do this because it is easier to compare investment returns if the time periods over which each investment has been made are expressed in equivalent terms. The geometric mean return when calculated for a one-year period is called an average annual return, compound annual return, or *annualized return*. If the multi-period compound return that we are annualizing is calculated for

	A	B	C	D	E
1	Year	1	2	2-Year	
2	Actual Return	9.000%	6.000%	15.54%	=(1+B2)*(1+C2)-1
3	Geometric Average Return	7.4895	7.4895	15.54	=((1+B3/100)*(1+C3/100)-1)*100

FIGURE 4.12   Using the Geometric Average Return

a period greater than one year, the rate is restated to an annual basis using the inverse of the compounding formula. The inverse of taking a number and raising it to a power n is to take the nth root of the number:

$$\left[\left(\sqrt[\text{\# of years}]{(1 + \text{Periodic rate})}\right) - 1\right] * 100$$

An investment that earned 19.1% over a three-year period can be quoted as an annual average return of 6% by finding the 3rd root of the cumulative growth rate:

$$(\sqrt[3]{1.19102}) * 100 = 6.00$$

Notice that we calculate the annualized return by first taking the root of the cumulative growth rate (1.19102) as opposed to taking the nth root of the cumulative return. The nth root of the growth rate is the geometric average growth rate. To transform the average growth rate into a geometric average return we subtract 1 and multiply by 100.

We often need to calculate an annualized return for cumulative periods that are not exact multiples of a year. To calculate annualized returns for such odd periods, we can calculate the actual number of calendar days in the cumulative period and divide by 365 to calculate an annualized equivalent:

$$\text{Annualized return} = \left[\left(\sqrt[\frac{\text{Number of days}}{365}]{\text{Linked growth rates}}\right) - 1\right] * 100$$

	A	B	C
1	Cumulative Percent Return	14.00000	
2	Cumulative Growth Rate	1.14000	=1+(B1/100)
3	End Date	4/30/2016	
4	Start Date	12/31/2014	
5	Number of Days	486.00000	=B3-B4
6	Days in a Year	365.00000	
7	Multiples of a Year	1.33151	=B5/B6
8	Annualized Growth Rate	1.10341	=B2^(1/B7)
9	Annualized Percent Return	10.34107	=(B8-1)*100

FIGURE 4.13   Geometric Average Return for Odd Period

	A	B	C
1	Cumulative Percent Return	14.00000	
2	Cumulative Growth Rate	1.14000	=1+(B1/100)
3	End Date	4/30/2016	
4	Start Date	12/31/2014	
5	Number of Days	486.00000	=B3-B4
6	Days in a Year	365.25000	
7	Multiples of a Year	1.33060	=B5/B6
8	Annualized Growth Rate	1.10349	=B2^(1/B7)
9	Annualized Percent Return	10.34851	=(B8-1)*100

FIGURE 4.14 Geometric Average Return for a Leap Year Period

For example, Figure 4.13 shows the annualized equivalent of a 14% return earned over 16 months equals 10.36%.

If the period crossed over a leap year, then we would use 365.25 days to annualize the return, as in Figure 4.14.

$$\text{Annualized return} = \left[\left(\sqrt[\frac{\text{Number of days}}{365.25}]{\text{Linked growth rates}} \right) - 1 \right] * 100$$

SUMMARY

In this chapter we outlined the procedures for creating periodic composite returns using the composite constituents (the portfolios that belong to a composite for each period), the returns, and the market value data for the constituent portfolios. The periodic composite returns for each period are then linked together to form the annual composite returns that must be included in a GIPS-compliant presentation. Composite returns for greater than a year can be presented, and these returns and the associated benchmark returns are often presented on an annual average basis.

Composite returns are arguably the most important statistics used by prospective clients to evaluate the past performance of an investment manager. In the next chapter, we will make use of the composite returns to create descriptive statistics about the composite and also to estimate the risk taken to earn the composite return.

CHAPTER 5

Dispersion and Risk Measurement

In the previous two chapters, we learned how to calculate portfolio returns and then combine the returns in a composite that represents the performance of an investment strategy. These returns quantify the performance record that will be marketed to prospective investors. But, was the composite return representative of the return actually realized by the average client who invested with the manager? What risks were taken in order to earn these returns? How did these risks compare to those taken by competing managers offering similar strategies? To help prospective investors answer these questions, the GIPS standards mandate that investment managers provide prospective investors with quantitative measures of composite dispersion and risk. These are the subjects taken up in this chapter.

INTERNAL DISPERSION

The GIPS standards require the reporting of an internal dispersion statistic together with the annual composite returns. As will be discussed in more detail in Chapter 6, the required statistic is calculated using as inputs the annual returns of only those portfolios that are included in the composite for the full annual period. A portfolio that participates in the composite for only a portion of the annual period is not considered in the internal dispersion calculation.

A firm must determine which internal dispersion statistic to include in compliant presentations. There are two types of dispersion statistics, equal weighted and asset weighted. *Equal weighted dispersion statistics* are indications of the variability in returns experienced by the portfolios within the composite. The most commonly presented measure of equal weighted dispersion is the standard deviation of portfolio returns. Alternatively, a firm can present asset weighted dispersion statistics. *Asset weighted dispersion statistics* illustrate the dispersion of returns for the average dollar invested in the composite. For example, if a composite had one very large portfolio and nine smaller portfolios, the asset weighted composite dispersion statistics would not be greatly influenced by the performance of the smaller accounts. Small and large portfolios have an equal influence on equal weighted statistics.

Regardless of which internal dispersion measure is selected, the firm must perform these two steps for each annual period:

1. Review the composite's constituents and determine which portfolios were included in the composite for the full year. Assuming a firm presents annual composite returns on a calendar-year basis, the firm will identify all portfolios that were included in the composite for every month from January through December.
2. For each portfolio included in the composite for the full year, calculate the annual portfolio-level return by linking the periodic returns. Assuming a firm calculates composite returns monthly, the firm will link the 12 monthly portfolio returns to determine the annual portfolio-level returns.

We will use the sample data provided in Table 5.1 to illustrate our explanation of the different internal dispersion measures. This example shows the annual returns for only those portfolios included in the composite for the entire year. (An intentionally wide range of returns is used here in order to illustrate the dispersion calculations.)

TABLE 5.1 Annual Portfolio-Level Returns for Sample Composite

Portfolio	Annual Return
A	10.00%
B	9.68%
C	13.48%
D	8.00%
E	10.00%
F	12.00%

EQUAL WEIGHTED DISPERSION

We can calculate dispersion statistics using each portfolio's return on an equal weighted basis. The equal weighted statistics measure the dispersion of performance around the average portfolio return. We measure equal weighted dispersion using standard descriptive statistics including:

- The equal weighted standard deviation of returns.
- The high, low, and range of returns.
- The first-quartile, median, and third-quartile returns.

The following subsections describe these statistics.

Equal Weighted Standard Deviation

Standard deviation is a measure of how widely the actual returns were dispersed from the average return. As illustrated in Figure 5.1, we can use the standard deviation together with the mean (assuming the returns are normally distributed, as well as making other statistical assumptions) to describe the distribution of the returns:

- About 68% of the observed returns will be within one standard deviation above or below the mean return.

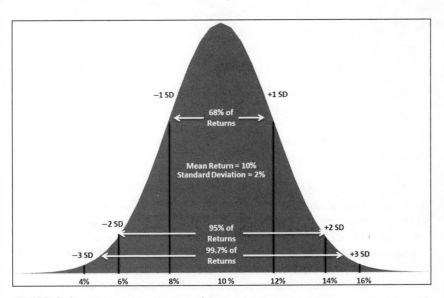

FIGURE 5.1 Normal Distribution of Returns

- About 95% of the returns will be within two standard deviations.
- Almost all of the returns will be within three standard deviations.

Figure 5.1 illustrates the use of mean and standard deviation where we'd expect that approximately 68% of the returns would fall between 8% and 12%, if we assume that the returns are normally distributed and we had a mean return equal to 10% and a standard deviation of 2%.

To calculate the standard deviation of annual portfolio returns follow these seven steps:

1. Gather the annual returns for portfolios that were members of the composite for the full year.
2. Calculate the arithmetic mean of the annual returns.
3. Calculate the difference between each portfolio return and the arithmetic mean of the portfolio returns.
4. Square the difference between each portfolio return and the arithmetic mean of the portfolio returns.
5. Sum the squared differences.
6. Divide the sum of the squared differences by the number of returns.
7. Take the square root of the result.

$$\text{Standard deviation} = \sqrt{\frac{\sum (RP_i - \overline{RP})^2}{N}}$$

where RP_i = individual return observations
$\overline{RP}$ = mean portfolio return
N = number of portfolio returns used

Figure 5.2 illustrates the calculation of equal weighted standard deviation for our sample composite.

With an average return of 10.53% and an equal weighted standard deviation of 1.76%, by adding and subtracting the standard deviation from the mean, we would expect the annual returns for approximately two-thirds of the portfolios invested in the strategy to fall between 8.77% and 12.29%.

Here we used the sample versus the population version of the standard deviation formula. Dividing by N gives the average when we are calculating statistics for the entire *population* of returns we want to describe. When we are using statistics such as the standard deviation to identify the characteristics of a complete data set, we use the population version of these statistics. Sometimes we calculate the statistics using a part of the population, or a *sample* set of returns. When we calculate risk statistics using a sample, but intend to use the statistics to make judgments about the entire population,

	A	B	C	D
1	**Portfolio**	**Annual Return**	**Difference to Average Return**	**Squared Difference to Average Return**
2	A	10.00%	(0.53)	0.2774
3	B	9.68%	(0.85)	0.7168
4	C	13.48%	2.95	8.7222
5	D	8.00%	(2.53)	6.3840
6	E	10.00%	(0.53)	0.2774
7	F	12.00%	1.47	2.1707
8			=(B7-C10)*100	=C7^2
9				
10	**Arithmetic Mean**		10.53%	=AVERAGE(B2:B7)
11	**Count of Portfolios**		6	=COUNT(B2:B7)
12	**Sum of Squared Differences**		18.55	=SUM(D2:D7)
13	**Standard Deviation**		1.76	=SQRT(C12/C11)

FIGURE 5.2 Equal Weighted Standard Deviation for Sample Composite

we divide by $N - 1$ instead of N. If we were to recalculate the examples in this chapter dividing by $N - 1$ instead of N we *would* get meaningfully different results. This is because we chose to use only a few observations in order to demonstrate the calculation of each measure. If we were to take statistics calculated using two different sources and then use them in a comparison, it would be useful to know whether the population or sample method was used. In practice, both the population and sample versions of the formula are acceptable for GIPS-required calculation purposes.

We can use Excel to calculate equal weighted standard deviation. Using Excel, the function stdevp() is used to calculate the population standard deviation and stdev() for the sample standard deviation.

The firm is free to choose whether gross- or net-of-fee returns are used to calculate the standard deviation. Common practice is to use gross-of-fee returns. Although not required, disclosing which returns are used in this calculation is also common practice.

Other Measures of Equal Weighted Dispersion

The standard deviation is by far the most commonly reported measure of internal dispersion for GIPS purposes. But firms can choose to present other internal dispersion measures based on equal weighted annual portfolio returns. Table 5.2 describes some alternatives, and Figure 5.3 shows the

TABLE 5.2 Equal Weighted Internal Dispersion Measures

Statistic	Description
High and Low Returns	The best and worst annual portfolio returns. Both the high and low annual return must be presented.
Range of Returns	The difference between the best and worst annual portfolio returns.
Median and Quartile Returns	If reported together, the median and quartile returns provide a further breakdown of dispersion. The *Median Return* is the "middle" return in an ordered list of the returns. If there is an even number of returns, the median equals the average between the two middle returns.
	The *First Quartile Return* is the midpoint between the highest return and the median return. Depending on the number of returns, the quartile return will be interpolated. Note that in investments the "first quartile" usually denotes the point where the top 25% of returns would lie. But the Excel quartile() function uses the reverse convention where the third quartile is the best quartile.
	The *Third Quartile Return* is the midpoint between the median return and the lowest return. Depending on the number of returns, the quartile return will be interpolated. Note that in investments the "third quartile" usually denotes the point where the bottom 25% of returns would lie. But the Excel quartile() function uses the reverse convention where the first quartile is the worst quartile.

calculation of these statistics for our sample composite. While these statistics are not commonly included as the required internal dispersion measure in GIPS presentations, they are good descriptive statistics summarizing the distribution of portfolio returns.

ASSET WEIGHTED DISPERSION

The internal dispersion measures described in the previous section do not reflect the relative size of the portfolios within the composite. This is because

	A	B	C	D	E
1	**Portfolio**	**Annual Return**	**Descriptive Statistics**		
2	A	10.00%	High Return	13.48%	=MAX(B2:B7)
3	B	9.68%	Low Return	8.00%	=MIN(B2:B7)
4	C	13.48%	Range of Returns	5.48%	=D2-D3
5	D	8.00%			
6	E	10.00%	First Quartile Return	11.50%	=QUARTILE(B2:B7,3)
7	F	12.00%	Median Return	10.00%	=MEDIAN(B2:B7)
8			Third Quartile Return	9.76%	=QUARTILE(B2:B7,1)
9	**Average Return**	10.53%			

FIGURE 5.3 Sample Composite Descriptive Statistics

they treat each portfolio the same, even if, for example, there was one very large portfolio and many smaller portfolios in the composite. Considering the size of each portfolio may be useful when measuring the dispersion of returns. The asset weighted standard deviation and quartile dollar dispersion statistics do this, and they are described next.

Asset Weighted Standard Deviation

We can calculate an asset weighted standard deviation that reflects the size of each portfolio. We do this by asset weighting the deviations from the mean return. The formula for calculating the asset weighted standard deviation is as follows:

$$\text{Asset weighted standard deviation} = \sqrt{\sum W_i \left(RP_i - \left(\sum W_i RP_i \right) \right)^2}$$

where W_i are the individual portfolio constituent weights and RP_i are the individual portfolio returns. To calculate the asset weighted standard deviation of portfolio returns:

1. Gather the annual returns and beginning market values for portfolios that were members of the composite for the full year.
2. Calculate an annual asset weighted mean, using only those portfolios that were members of the composite for the full year.
3. Calculate the difference between each portfolio return and the annual asset weighted mean.
4. Square the difference between each portfolio return and the annual asset weighted mean.

	A	B	C	D	E	F	G	H
1	Portfolio	BMV	Annual Return	Weight (BMV)	Contribution (BMV)	Difference to Average Return	Squared Difference	Weighted Squared Difference
2	A	1,000	10.00%	10.00%	1.00%	(0.58)	0.3364	0.0336
3	B	2,000	9.68%	20.00%	1.94%	(0.90)	0.8100	0.1620
4	C	3,000	13.48%	30.00%	4.04%	2.90	8.4100	2.5230
5	D	2,500	8.00%	25.00%	2.00%	(2.58)	6.6564	1.6641
6	E	1,000	10.00%	10.00%	1.00%	(0.58)	0.3364	0.0336
7	F	500	12.00%	5.00%	0.60%	1.42	2.0164	0.1008
8				=B7/B9	=D7*C7	=(C7-E9)*100	=F7^2	=D7*G7
9	Asset Weighted Mean	10,000		100.00%	10.58%			4.517
10								
11			Arithmetic Mean	10.53%	=AVERAGE(C2:C7)			
12			Count of Portfolios	6	=COUNT(C2:C7)			
13		Sum of Squared Differences		18.566	=SUM(G2:G7)			
14		Equal Weighted Standard Deviation		1.76	=SQRT(D13/D12)			
15		Asset Weighted Standard Deviation		2.13	=SQRT(H9)			

FIGURE 5.4 Asset Weighted Standard Deviation for Sample Composite

5. Multiply the squared differences by the weight of the portfolio in the composite.
6. Sum the weighted squared differences.
7. Take the square root of the result.

Figure 5.4 illustrates the calculation of the asset weighted standard deviation for the sample composite.

The asset weighted standard deviation is 2.13%. Because this standard deviation is asset weighted, larger portfolios contribute more to this variability measure than smaller portfolios. For example, Portfolio C has the best return, 13.48%, the return furthest from the average or arithmetic mean return, and is a large portfolio that represents 30% of the assets that are included in the calculation. The effect of Portfolio C's return is increased because the squared return deviation is weighted by the portfolio's asset size. The higher the asset weighted standard deviation, the more variability there was in the return to the average *dollar* (as opposed to the average *portfolio*) invested in the strategy. With a composite proxy return of 10.58% and an asset weighted standard deviation of 2.13%, by adding and subtracting the standard deviation from the asset weighted mean, we would expect the annual returns for approximately two-thirds of the dollars invested in the strategy to fall between 8.45% and 12.71%.

Note that the actual annual return of the composite is not a component of this calculation. The asset weighted mean is a *proxy* composite return, using only those portfolios included in the composite for the full year.

Figure 5.4 showed how to calculate the asset weighted standard deviation for the year, and each portfolio's contribution to the standard deviation calculation used the beginning of period weight. Using the beginning-of-year market value as each portfolio's weight does make an assumption that each portfolio's relative market value stays consistent throughout the year. We could instead choose to calculate each portfolio's average invested balance during the year, and weight cash flows based on the date of the cash flow during the year. However, this work is usually not worth the effort, so most firms that choose to report an asset weighted standard deviation weight portfolios by the beginning-of-year market values.

Quartile Dollar Dispersion

In addition to the asset weighted standard deviation, we can further describe the asset weighted distribution of returns by calculating asset weighted first and third quartile returns. While not commonly used in GIPS-compliant presentations, *quartile dollar dispersion* (QDD) is the rate of return for the best and worst performing 25% of dollars invested in the composite during the period. The return of the best performing 25% of dollars is sometimes called quartile dollar dispersion 1, or QDD1. The return of the worst performing 25% of dollars is quartile dollar dispersion 4, or QDD4. To calculate the Best QDD, we:

1. Select the portfolios that were in the composite for the whole year.
2. Order the annual portfolio returns from high to low.
3. Calculate a quarter of the composite market value using either beginning market value or the average invested balance. (While beginning market value would be easier in practice for the reasons discussed in the previous section, for purposes of illustrating the calculation we will use average invested balance here.)
4. Starting with the best performing portfolio:
   a. Accumulate the market values for each portfolio up to the quarterly value from step 3.
   b. Weight the portfolio returns by their percentage of the quarterly market value. For the portfolio that puts the accumulated market value over the quarterly market value, use only the portion of the market value required to sum to the quarterly market value.
   c. Calculate the QDD by summing the weighted returns.

We calculate the Worst QDD in the same way, except that we use the mirror of the process to accumulate the worst performing portfolio returns.

	A	B	C	D	E
1	Portfolio	Average Invested Balance	Weight (ABAL)	Annual Return	
2	C	2,967	29.57%	13.48%	
3	F	500	4.98%	12.00%	
4	A	1,000	9.97%	10.00%	
5	E	1,000	9.97%	10.00%	
6	B	2,067	20.60%	9.68%	
7	D	2,500	24.92%	8.00%	
8					
9	Asset Weighted Mean	10,034	100.00%	10.56%	
10					
11	Quarter of Composite Market Value:			2,508.50	=B9/4
12					
13	Best Performing Portfolios down to quarter value:				
14	Portfolio	Market Value	Weight	Return	Contribution to QDD
15	C	2,508.50	100.00%	13.48%	13.48%
16				Best Performing QDD:	13.48%
17					
18	Worst Performing Portfolios up to quarter value:				
19	D	2,500	99.66%	8.00%	7.97%
20	B	8.50	0.34%	9.68%	0.03%
21		2,508.50		Worst Performing QDD:	8.01%

FIGURE 5.5 Quartile Dollar Dispersion for Sample Composite

Figure 5.5 shows the calculation of the best and worst quarter dollars under management for our sample composite for the year.

How do we interpret this example? The best performing 25% of dollars invested in the strategy earned a 13.48% return during the period. This equals Portfolio C's return because Portfolio C comprised more than a quarter of the value of the composite. Notice that in our example, the Worst QDD equals the contribution of the worst performing portfolio plus a portion of the next-to-worst performing portfolio. We interpret this to mean that the worst performing quarter of the assets in the composite (as opposed to the portfolios in the composite) earned a return of 8.01% for the year.

RISK

Risk produces return. If we do not take on risk, we should not expect to earn a return greater than the return that compensates for the time value of money. Given a diversified portfolio and long time horizon, we expect to achieve a higher return for taking on risk. But how do we measure risk? The techniques for measuring investment risk are not intuitive to many investment professionals. There are literally dozens of statistics that can be used to quantify risk. Recognizing that risk is a major component of performance, the GIPS standards require the disclosure of the *ex-post*, or trailing, three-year annualized composite and benchmark standard deviation. If the firm decides that standard deviation is not a relevant or appropriate risk measure for the strategy, then an additional risk measure must be presented. In this section, we first summarize the theoretical basis for the risk measures that we use. Then we discuss standard deviation and the issues with calculating it. Finally, we present several common alternative measures for quantifying the risk of an investment strategy.

Risk Measurement in Investment Management

Capital market theory and history indicate that there is a trade-off between risk taken and the returns achieved. To most of us, the return and the measurement of return through observing the change in market value over time are intuitive concepts. This is not the case for risk. Our awareness of what is risky depends on our individual situation, and the methods used to quantify risk might not be self-evident.

Different investments or combinations of investments have different levels of uncertainty associated with them. Two composites might have had a similar average annual return, for example 5%. But there is a clear difference in the two strategies if Composite A had steady returns of 5% a year and Composite B had a history where half of the time the returns were 0% and the other half of the time they were 10%.

In performance measurement, we are interested in quantifying past performance. So how can we relate a concept of risk defined as future uncertainty when we are actually measuring past activity? This is a valid question. Some would say there is no risk in past returns because these returns have already happened and we know what they were! In fact, to quantify ex-post risk we need to come up with a measure of uncertainty. When we turn to the measurement of past risk we use as our proxy for uncertainty the volatility of the periodic returns. Return volatility is the variability of the periodic returns over time.

Three-Year Annualized Standard Deviation

The 2010 edition of the GIPS standards includes a new requirement to present the three-year annualized ex-post standard deviation of both the composite and the benchmark. This standard deviation must be presented for annual periods that end after January 1, 2011. A firm that prepares compliant presentations that include annual returns as of December 31 would first need to do this calculation as of December 31, 2011. Prospectively a firm must add this measure to the compliant presentation each time an additional annual period is added.

There are many measures of risk, so why do the GIPS standards require standard deviation as its chosen measure of risk? One approach to risk is measuring the variability of returns. One indication of variability is the range between the highest periodic return achieved and the lowest. But using the range of returns to estimate risk leaves out information as to the historical probability of achieving a particular return. We can estimate this probability by taking the arithmetic average of the periodic returns. The average provides the center around which the periodic observed returns are distributed.

Let's consider monthly composite returns. Each periodic, that is, monthly, composite return over a given period differs to some extent from the arithmetic mean of these returns. In some months, the composite performs better than its own average and in some months worse. The average degree of this variation in the performance history is what we seek to summarize when we measure absolute investment risk. A composite with a smaller degree in variation of monthly returns around its mean exhibits less risk than a composite with a greater variation.

We call the differences between the periodic returns and the mean return *return deviations*. An intuitive way to attempt to encapsulate in a single statistic the total variability of a series of returns would be to take the average of all of the return deviations. But we cannot take the simple average because the sum of the return deviations is zero. To correct for this, we can instead take the absolute value of the deviations and then average them. This average is called the *mean absolute deviation* (MAD).

While the mean absolute deviation is a functional description of the variability in a series of returns, it is not commonly used in performance analysis. This is because there are measures of variability with better statistical properties than the mean absolute deviation. But we use the deviations from the mean in the calculation of the most commonly used statistic representing return dispersion, the standard deviation of returns.

Let's review how to calculate the three-year annualized ex-post standard deviation (in this calculation, the periodic returns are the monthly returns for the composite):

1. Obtain the 36 monthly composite returns and calculate the arithmetic mean return.
2. Square each difference between the periodic returns and the arithmetic mean return.
3. Sum the squared differences.
4. Divide the sum of the squared differences by the number of returns.
5. Take the square root of the result.

The formula that accomplishes this is as follows:

$$\text{Standard deviation of periodic returns} = \sqrt{\frac{\sum (RP_i - \overline{RP})^2}{N}}$$

where RP_i are the individual return observations, $\overline{RP}$ is the mean composite return, and N is the count of composite returns used. As discussed previously, in these examples we use the population (N) version of the standard deviation calculation. The sample version ($N - 1$) is an acceptable formula for this GIPS-required calculation, and would be used when we are using historical data to make inferences about future volatility. Note that while the formula for calculating the standard deviation of the time series of monthly composite returns is exactly the same as the formula for calculating the standard deviation of the portfolio returns within a composite, the inputs and purpose are completely different. In the previous section, we were concerned with measuring the dispersion, or spread, of portfolio returns around the mean return. Here we are measuring the variability in composite monthly returns over time.

For the same reason that stating returns in annual equivalents is helpful, we can state risk on an annualized basis. The method we use to annualize risks is different than that used to annualize returns. The annualized version of the standard deviation statistic is sometimes called *volatility*. To annualize the standard deviation, we multiply the standard deviation by the square root of the number of returns in a year, given the periodicity of the data, as shown:

$$\text{Annualized standard deviation} = \sqrt{\frac{\sum (RP_i - \overline{RP})^2}{N}} * \sqrt{P}$$

	A	B	C	D	E	F	G	H	I
1	Month	Return	Deviation from Mean	Squared Deviation		Month	Return	Deviation from Mean	Squared Deviation
2	1	2.00%	0.00%	0.00%		19	5.00%	3.00%	0.09%
3	2	4.00%	2.00%	0.04%		20	-1.00%	-3.00%	0.09%
4	3	3.00%	1.00%	0.01%		21	-3.00%	-5.00%	0.25%
5	4	7.00%	5.00%	0.25%		22	-6.00%	-8.00%	0.64%
6	5	0.00%	-2.00%	0.04%		23	-1.00%	-3.00%	0.09%
7	6	3.00%	1.00%	0.01%		24	2.00%	0.00%	0.00%
8	7	9.00%	7.00%	0.49%		25	1.00%	-1.00%	0.01%
9	8	8.00%	6.00%	0.36%		26	4.00%	2.00%	0.04%
10	9	-6.00%	-8.00%	0.64%		27	1.00%	-1.00%	0.01%
11	10	9.00%	7.00%	0.49%		28	-3.00%	-5.00%	0.25%
12	11	1.00%	-1.00%	0.01%		29	-2.00%	-4.00%	0.16%
13	12	1.00%	-1.00%	0.01%		30	3.00%	1.00%	0.01%
14	13	16.00%	14.00%	1.96%		31	4.00%	2.00%	0.04%
15	14	8.00%	6.00%	0.36%		32	1.00%	-1.00%	0.01%
16	15	1.00%	-1.00%	0.01%		33	2.00%	0.00%	0.00%
17	16	-1.00%	-3.00%	0.09%		34	1.00%	-1.00%	0.01%
18	17	-5.00%	-7.00%	0.49%		35	1.00%	-1.00%	0.01%
19	18	1.00%	-1.00%	0.01%		36	2.00%	0.00%	0.00%
20	=B19-F21								
21			Average Monthly Return			2.00%	=AVERAGE(B2:B19,G2:G19)		
22			Count of Returns			36.00	=COUNT(B2:B19,G2:G19)		
23			Sum of Squared Deviations			6.98%	=SUM(D2:D19,I2:I19)		
24			Monthly Standard Deviation			4.40%	=SQRT(F23/F22)		
25			Annualized Standard Deviation			15.25%	=F24* SQRT(12)		

FIGURE 5.6 Standard Deviation for a Sample Composite

where P is the number of returns in a year, given the periodicity of the data. Figure 5.6 shows the calculation of the monthly and annualized standard deviation for the sample composite.

Since our example uses monthly data, we multiply the standard deviation of the monthly returns (4.40%) by the square root of 12, which is approximately 3.46, in order to annualize the standard deviation. The annualized standard deviation of our sample composite is 15.25%. Note that we multiply a monthly standard deviation by the square root of 12 regardless of the length of the total time period. We then perform the same calculation for the composite's benchmark.

We can compare the standard deviation of the composite to the standard deviation of the benchmark. Given the same average return, a composite that has twice the standard deviation of the benchmark has twice the volatility of that benchmark. We can also compare the standard deviation of two composites with similar returns to understand which composite had more volatility.

What should we report in a GIPS-compliant presentation for situations where we do not have a history of 36 monthly returns? If the composite history goes back three years, but quarterly and not monthly returns were calculated at some point over those three years, we cannot mix frequencies. Instead, the standard deviation is not included in the presentation until 36 monthly returns are available, and the firm must disclose that this was the reason for not reporting it.

Alternative Risk Measures

All compliant presentations must include the three-year annualized standard deviation for the composite and the benchmark for annual periods ended after January 1, 2011. However, what does a firm do if it believes that the required annualized standard deviation is not an appropriate or relevant risk measure for a specific composite? Even if the firm believes that the three-year annualized ex-post standard deviation is not relevant or appropriate for a specific composite, the firm is still required to present this risk measure in the compliant presentation. However, the firm must also present an additional three-year ex-post risk measure. The additional risk measure must:

- Be calculated over a 36-month period.
- Use the same periodicity of input returns for the composite and the benchmark.

The firm must describe why the standard deviation is irrelevant or inappropriate. The firm must also describe the additional risk measure selected, including why it was selected as an appropriate risk measure.

A variety of risk measures are available, so how does a firm decide which additional risk measure should be presented? There are three main classes of historical risk statistics: absolute risk measures, downside risk measures, and benchmark relative risk measures. There are also various ratios relating risk and return. The sections that follow discuss the most commonly used statistics. In addition to past volatility, there are additional techniques for estimating risk that depend on the asset class and investment strategy. For example, if we had a fixed income strategy, we could calculate the composite's average duration, credit quality, and other risk factors specific to fixed income securities. These would give us an indication as to the risk of loss due to unexpected interest rate changes or quality downgrades. For an equity strategy, we could present the average price–earnings (P/E) ratio, market capitalization, country exposure, industry exposure, and other equity risk factors. Why are exposures a measure of risk? As an example, a concentrated investment in technology stocks is expected to be more volatile than a more diversified portfolio.

Some risk measures, such as tracking error, are calculated using both composite and benchmark returns as inputs. When using the two sets of returns to perform these calculations, firms must take care to ensure the same periodicity is used for both series and across statistics. For example, if a firm calculates the composite's Sharpe ratio using monthly returns for the 36-month period, the firm must calculate the benchmark's Sharpe ratio using monthly returns. Likewise, if the firm chooses to use daily composite returns, then benchmark daily returns would be required as an input to the benchmark's calculation.

Absolute Risk Measures

Absolute risk is defined as the total variability in returns. By total variability we mean two things: first, it is the total dispersion of returns that we are interested in measuring; second, when we measure the risk of a composite by using standard deviation, we include both the variability inherent in the underlying asset class, as represented by the benchmark, as well as any non-benchmark-specific volatility introduced by an active manager. The primary measure of absolute risk is the standard deviation of periodic short-term returns.

Downside Risk Measures

There are investment strategies specifically designed to reduce the risk of extreme losses, as well as strategies with a higher than average risk of extreme losses. An example of a strategy with a risk of extreme losses would be one that employs leverage by borrowing money to invest. Several risk measures exist to isolate this downside risk. Downside risk measures can also provide a better indication of risk when the assumptions underlying the use of standard deviation do not hold.

If we accept that we can equate the variability in returns around the mean return with "risk," then the standard deviation of returns is an acceptable measure of risk. But the variability of returns around the mean return might not be how we would all conceptualize the risk of investing. There are two reasons why this may not seem logical:

1. The center around which standard deviation is calculated is the mean historical return.
2. Standard deviation treats positive and negative return deviations from the mean with equal weight.

The first criticism reflects the fact that the return deviations that comprise the standard deviation are calculated using the mean return as a reference return. The mean return is a measure of the average return in the return history. The concept of standard deviation treats as a contribution to risk any returns that fall on either side of this mean return. Investors may, however, have a different focal point for riskiness, for example zero or all negative returns. The second criticism is that standard deviation treats positive return deviations in the same way as negative deviations. For many of us, it is counterintuitive that above-average returns can make a positive contribution toward a measure of riskiness.

The volatility created by losses certainly has more of an impact on how we feel about an investment than the volatility created by gains in excess of the mean return. This second criticism is tempered when the returns are normally distributed: If half of the returns are above the mean return and half below the mean return, any ranking of composites based on upside and downside risks will be the same. But this is not the case if the returns are not normally distributed or if the investor has a target return that is different than the mean return.

Downside risk statistics function by counting as risky only those returns that are below a specified reference return. Downside risk statistics are based on the concept of partial, or semideviation. *Semideviation*, or *downside deviation*, is the standard deviation of the returns that fall below the average return. You can use the average return, or some minimally acceptable or target rate of return, in the following formula:

$$\text{Annualized downside deviation} = \sqrt{\frac{\sum (RP_i - T)^2 \text{ where } RP_i < T}{N}} * \sqrt{P}$$

where T equals the minimally acceptable return for the period. Figure 5.7 demonstrates the calculation of downside deviation for our sample

	A	B	C	D	E	F	G	H	I	J	K
1	Month	Return	Risk-Free Rate	Return Shortfall	Return Shortfall Squared		Month	Return	Risk-Free Rate	Return Shortfall	Return Shortfall Squared
2	1	2.00%	0.06%				19	5.00%	0.16%		
3	2	4.00%	0.08%				20	-1.00%	0.08%	-1.08%	0.01%
4	3	3.00%	0.14%				21	-3.00%	0.14%	-3.14%	0.10%
5	4	7.00%	0.12%				22	-6.00%	0.12%	-6.12%	0.37%
6	5	0.00%	0.15%	-0.15%	0.00%		23	-1.00%	0.08%	-1.08%	0.01%
7	6	3.00%	0.08%				24	2.00%	0.06%		
8	7	9.00%	0.05%				25	1.00%	0.02%		
9	8	8.00%	0.05%				26	4.00%	0.14%		
10	9	-6.00%	0.14%	-6.14%	0.38%		27	1.00%	0.06%		
11	10	9.00%	0.02%				28	-3.00%	0.15%	-3.15%	0.10%
12	11	1.00%	0.14%				29	-2.00%	0.05%	-2.05%	0.04%
13	12	1.00%	0.13%				30	3.00%	0.12%		
14	13	16.00%	0.15%				31	4.00%	0.12%		
15	14	8.00%	0.12%				32	1.00%	0.15%		
16	15	1.00%	0.14%				33	2.00%	0.14%		
17	16	-1.00%	0.06%	-1.06%	0.01%		34	1.00%	0.05%		
18	17	-5.00%	0.12%	-5.12%	0.26%		35	1.00%	0.15%		
19	18	1.00%	0.15%				36	2.00%	0.05%		
20											
21					Count of Returns		36.00	=COUNT(B2:B19,H2:H19)			
22				Sum of Squared Return Shortfalls			0.0129	=SUM(E2:E19,K2:K19)			
23					Downside Deviation		1.89%	=SQRT(G22/G21)			
24				Annualized Downside Deviation			6.55%	=G23*SQRT(12)			

FIGURE 5.7 Annualized Downside Deviation for Sample Composite

composite, where the minimally acceptable return is set as the risk-free return for the period.

Note that even though we used only the returns that fell short of the target return in the calculation in this figure, we still divide the sum of the squared return shortfalls by the total number of returns (36 in this example).

Relative Risk Measures

Given the relationship between risk and return, we are also interested in whether the risk level of the portfolio differs from the benchmark. If the benchmark was selected based on the investor's appetite for risk, the risk of the composite relative to that of the benchmark is what we are interested in measuring.

Where absolute risk is proxied by the standard deviation of returns, relative risk is measured by looking at how the composite returns and the benchmark returns vary together. Measures of the association between the composite and the benchmark return series give us an understanding as to how much benchmark relative risk was exhibited by the composite. This degree of covariability is called *covariance*, which is a statistical measure of the tendency for two data series to move together. Covariance measures the direction and degree of association of the composite and benchmark returns, as well as the magnitude of the variability in the composite and benchmark returns.

Covariance is difficult to interpret and we can transform it into the correlation coefficient, which is more useful for investment comparisons. The *correlation coefficient* is a measure of the amount by which two investments vary together. It measures the direction and degree of association in the composite and benchmark returns. A correlation of +1.0 indicates that the returns are perfectly positively correlated, while a correlation of −1.0 indicates the returns are perfectly negatively correlated. As values get closer to zero there is less of a correlation between the returns.

We can have a composite and benchmark with similar average returns and standard deviations, but imperfect correlation. Many investment strategies are designed to minimize return differences to the benchmark. The historical tracking risk, or *annualized tracking error*, of a composite or strategy equals the standard deviation of the difference between the periodic composite and benchmark returns and is calculated as follows:

$$\text{Annualized tracking error} = \sqrt{\frac{\sum (D_i - \overline{D})^2}{N}} * \sqrt{P}$$

where D represents the periodic differences between the composite and benchmark returns. Tracking error is useful in expressing the concept of correlation because it is expressed in units of return. Figure 5.8 shows the calculation for our sample composite and its benchmark.

Risk-Adjusted Return Measures

Given that standard deviation and similar statistics are measures of return variability, wanting to compare two investments to determine whether one is more volatile than the other is natural. We can compare returns across composites—for example, ignoring risk, a composite that has a 10% return did better than one with an 8% return. But can we compare risk measures across composites? One barrier to communicating risk is that we cannot

	A	B	C	D	E	F	G	H	I
1	Month	Return	Benchmark Return	Value Added		Month	Return	Benchmark Return	Value Added
2	1	2.00%	3.00%	-1.00%		19	5.00%	9.00%	-4.00%
3	2	4.00%	1.00%	3.00%		20	-1.00%	2.00%	-3.00%
4	3	4.00%	-3.00%	7.00%		21	-3.00%	1.00%	-4.00%
5	4	7.00%	-2.00%	9.00%		22	-5.00%	7.00%	-12.00%
6	5	0.00%	5.00%	-5.00%		23	-1.00%	3.00%	-4.00%
7	6	3.00%	4.00%	-1.00%		24	1.00%	1.00%	0.00%
8	7	9.00%	1.00%	8.00%		25	1.00%	-1.00%	2.00%
9	8	8.00%	2.00%	6.00%		26	4.00%	-5.00%	9.00%
10	9	-6.00%	1.00%	-7.00%		27	1.00%	1.00%	0.00%
11	10	9.00%	1.00%	8.00%		28	-3.00%	1.00%	-4.00%
12	11	2.00%	2.00%	0.00%		29	-2.00%	-4.00%	2.00%
13	12	1.00%	-1.00%	2.00%		30	3.00%	4.00%	-1.00%
14	13	16.00%	4.00%	12.00%		31	4.00%	4.00%	0.00%
15	14	8.00%	1.00%	7.00%		32	1.00%	2.00%	-1.00%
16	15	1.00%	1.00%	0.00%		33	2.00%	3.00%	-1.00%
17	16	-1.00%	0.00%	-1.00%		34	1.00%	-4.00%	5.00%
18	17	-5.00%	-6.00%	1.00%		35	1.00%	2.00%	-1.00%
19	18	1.00%	5.00%	-4.00%		36	2.00%	3.00%	-1.00%
20									
21			Monthly Tracking Error			5.03%	=STDEVP(D2:D19,I2:I19)		
22			Annualized Tracking Error			17.43%	=F21* SQRT(12)		

FIGURE 5.8   Annualized Tracking Error for Sample Composite

properly compare standard deviations and other risk statistics without referencing other statistics like the mean return. Analysts have surmounted this barrier by deriving various ratios that relate risk and return.

We can divide the average return over a period by the risk taken during the period to derive the return per unit of risk. While this statistic can be used to rank the risk and return efficiency of composites, it is not often reported. The *Sharpe Ratio* is a modification to this risk-adjusted return. The modification is based on the idea that we should not be able to earn returns over and above a risk-free return without taking on risk. Given standard deviation as a proxy for risk, theoretically there should be no standard deviation of returns for the risk-free investment. So it is the excess return that we earn in exchange for taking on risk. The Sharpe Ratio—named for

William Sharpe, who is associated with the Capital Asset Pricing Model (CAPM)—takes these theoretical constructs into account by relating the excess composite return to risk. Two managers with similar returns can be differentiated on a risk-adjusted basis using the Sharpe Ratio. The higher the Sharpe Ratio, the more return the composite has provided per unit of risk. Calculating the Annualized Sharpe Ratio uses the following formula:

$$\text{Annualized Sharpe Ratio} = \frac{(\overline{RP} - \overline{RF})}{\text{Standard deviation}\,(RP_i) \,*\, \sqrt{P}}$$

where $\overline{RP}$ and $\overline{RF}$ are the average composite returns and risk-free returns. Figure 5.9 shows the calculation for our sample composite.

What is the appropriate risk-free rate to use when calculating measures like the Sharpe Ratio? The risk-free rate is a hurdle rate, or benchmark for risk, in that we can earn this rate without taking on risk. A risk-free investment is one where the actual return equals the expected return, that is, there is no variance around the expected return. In practice, we use the rates on short-term government securities to represent the risk-free investment because they do not suffer from credit risk. The return on a risk-free investment represents the pure time value of money. All other investments that incur other risks, such as the risk of default or the risk of losing principal, should return a premium to the risk-free rate. To select the risk-free rate, we choose an instrument with a time to maturity that has no reinvestment risk; that is, we use the return on a 30-day T-bill for comparison to one-month returns on risky investments. The risk-free rate should also be selected based on the currency of the composite (e.g., the euro rate for euro-denominated composites).

We can adjust the Sharpe Ratio to use the appropriate measure of risk for the situation. For example the *Sortino Ratio*—named for Frank Sortino, who is associated with the Pension Research Institute—demonstrated in Figure 5.10, measures the return in excess of a target return, over the risk of returns falling below that target return.

$$\text{Annualized Sortino Ratio} = \frac{\text{Annualized return in excess of a target return}}{\text{Annualized downside deviation}}$$

Finally, the *Information Ratio* is a measure of the benchmark relative return gained for taking on benchmark relative risk. It is analogous to the role that the Sharpe Ratio takes in measuring absolute risk-adjusted returns. The Information Ratio presents in a single statistic the units of incremental return given the amount of benchmark relative risk taken to earn it.

▲	A	B	C	D	E	F	G	H	I
1		Month	Return	Risk-Free Rate		Month	Return	Risk-Free Rate	
2		1	2.00%	0.06%		19	5.00%	0.16%	
3		2	4.00%	0.08%		20	-1.00%	0.08%	
4		3	3.00%	0.14%		21	-3.00%	0.14%	
5		4	7.00%	0.12%		22	-6.00%	0.12%	
6		5	0.00%	0.15%		23	-1.00%	0.08%	
7		6	3.00%	0.08%		24	2.00%	0.06%	
8		7	9.00%	0.05%		25	1.00%	0.02%	
9		8	8.00%	0.05%		26	4.00%	0.14%	
10		9	-6.00%	0.14%		27	1.00%	0.06%	
11		10	9.00%	0.02%		28	-3.00%	0.15%	
12		11	1.00%	0.14%		29	-2.00%	0.05%	
13		12	1.00%	0.13%		30	3.00%	0.12%	
14		13	16.00%	0.15%		31	4.00%	0.12%	
15		14	8.00%	0.12%		32	1.00%	0.15%	
16		15	1.00%	0.14%		33	2.00%	0.14%	
17		16	-1.00%	0.06%		34	1.00%	0.05%	
18		17	-5.00%	0.12%		35	1.00%	0.15%	
19		18	1.00%	0.15%		36	2.00%	0.05%	
20									
21		Average Monthly Return				2.00%	=AVERAGE(C2:C19,G2:G19)		
22		Annual Average Return				24.00%	=F21*12		
23		Average Risk Free Rate				0.10%	=AVERAGE(D2:D19,H2:H19)		
24	Annual Average Risk Free Rate					1.25%	=F23*12		
25		Monthly Standard Deviation				4.40%	=STDEVP(C2:C19,G2:G19)		
26		Annualized Sharpe Ratio				1.49	=(F22-F24)/(F25*SQRT(12))		

FIGURE 5.9   Annualized Sharpe Ratio for Sample Composite

	A	B	C	D	E	F	G	H	I	J	K	L	M
1		Month	Return	Risk Free Rate	Return Shortfall	Return Shortfall Squared		Month	Return	Risk Free Rate	Return Shortfall	Return Shortfall Squared	
2		1	2.00%	0.06%				19	5.00%	0.16%			
3		2	4.00%	0.08%				20	-1.00%	0.08%	-1.08%	0.01%	
4		3	3.00%	0.14%				21	-3.00%	0.14%	-3.14%	0.10%	
5		4	7.00%	0.12%				22	-6.00%	0.12%	-6.12%	0.37%	
6		5	0.00%	0.15%	-0.15%	0.00%		23	-1.00%	0.08%	-1.08%	0.01%	
7		6	3.00%	0.08%				24	2.00%	0.06%			
8		7	9.00%	0.05%				25	1.00%	0.02%			
9		8	8.00%	0.05%				26	4.00%	0.14%			
10		9	-6.00%	0.14%	-6.14%	0.38%		27	1.00%	0.06%			
11		10	9.00%	0.02%				28	-3.00%	0.15%	-3.15%	0.10%	
12		11	1.00%	0.14%				29	-2.00%	0.05%	-2.05%	0.04%	
13		12	1.00%	0.13%				30	3.00%	0.12%			
14		13	16.00%	0.15%				31	4.00%	0.12%			
15		14	8.00%	0.12%				32	1.00%	0.15%			
16		15	1.00%	0.14%				33	2.00%	0.14%			
17		16	-1.00%	0.06%	-1.06%	0.01%		34	1.00%	0.05%			
18		17	-5.00%	0.12%	-5.12%	0.26%		35	1.00%	0.15%			
19		18	1.00%	0.15%				36	2.00%	0.05%			
20													
21		Count of Returns			36	=COUNT(C2:C19,I2:I19)		Sum of Squared Return Shortfalls			1.29%	=SUM(F2:F19,L2:L19)	
22		Average Composite Return			2.00%	=AVERAGE(C2:C19,I2:I19)		Downside Deviation			1.89%	=SQRT(L21/E21)	
23		Annual Average Composite Return			24.00%	=E22*12		Annualized Downside Deviation			6.55%	=L22*SQRT(12)	
24		Average Risk Free Rate			0.10%	=AVERAGE(D2:D19,J2:J19)							
25		Annual Average Risk Free Rate			1.25%	=E24*12		Sortino Ratio			3.47	=E26/L23	
26		Annual Average Excess Return			22.75%	=E23-E25							

FIGURE 5.10 Annualized Sortino Ratio for Sample Composite

The measure of return that we use in the Information Ratio is the average periodic value added. We divide this by the tracking error to relate the benchmark relative return and risk, as demonstrated in the following formula:

$$\text{Annualized Information Ratio} = \frac{\left(\frac{\sum(RP_i - RM_i)}{N}\right) * \sqrt{P}}{\text{Standard deviation}\,(RP_i - RM_i) * \sqrt{P}}$$

where RP_i are the periodic composite returns and RM_i are the periodic returns for the market, or benchmark. Figure 5.11 shows the calculation for our sample composite.

Capital Asset Pricing Model (CAPM) Statistics

Alpha and beta are two risk statistics commonly reported by investment managers. They relate to a theoretical model of the relationship between investment risk and return, the Capital Asset Pricing Model, or CAPM.

	A	B	C	D	E	F	G	H	I
1	Month	Return	Benchmark Return	Value Added		Month	Return	Benchmark Return	Value Added
2	1	2.00%	3.00%	-1.00%		19	5.00%	9.00%	-4.00%
3	2	4.00%	1.00%	3.00%		20	-1.00%	2.00%	-3.00%
4	3	4.00%	-3.00%	7.00%		21	-3.00%	1.00%	-4.00%
5	4	7.00%	-2.00%	9.00%		22	-5.00%	7.00%	-12.00%
6	5	0.00%	5.00%	-5.00%		23	-1.00%	3.00%	-4.00%
7	6	3.00%	4.00%	-1.00%		24	1.00%	1.00%	0.00%
8	7	9.00%	1.00%	8.00%		25	1.00%	-1.00%	2.00%
9	8	8.00%	2.00%	6.00%		26	4.00%	-5.00%	9.00%
10	9	-6.00%	1.00%	-7.00%		27	1.00%	1.00%	0.00%
11	10	9.00%	1.00%	8.00%		28	-3.00%	1.00%	-4.00%
12	11	2.00%	2.00%	0.00%		29	-2.00%	-4.00%	2.00%
13	12	1.00%	-1.00%	2.00%		30	3.00%	4.00%	-1.00%
14	13	16.00%	4.00%	12.00%		31	4.00%	4.00%	0.00%
15	14	8.00%	1.00%	7.00%		32	1.00%	2.00%	-1.00%
16	15	1.00%	1.00%	0.00%		33	2.00%	3.00%	-1.00%
17	16	-1.00%	0.00%	-1.00%		34	1.00%	-4.00%	5.00%
18	17	-5.00%	-6.00%	1.00%		35	1.00%	2.00%	-1.00%
19	18	1.00%	5.00%	-4.00%		36	2.00%	3.00%	-1.00%
20									
21				Average Value Added		0.72%	=AVERAGE(D2:D19,I2:I19)		
22				Annualized Value Added		8.67%	=F21*12		
23				Monthly Tracking Error		5.03%	=STDEVP(D2:D19,I2:I19)		
24				Annualized Tracking Error		17.43%	=F23* SQRT(12)		
25				Monthly Information Ratio		0.14	=F21/F23		
26				Annualized Information Ratio		0.50	=F22/F24		

FIGURE 5.11   Annualized Information Ratio for Sample Composite

Originally developed to explain the difference in returns produced by investments in individual common stocks, CAPM has been put into service to carry out a risk-adjusted performance assessment of investment portfolios (and composites). The CAPM is one of the fundamental building blocks of Modern Portfolio Theory, or MPT. The regression coefficients we derive using CAPM are sometimes called MPT statistics. We will first discuss the theoretical background behind these statistics, and then show how they are calculated.

The CAPM is concerned with explaining the differences in returns earned on different investments. The CAPM equation rests on several principles, including these three:

1. An investment that has no risk will earn the risk-free return.
2. The volatility in returns can be broken down into two types of risk:
   a. *Systematic risk*, the degree to which portfolio returns vary with market returns.
   b. *Unsystematic risk*, the volatility that is unique to the asset and can be eliminated via portfolio diversification.
3. Investments are awarded a degree of return over the risk-free rate—a *risk premium*—based only on the degree of market risk taken.[1]

Given these assumptions, we can derive the CAPM regression equation as follows:

$$RP_i = RF_i + [\text{CAPM beta} * (RM_i - RF_i)]$$

The equation can be interpreted as saying that investment returns (RP_i) should be equal to the risk-free rate (RF_i) plus a risk premium, where the risk premium is calculated by looking at the amount by which investment returns vary in proportion (CAPM beta) to the variability in the underlying market excess return ($RM_i - RF_i$).

CAPM Beta

The *CAPM beta* represents the degree of market risk exposure. The CAPM beta is equal to the covariance of the composite and benchmark excess returns divided by the variance of the benchmark excess returns. This can be transformed into this formula:

$$\text{CAPM beta} = \text{Correlation}\,(ERP_i, ERM_i) * \left(\frac{\text{Stdevp}\,(ERP_i)}{\text{Stdevp}\,(ERM_i)} \right)$$

where ERP_i are the periodic composite portfolio excess return values and ERM_i are the periodic market excess return values.

---

[1]For a history of modern finance including the development of the CAPM, see Peter Bernstein, *Capital Ideas: The Improbable Origins of Modern Wall Street* (New York: The Free Press, 1992).

Jensen's Alpha

Using the CAPM equation, what if an investment has a higher return than that predicted by the degree of market risk taken? We could hypothesize that this difference is due to the *value added* by the investment manager. The magnitude of this outperformance represents value added over the benchmark, on a risk-adjusted basis. The CAPM alpha, or *Jensen's alpha*, is the factor of return that reconciles actual returns to those predicted by the CAPM. Jensen's alpha is frequently used as a measure of the risk-adjusted return earned by a portfolio. Michael Jensen developed this extension to the CAPM as a tool for evaluating mutual fund managers.

Jensen's alpha can be calculated by adding a term to the CAPM equation used to predict the (theoretical) composite return. Jensen's alpha is commonly expressed in annual equivalents. *Annual Jensen's alpha* is the average monthly alpha times the number of periods per year:

$$\text{Annual Jensen's alpha} = [(\overline{RP} - \overline{RF}) - (\text{CAPM beta} * (\overline{RM} - \overline{RF}))] * 12$$

Figure 5.12 shows the calculation of CAPM beta and Jensen's alpha for our sample composite. (Note that this example uses the same composite, portfolio, and risk-free returns used in the previous examples. The excess return series are calculated by taking the difference between the periodic composite and benchmark returns and the risk-free rate).

A beta of 1 would indicate that the composite returns varied to the same degree as the benchmark returns. Our example beta of .18 (this example uses extreme values to illustrate the calculations) is close to 0. This indicates that the returns of this composite are not related to the variability in returns of the market portfolio. Using CAPM, if beta equals 0 then the composite return should equal the risk-free rate. If beta equals 1 then CAPM predicts that the composite return will equal the market return. If beta is greater than 1, the theory expects the composite to earn a return greater than the benchmark return. Because the beta is so low, and the returns are substantially larger than 0, the CAPM equation results in the large Jensen's alpha of 19.49%.

	A	B	C	D
1	Average Monthly Excess Return	1.95%	=AVERAGE(PortfolioExcessReturns)	
2	Average Monthly Benchmark Excess Return	1.23%	=AVERAGE(BenchmarkExcessReturns)	
3	Average Risk-Free Rate	0.10%	=AVERAGE(RiskFreeRates)	
4	Correlation	0.1300	=CORREL(PortfolioExcessReturns, BenchmarkExcessReturns)	
5	Portfolio Excess Return Standard Deviation	4.37%	=STDEVP(PortfolioExcessReturns)	
6	Benchmark Excess Return Standard Deviation	3.13%	=STDEVP(BenchmarkExcessReturns)	
7	CAPM Beta	0.18	=B4*(B5/B6)	
8	Annualized Jensen's Alpha	19.49%	=((B1-B3)-(B7*B2))*12	

FIGURE 5.12   CAPM Statistics

Regression Analysis

Note that Jensen's alpha and CAPM beta are derived from a *theoretical* model of the relationship between investment risk and return. Sometimes alpha and beta are calculated to represent the purely statistical regression analysis–based relationship between the composite and benchmark returns. To do this, we perform a regression analysis to describe the relationship between the benchmark and composite return series.

Regression beta is the product of the correlation between the composite and benchmark returns multiplied by the ratio of the standard deviations of the composite and benchmark returns or

$$\text{Regression beta} = \text{Correlation}\,(RP_i,\,RM_i) * \left(\frac{\text{Stdevp}\,(RP_i)}{\text{Stdevp}\,(RM_i)} \right)$$

Regression alpha equals the value of the composite return when the benchmark return is equal to 0 as modeled by the regression equation. Alpha is calculated using the average composite and benchmark returns adjusted by the Regression beta. We annualize the alpha by multiplying the monthly alpha by 12:

$$\text{Annualized Regression alpha} = [(\overline{RP} - (\text{Regression beta} * \overline{RM})) * 12]$$

Notice that this is different from the Jensen's alpha formula. Jensen's alpha uses excess returns (returns adjusted by the risk-free rate); this formula does not. Figure 5.13 shows the calculation of Regression alpha and beta for our sample composite.

Notice that the Regression alpha (21.76%) is higher than the CAPM Jensen's alpha (19.49%). This is because the Regression alpha has not been adjusted to reflect the theoretical market relationships implied by CAPM.

	A	B	C
1	Average Monthly Return	2.06%	=AVERAGE(PortfolioReturns)
2	Average Monthly Benchmark Return	1.33%	=AVERAGE(BenchmarkReturns)
3	Correlation	0.1306	=CORREL(PortfolioReturns, BenchmarkReturns)
4	Portfolio Standard Deviation	4.36%	=STDEVP(PortfolioReturns)
5	Benchmark Standard Deviation	3.14%	=STDEVP(BenchmarkReturns)
6	Regression Beta	0.18	=B3*(B4/B5)
7	Annualized Regression Alpha	21.76%	=(B1-(B6*B2))*12

FIGURE 5.13 Regression Statistics

Defining Alpha

Investment managers are frequently judged on their ability to add "alpha." But one problem with the term alpha is that it has several different meanings. Sometimes alpha is used in the way we have been describing value added, or the difference between the composite return and the benchmark return. Used in this way, alpha measures outperformance unadjusted for the risk taken. Both the Regression alpha and Jensen's alpha adjust for the risk taken by levering the market return up or down by the beta. But sometimes a composite's alpha or beta will be reported without reference to whether the alpha or beta was calculated using a regression analysis of the returns or using a CAPM equation with excess return inputs. As the regression and CAPM coefficients have different values and interpretation, differentiating between them when calculating and reporting risk statistics is important. The regression coefficients are a statistical description of a portfolio's expected return given the market return as represented by the benchmark. The CAPM return and alpha coefficient are theoretical estimates of expected return and excess return due to portfolio management. Table 5.3 summarizes different definitions of alpha, where

$$A = \text{alpha}$$

$$RP = \text{portfolio return}$$

$$RF = \text{risk-free return}$$

$$RM = \text{market return}$$

TABLE 5.3 Definitions of Alpha

Alpha Definition	Calculated As	Term Used Here	Not Measured
Difference of portfolio (or composite) and risk-free return	$A = RP - RF$	Excess return	Adjustment for market risk
Difference of portfolio and benchmark return	$A = RP - RM$	Value added	Adjustment for risk taken
Intercept of the linear regression equation	$A = RP - (B * RM)$	Regression alpha	Adjustment for the risk-free return
Excess return not predicted by the CAPM equation	$A = (RP - RF) - B * (RM - RF)$	Jensen's alpha	

Ex-Post versus Ex-Ante Risk Measures

The risk statistics we reviewed here all use past returns as inputs. However, historical risk statistics may not be adequately relevant to the forecasting of future risk. Portfolio composition, manager style, capital market relationships, and other factors change over time. As an extreme example, the backward-looking risk statistics for a portfolio of fixed income instruments would not be meaningful at all going forward if the bonds were sold and stocks were purchased to replace them.

The same caveat about past returns not necessarily providing a good indication as to future returns applies to risk measurement as well. To move beyond the information provided by the historical returns, we need more information as to the current and proposed portfolio holdings, as well as a different set of forward-looking, or *ex-ante*, risk measurement tools. Instead of reporting the actual standard deviation and tracking error, these tools project these and other statistics.

Forward-looking risk is a different subject than backward-looking risk. While ex-ante return and risk estimation techniques use historical returns as inputs, they are estimates and therefore are not the focus of a GIPS presentation. A GIPS-compliant presentation must contain ex-post measures. A manager can, however, include ex-ante risk statistics in the compliant presentation if the firm feels that they are important factors for the prospect to understand when considering a potential investment. These ex-ante risk measures must be clearly identified as supplemental information.

SUMMARY

A GIPS-compliant presentation requires that firms provide information about the dispersion of portfolio returns within the composite, as well as information about the risk taken in order to achieve the composite returns. The most commonly used measures of dispersion and risk used in GIPS-compliant presentations are the standard deviation of the portfolios within a composite (or internal dispersion) and the newly required annualized standard deviation of three years of monthly composite and benchmark returns (external dispersion).

Differentiating between the two types of standard deviation commonly reported in a GIPS-compliant presentation is important. The first is a measure of dispersion used to explain the variability in portfolio returns earned by clients invested in the strategy. The second is a measure of the volatility of the strategy, intended to measure the risk of investing in the strategy.

In this chapter, we reviewed the requirements for these as well as alternate measures of dispersion and commonly reported absolute, downside, and benchmark-relative risk statistics used by investment firms to quantify the risk taken to earn portfolio returns. These statistics are not always useful in projecting the volatility of a portfolio or composite going forward, but they are comparable across investment managers managing portfolios with a similar strategy.

PART Three

Reporting and Maintaining Compliance with the GIPS Standards

CHAPTER 6

Disclosing and Advertising Composite Performance

Once a firm claims compliance with the GIPS standards, it must inform all prospective clients of this fact. The firm accomplishes this by providing the prospective client a *compliant presentation* for the composite that is of interest. The compliant presentation is a document that contains all of the information for a specific composite that is required by the GIPS standards. This chapter provides guidance for preparing compliant presentations. It also provides guidance for preparing an advertisement in accordance with the GIPS Advertising Guidelines.

REQUIRED NUMERICAL INFORMATION

Section 5 of the GIPS standards contains the requirements related to performance and other numerical information for the composite that must be presented in a compliant presentation. The numerical information is typically included in a table followed by accompanying disclosures. Details regarding these disclosures are covered in Section 4 of the GIPS standards. Table 6.1 is an extract from a typical compliant presentation for a composite. However, it includes only an excerpt of the numerous disclosures usually included in a compliant presentation.

Since there is no explicit requirement to present the required numerical information in a tabular format, a firm could choose to include all such data in a series of disclosures. However, a tabular format allows the reader to more easily understand the data.

The period of time that must be included in the compliant presentation depends on the period for which the firm claims compliance, as well as the length of the composite's history. A compliant presentation must initially include a minimum of five years of annual performance, although the period

TABLE 6.1 Sample Compliant Presentation Excerpt: The Growth Equity Composite of Firm A from March 1, 2000 through December 31, 2009

Year	Gross Return (%)	Net Return (%)	Benchmark Return (%)	Internal Dispersion (%)	Number of Portfolios	As of December 31 Composite Assets ($ millions)	As of December 31 Total Firm Assets ($ millions)
2009	33.08	31.78	26.46	1.3	46	124	1,028
2008	−35.35	−36.23	−37.00	1.2	38	100	780
2007	4.77	3.89	3.21	0.9	36	129	941
2006	16.42	15.66	15.99	0.7	34	125	893
2005	−14.22	−15.00	−21.51	1.1	30	130	866
2004	−9.45	−10.04	−11.71	1.0	31	141	1,007
2003	7.12	6.10	6.08	1.2	32	127	907
2002	14.22	13.11	12.75	0.9	28	116	1,054
2001	17.01	16.22	14.68	0.8	27	115	958
2000[a]	28.02	27.13	29.98	1.0	25	110	846

[a] Returns are for the period from March 1, 2000 (inception) through December 31, 2000.

Firm A claims compliance with the Global Investment Performance Standards (GIPS®) and has prepared and presented this report in compliance with the GIPS standards. Firm A has been independently verified for the period from March 1, 2000 through December 31, 2009. The verification report is available upon request. Verification assesses whether (1) the firm has complied with all the composite construction requirements of the GIPS standards on a firmwide basis, and (2) the firm's policies and procedures are designed to calculate and present performance in compliance with the GIPS standards. Verification does not ensure the accuracy of any specific composite presentation.

Firm A is an independent investment advisor registered under the Investment Advisers Act of 1940. A list of composite descriptions, as well as policies for valuing investments, calculating performance, and preparing compliant presentations are available upon request. All returns are expressed in U.S. dollars.

The Growth Equity Composite includes all institutional, tax-exempt portfolios benchmarked to the XYZ Growth Benchmark. The composite was created in April 2000.

presented may be shorter if the composite has been in existence less than five years. After the firm initially presents the minimum five-year history, on a prospective basis the firm must add an annual year of performance until the firm has created a 10-year track record for the composite. Once the composite has at least 10 years of history, the compliant presentation must include those 10 years at a minimum. As additional years are added to the composite's history, a firm can continue to increase the number of years that are presented in the compliant presentation above and beyond the 10-year minimum. While no explicit requirement prevents a firm from adding or dropping additional periods beyond the required minimum periods, firms should not drop periods due to poor performance or add periods because of good performance. Alternatively, a firm can choose to roll forward the 10-year period, so that only the most recent 10 years are presented.

A firm may choose the annual period that is presented in the compliant presentation. The annual period often ends as of December 31, but there is no requirement to choose a calendar year.

Required Numerical Information for all Composites

For all composites, for each year presented, the compliant presentation must include all of the information discussed in this section.

Annual Composite Returns   A firm may choose to present gross-of-fees returns only, net-of-fees returns only, or both gross and net returns. Gross returns are recommended, as gross returns allow for better comparability between firms. Net returns are typically included due to regulatory requirements. Common practice is to include both gross and net returns. Whichever returns are presented, the firm must clearly identify them as gross- or net-of-fees. This is typically accomplished by clearly labeling the column headings in the table as gross-of-fees or net-of-fees. Returns could also be identified as gross or net through disclosure in the notes to the presentation. This alternative makes more sense when only one of the streams of composite returns is presented.

If the composite's first year of history is not a complete annual period, the firm cannot ignore the initial partial year of performance. While many firms include the initial partial year of performance (as for the year 2000 in Table 6.1), in the past some firms did not. The 2010 edition of the GIPS standards explicitly states the requirement to disclose the first partial year return of a composite. The requirement to show the initial partial year return is applicable only for those composites that have an inception date on or after January 1, 2011. However, because this requirement is simply making explicit what was always intended, the initial partial year return for all composites, regardless of inception date, should be shown.

The same concept applies for a composite that terminates, and whose last year is a partial year. If a composite terminates after January 1, 2011, the final compliant presentation for a terminated composite must include the final partial year of performance.

Benchmark Returns   Benchmark total returns for each year must be presented. The benchmark must reflect the composite's investment mandate, objective, or strategy. The benchmark's return must be a total return, and cannot be a price-only return if a total return exists for the benchmark.

There may be composites for which no appropriate benchmark exists. While rare, there are some strategies for which a firm could justify why no benchmark is appropriate. Examples of such composites could include tactical asset allocation overlay or portable alpha strategies. When no appropriate benchmark exists, benchmark returns must not be presented. In such a case firms are required to disclose why benchmark returns are not presented.

A single benchmark's returns must be presented for each annual period. But a firm may choose to present the returns of additional benchmarks in the compliant presentation.

Where the composite returns presented are for a partial year, due to either composite inception or termination, care should be taken to present a partial benchmark return for the same time periods.

A Measure of Internal Dispersion   An internal dispersion measure helps the prospective client understand how consistently portfolios within a composite are managed. The inputs to the calculation are the annual returns of those portfolios within the composite for the full year. The use of gross returns in this calculation is common practice, but either gross or net returns may be used. If a portfolio is not included in the composite for the full year, it is not included in the dispersion calculation. For example, assume the Core Fixed Income Composite had nine portfolios that were members at some point during 2010, as illustrated in Table 6.2. The shaded cells indicate that the portfolio is included in the composite for that month. In this example, portfolios 5, 6, 8, and 9 would not be included in the calculation of internal dispersion for 2010.

The firm may choose which measure of internal dispersion to present. Options include standard deviation, high/low returns, and range of returns. Standard deviation is the most widely used measure. There are two options for standard deviation. *Equal weighted standard deviation*, which represents the dispersion of the annual portfolio returns, is a measure of how similarly

TABLE 6.2 Composite Membership: The Core Fixed Income Composite Membership for 2010

Portfolio	January	February	March	April	May	June	July	August	September	October	November	December
1	X	X	X	X	X	X	X	X	X	X	X	X
2	X	X	X	X	X	X	X	X	X	X	X	X
3	X	X	X	X	X	X	X	X	X	X	X	X
4	X	X	X	X	X	X	X	X	X	X	X	X
5	X	X	X	X		X	X	X	X	X	X	X
6	X	X	X	X	X	X		X	X	X	X	X
7	X	X	X	X	X	X	X	X	X	X	X	X
8			X	X	X	X	X	X	X	X	X	X
9	X	X	X	X	X	X	X	X	X		X	X

portfolios have been managed during the year, regardless of their size. Firms can also present an *asset weighted standard deviation*, where the size of the portfolio is factored into the calculation. This measures the dispersion of portfolio returns relative to a proxy asset weighted composite return (based on beginning of year values) using only those portfolios in the composite for the full year.

The equal and asset weighted standard deviations convey different information. Some argue that asset weighted dispersion is a better measure of dispersion because the composite return is asset weighted. But if the goal is to show the prospective investor the dispersion of the actual portfolio returns, then the equal weighted standard deviation is a better measure of the dispersion of portfolio returns within the composite. The calculation of both asset weighted and equal weighted standard deviation are demonstrated in Chapter 5.

If there are fewer than six portfolios included in the composite for the full year, no measure of internal dispersion is required. A firm may still choose to show a measure of internal dispersion for that year, but this is optional. There is no requirement to discuss the reason for the omission if the manager does not present this measure due to the small number of portfolios in the composite for the year, but it is common practice to do so.

A firm is not required to present the same internal dispersion measure for all composites. It could decide to present equal weighted standard deviation for some composites and high/low returns for others. In addition, a firm is not required to present the same internal dispersion measure for a specific composite forever. A firm may change the internal dispersion measure that is presented for a composite if it decides that this shift is appropriate. For example, a firm could transition from presenting the asset weighted standard deviation to the equal weighted standard deviation as of a certain date, and make the change prospectively only.

Composite Market Value as of Year End   This is the sum of the ending market value of portfolios included in the composite as of year end. All portfolios in the composite are included in this calculation. Note that this is different from the dispersion calculation, where only portfolios that belonged to the composite for the whole year were included.

The Number of Portfolios in the Composite as of Year End   This is the number of portfolios used in the calculation of composite market value as of year end. Note that the requirement is for the number of portfolios and not the number of clients. If a client has two portfolios managed according to the same strategy, then they are counted as two portfolios for the purpose of all GIPS-required calculations. The GIPS standards do not include a requirement for disclosing the number of clients.

Total Firm Assets or the Percentage of Firm Assets the Composite Represents as of Year End   A firm has the option of disclosing either or both of these items. In the past, both were required, so many firms continue to show both since the format for their compliant presentation has been set up to include both. Total firm assets is the sum of the ending market values for all portfolios within the firm (as defined for GIPS compliance purposes).[1] It includes the market value of all portfolios, whether portfolios are included in a composite or not. If the firm hires subadvisors to manage a portion of the assets, then total firm assets includes the assets that are managed by a subadvisor.

When calculating total firm assets, care must be taken to ensure assets are not double-counted. For example, assume Firm B manages balanced portfolios. All balanced portfolios are included in the appropriate

---

[1]The 2010 edition of the GIPS standards requires portfolios to be fair valued versus market valued, as was required in prior editions of the GIPS standards. We use the generic term market value, which is intended to capture all assets that are valued using either fair value or market value.

balanced composite. Also assume that the equity and fixed income segments of the balanced portfolios are managed as subportfolios, and that each subportfolio is managed with its own cash balance. Firm B also includes each equity subportfolio in its respective equity composite. If Firm B calculates total firm assets by summing the market values of all composites, firm assets would be overstated because of the double-counting of the equity assets.

Double-counting is not always so obvious. For example, consider the common situation of a firm managing both pooled funds and portfolios that may invest a portion of their portfolio in the pooled funds. Assume Firm C manages a money market fund and many segregated institutional portfolios. Each institutional portfolio makes use of the money market fund for investing excess cash. Because of this, summing the total market value of all portfolios results in double-counting. In this case and others like it, Firm C must subtract the money market fund assets held in segregated portfolios when calculating total firm assets.

Total firm assets is the denominator in the calculation of the percentage of firm assets represented by the composite. The numerator is the market value of the composite as of year end. This measure helps potential investors understand the significance of a particular strategy/composite to the firm. Whether a particular investment strategy represented 25% or 0.25% of the firm's assets under management would be helpful for a prospective client to know. However, even if this measure is not presented, it can be easily calculated, as both the numerator and the denominator for this calculation would be presented in the compliant presentation.

Three-Year Annualized Ex-Post Standard Deviation of the Composite and the Benchmark   Standard deviation, intended as a measure of risk, is newly required by the 2010 edition of the GIPS standards. This measure must be disclosed for annual periods that end after January 1, 2011. The inputs to the calculation are the monthly returns of the composite and the benchmark for the last 36 months. For example, if the composite's presentation is being prepared as of December 31, 2011, the inputs to this calculation for the composite are the monthly composite returns for the period from January 2009 through December 2011. The calculation is explained in detail in Chapter 5. The same standard deviation calculated for the composite is also calculated using the benchmark returns.

If a composite has less than 36 months of history, the composite standard deviation calculation is not required. For example, assume Firm D's Equity Composite has an inception date of July 1, 2011, and Firm D presents performance in compliant presentations for all composites as of December 31 and updates compliant presentations annually. When Firm D prepares the compliant presentation for the Equity Composite as of December 31, 2011, the composite will have only six monthly returns. Therefore, no composite standard deviation is required. For this composite, the first time standard deviation will be required to be presented for both the composite and the benchmark is for the three-year period ended December 31, 2014.

Through December 31, 2009, firms were allowed to calculate composite returns quarterly. Assuming calender year returns are presented, until December 31, 2013, some firms may have a 36-month period that reaches back to a time when only quarterly composite returns are available. In these cases, the composite standard deviation is not required until 36 monthly returns are available.

Some benchmarks may not have monthly returns available. The firm must present the standard deviation for the benchmark only if 36 monthly returns are available. If 36 monthly returns are not available, then no benchmark standard deviation is required.

The firm may decide that standard deviation is not a relevant or appropriate measure of risk for the composite/strategy. The firm is still required to show the three-year standard deviation, even if the firm believes this measure is not relevant or appropriate. If this is the case, the firm must also present an additional three-year ex-post measure of risk. If the measure is not already benchmark-relative (such as tracking error) then the additional risk measure must be presented for both the composite and benchmark. Care must be taken to ensure that the periodicity used in the additional risk measure is the same for both the composite and the benchmark. For example, if daily returns are used for the composite risk calculation, the benchmark risk calculation must also use daily returns. A firm may also present additional ex-post risk measures if it wishes to do so.

Ex-ante risk measures may also be included in the compliant presentation, but they are considered supplemental information and need to be clearly labeled as such. Ex-ante risk measures do not satisfy the requirement to show an additional three-year ex-post risk measure if the firm determines that the standard deviation is not relevant or appropriate.

Finally, either gross or net composite returns may be used for the standard deviation and other risk measure calculations. Gross returns are most commonly used, but the firm does have a choice. Even if both gross and net returns are included in the compliant presentation, only one composite standard deviation needs to be presented.

Additional Numerical Items, if Applicable

Some additional numerical items are required only if they are applicable to the specific composite. If the item is not applicable to the specific composite then no disclosure is required.

Percentage of the Composite Composed of Non-Fee-Paying Portfolios as of Year End. If a composite includes any non-fee-paying portfolios, the percentage of the composite represented by those non-fee-paying portfolios as of each year end must be disclosed. If a composite does not include any non-fee-paying portfolios, there is no requirement to add a column for non-fee-paying portfolios to explain that 0% of the composite's assets are non-fee-paying portfolios.

Some firms have a policy whereby portfolios of the firm's management are not charged a management fee, but instead pay a small fee to cover a portion of the costs incurred to manage the portfolio. Such fees are not representative of ordinary management fees. These portfolios should be considered non-fee-paying for purposes of this non-fee-paying assets disclosure.

Percentage of the Composite Composed of Carve-Outs as of Year End. If a composite includes carve-out portfolios, the percentage of the composite represented by carve-out portfolios in existence at year end must be disclosed. This item must be disclosed only for annual periods ended from January 1, 2006 through December 31, 2010. However, because this disclosure was previously required by the AIMR-PPS standards, managers commonly make this disclosure for every period end, including annual periods ended prior to January 1, 2006. This disclosure is not required for periods ended after January 1, 2011.

Percentage of the Composite Composed of Portfolios with Bundled Fees as of Year End. In a bundled fee arrangement, a single fee is charged that combines several fees, and normally includes custody, trading fees, portfolio management, and potentially other fees and expenses. Bundled fees are used in certain markets or for specific portfolio types. For example, universal banks in Europe typically charge clients a bundled fee that includes custody, transaction, and portfolio management fees. And wrap, or SMA, accounts in the United States typically pay fees that include brokerage and management fees. Wrap fees are considered a type of bundled fee. If a composite includes any portfolios where bundled fees are being assessed, then the percentage of the composite represented by those portfolios with bundled fees must be disclosed as of each year end.

REQUIRED DISCLOSURES

In addition to the numerical items described in the previous section, this section discusses disclosures required by the GIPS standards for the purpose of helping prospective clients understand the composite performance.

Required Disclosures for all Composites

The disclosures discussed in this section must be included in all compliant presentations.

Claim of Compliance and Verification Status   A firm must use one of the following claims of compliance with the GIPS standards. Selecting the appropriate version to use for a specific composite's compliant presentation first depends on whether the firm is verified or not. Relevant language is also added to the claim of compliance if the specific composite has been examined.

The first part of the claim of compliance is the same for all compliant firms:

> [Name of firm] claims compliance with the Global Investment Performance Standards (GIPS®) and has prepared and presented this report in compliance with the GIPS standards.

Immediately following this sentence is the firm's disclosure about its verification status. (Verification is discussed in Chapter 9.) For a firm that has never been verified, the claim of compliance in its entirety would be:

> [Name of firm] claims compliance with the Global Investment Performance Standards (GIPS®) and has prepared and presented this report in compliance with the GIPS standards. [Name of firm] has not been independently verified.

For a firm that has been verified, the claim of compliance in its entirety would be:

> [Name of firm] claims compliance with the Global Investment Performance Standards and has prepared and presented this report in compliance with the GIPS standards. [Name of firm] has been independently verified for the periods [insert dates]. The verification report(s) is/are available upon request.
>
> Verification assesses whether (1) the firm has complied with all the composite construction requirements of the GIPS standards on a firmwide basis and (2) the firm's policies and procedures are designed to calculate and present performance in compliance with the GIPS standards. Verification does not ensure the accuracy of any specific composite presentation.

The language in the second paragraph describing the scope of verification is intended to ensure that the reader does not assume a higher level of assurance than is actually provided by a verification report. While a verification does not, in any way, provide assurance on the results of a specific composite, a firm may choose to have a performance examination conducted for a specific composite, which does provide assurance about the results of that composite. If a firm has chosen to have a performance examination conducted on specific composites, the entire claim of compliance for those examined composites would be:

> [*Insert name of firm*] *claims compliance with the Global Investment Performance Standards (GIPS®) and has prepared and presented this report in compliance with the GIPS standards. [Insert name of firm] has been independently verified for the periods [insert dates].*
>
> *Verification assesses whether (1) the firm has complied with all the composite construction requirements of the GIPS standards on a firmwide basis and (2) the firm's policies and procedures are designed to calculate and present performance in compliance with the GIPS standards. The [insert name of composite] composite has been examined for the periods [insert dates]. The verification and performance examination reports are available upon request.*

These are the three claims of compliance options included in the GIPS standards. A fourth option was subsequently added via a Q&A to address the situation where the performance examination period is not current. The fourth option is used for an examined composite of a verified firm, but the end date of the performance examination period is more than 24 months from the end date that is included in the composite's compliant presentation. For example, assume Firm E has been verified for the period from January 1, 2005 through December 31, 2009, and has had its Equity Value Composite examined for the period from January 1, 2005 through December 31, 2007. When preparing the compliant presentation for this composite as of December 31, 2010, the end date of the performance examination period (December 31, 2007) is more than 24 months from the end date of the compliant presentation (December 31, 2010), therefore Firm E must use the following claim of compliance if it wishes to disclose the fact that the composite has been examined:

> [*Insert name of firm*] *claims compliance with the Global Investment Performance Standards (GIPS®) and has prepared and presented this report in compliance with the GIPS standards. [Insert name of firm] has been independently verified for the periods [insert dates].*

Verification assesses whether (1) the firm has complied with all the composite construction requirements of the GIPS standards on a firm-wide basis and (2) the firm's policies and procedures are designed to calculate and present performance in compliance with the GIPS standards. Verification does not ensure the accuracy of any specific composite presentation. The [insert name of composite] composite has been examined for the periods [insert dates]. The verification and performance examination reports are available upon request.

A firm may also choose not to refer to the fact that the composite has been examined and could instead use the claim of compliance for a verified firm.

Definition of the Firm   The firm must disclose how it has been defined for the purpose of complying with the GIPS standards. As described in Chapter 2, a small, independent firm's disclosure could be as simple as stating the firm's name. A long disclosure may be required to clarify the specific division of a large, multi-location, complex financial services conglomerate that is held out to the public as a separate and distinct business entity.

Composite Description   The firm must describe the composite's strategy. This description must include general information about the strategy, and does not need to be extremely detailed. However, all key features of the strategy must be included in the description. Each firm must independently determine what is considered a key feature. For example, any factor that differentiates one composite from another might be considered a key feature, as might risks related to the use of certain instruments.

Benchmark Description   This disclosure (new in the 2010 edition of the GIPS standards) requires the firm to describe the investments, structure, and/or characteristics of the benchmark. If the benchmark is widely known, then the benchmark name will suffice. For example, the GIPS standards do not require a detailed description of the S&P 500 Index. But many firms do include a brief description of the benchmark even if it is widely known. If the benchmark is not widely known, or if its recognizability is not certain, then the description of the benchmark must be included.

Availability of the List of Composite Descriptions   This is a slight modification of the language from the 2005 edition of the GIPS standards, which required that a complete list and description of composites be provided upon request. Some firms interpreted the words "list and description of composites" as meaning that the list of composites was a separate document from composite descriptions, and that only a list of the composite names had to be provided upon request. This was not the intention, as can be seen by the sample list and description of composites included in the 2005 edition as Appendix B. Remember that this list must include all current composites as well as composites that have terminated within the past five years. One way to keep track of which terminated composites need to be included on this list is to include the date of termination at the end of the composite description. With that the firm would easily know the point in time when a terminated composite can be removed from the list of composite descriptions.

Availability of Policies for Valuing Portfolios, Calculating Performance, and Preparing Compliant Presentations A firm must disclose that this information is available upon request. A slightly shortened version of the disclosure, which required a firm to offer to provide additional information regarding policies for calculating and reporting returns, was included in the 2005 edition of the GIPS standards. Up to that point, disclosure creep had found its way into many presentations. Firms kept adding more and more disclosures concerning details of performance calculations, as they either felt it was required to disclose such details, or they were being advised to do so. At the same time, compliant presentations were getting longer and longer, and the compliance burden was growing. While the GIPS standards never required a firm to disclose the detailed methodology used to perform the return calculations, this provision was added to the GIPS standards to address the misperception that detailed disclosures describing return calculations were required.

In the 2010 edition, this disclosure was expanded and now requires a firm to look beyond the performance calculations and consider the firm's policies for creating the entire compliant presentation. For example, this expanded language requires that a firm stand ready to provide policies about how it constructs composites. These policies should already be documented in the firm's GIPS Manual. The firm must now disclose that policies for valuing portfolios, calculating performance, and preparing compliant presentations are available upon request. A firm may choose to disclose any of these policies if it wishes to do so, but disclosure is not required.

Take note that this disclosure requires a firm to provide information about policies, not procedures. As described in Chapter 1, a *policy* is the rule a firm has adopted. A *procedure* is a process by which a firm makes sure the policy is followed. Only policies are required to be provided upon request. The procedures are not required to be provided upon request. The summary of a firm's policies should be an extract from the GIPS Manual. However, if a firm wishes to do so, it could provide the complete GIPS

Manual, including both policies and procedures, to satisfy any request for this information.

Currency Used to Express Performance   While this disclosure seems unimportant to firms in the United States that are marketing only to prospective U.S. clients, this can be an important disclosure for firms marketing in areas that employ multiple currencies and hold no widespread assumption that a particular base currency is used. This disclosure requirement can be met with brief text such as, "Returns are expressed in Canadian dollars." If the composite includes portfolios managed in multiple base currencies that are different from the composite's reporting currency, there is no requirement to go into any more detail about how the firm converted and then aggregated the portfolio returns to determine the composite return, but a firm could disclose this information if it wished to do so.

The manager may wish to express a composite return in multiple currencies. For example, a Canadian money manager may manage client portfolios for both U.S. and Canadian clients and want to present the composite returns in both U.S. and Canadian dollars. If a firm converts composite returns to another currency, all other information, such as composite assets and firm assets, must also be converted and reported in the other currency.

Which Measure of Internal Dispersion Is Used   As described previously, a firm may choose which measure of internal dispersion to present. However, due to the variety of options, the firm must disclose which measure is presented. While this disclosure does not need to include details about the method used to calculate the internal dispersion, firms commonly do so. For example:

> *Dispersion is measured by the standard deviation of the equal weighted annual portfolio gross returns of those portfolios included in the composite for the full year. For periods with six or fewer portfolios included in the composite for the full year, no dispersion measure is required to be presented.*

If the firm decides to change the internal measure that is presented, the firm must explain which measure is presented for which periods.

Fee Schedule   Firms must disclose the fee schedule that is appropriate to the compliant presentation. For U.S. firms that are registered with the SEC, the fee schedule is typically the product fee schedule that is included in Form ADV. Form ADV is the form used to register as an investment adviser with the SEC. This disclosure needs to be done carefully for firms offering the strategy via multiple portfolio types, such as institutional portfolios, commingled funds, and mutual funds. Further complications result when a firm offers different fee structures for different types of clients (e.g., domestic versus international clients) or when different compensation options are available (e.g., asset-only-based fees versus asset-based fees plus a performance fee component). The GIPS standards do not require disclosure of each and every fee schedule offered to every type of prospect. But the firm does have to carefully consider the appropriate fee schedule to present for each composite. Where multiple fee options exist, the firm should offer to provide information about the additional fee schedules.

Composite Creation Date *Composite creation date* is the date when the firm first combined portfolios to create the composite. This disclosure is intended to inform the reader if a composite is newly created. For example, assume a composite has a track record from April 2004 through December 2010. If the composite creation date was in 2009, this would indicate that the composite was created more recently, and may have been created with the benefit of hindsight. It should also raise the question: Where were the portfolios in this composite before this composite was created? A composite creation date in 2004 would not raise any such questions.

The composite creation date is not the same as the *composite inception date*. The inception date is the initial date of the composite's track record. In the example above, the composite inception date is April 1, 2004. There is no requirement to disclose the composite inception date.

Finally, note that a month and year, or even just the year for historical periods, will suffice for the composite creation date. No one is expected to determine the specific day when a composite was created.

Required Disclosures, if Applicable

Each of the disclosures described in the previous section must be included in all compliant presentations. The following disclosures must also be included in a compliant presentation if they are applicable to the specific composite. If the disclosure is not applicable to the specific composite, then no disclosure related to the item is required.

If Gross Returns Reflect the Deduction of Any Fees Other Than Trading Expenses
Gross returns must reflect the deduction of all trading expenses, such as brokerage fees. If trading expenses are not reflected in the calculation of gross return, this is not a GIPS-compliant gross return. In addition to trading expenses, investment portfolios may also incur other fees, such as management and custodian fees. The assumption in the GIPS standards is

that gross returns reflect only the deduction of trading expenses. Other fees may be deducted. If other fees are deducted, the firm must disclose this fact.

This is often the scenario when a firm relies on a return that is calculated by a third-party administrator. Assume a firm manages both mutual funds and institutional portfolios. The mutual funds are administered at a custodian bank, and returns based on a *net asset value* (NAV) are provided to the firm by the custodian bank.

To make a mutual fund return consistent with the return of an institutional portfolio, the mutual fund's NAV-based returns, which are net of all fees and expenses, can be "grossed up." Some firms will gross up the net return by the entire expense ratio, while others gross up only for the management fee. If the net return is grossed up only by the management fee, this would result in a gross return that is net of more than just trading expenses. A sample disclosure for this situation might be, "All returns reflect the deduction of trading expenses. Gross returns for pooled funds that are included in the composite also reflect the deduction of custodian, accounting, and other administrative expenses."

If gross returns reflect the deduction of only trading expenses, no disclosure is required.

If Net Returns Reflect the Deduction of Any Fees Other Than Trading Expenses and Investment Management Fees

Net returns must reflect the deduction of all trading expenses and investment management fees. As described above, if trading expenses are not reflected in the net return calculation, this is not a GIPS-compliant net return. The assumption is that net returns reflect the deduction of only trading expenses and investment management fees, and no other fees are deducted. Other fees or expenses may be deducted, and if they are, then the firm must disclose these other deductions. If a firm places reliance on an NAV-based return, and makes no adjustment to this NAV return, the net return will reflect the deduction of additional expenses. This net return is acceptable for GIPS purposes. There is no requirement to gross up the NAV-based return. A firm simply has to disclose additional information about the net returns.

If net returns reflect the deduction of only trading expenses and investment management fees, no disclosure that these are the only items deducted is required.

If Net Returns Are Net of Model or Actual Investment Management Fees

When calculating returns that are net of investment management fees, a firm may calculate net returns using either actual fees or model fees. When net returns are presented, the firm must disclose which method has been used. The disclosure can be as brief as:

Net returns reflect the deduction of actual investment management fees.

Or,

Net returns reflect the deduction of model investment management fees.

Many firms choose to add additional language to explain how net returns are calculated. For example:

Net returns are calculated by deducting .0833%, which is 1/12th of the highest tier of the fee schedule (1.00%), from the monthly gross composite return.

If Net Returns Are Net of Any Performance-Based Fees When net returns are presented, the firm must disclose if any performance-based fees are reflected in the net returns. For example:

Net returns reflect the deduction of actual management fees. Most portfolios included in the composite pay a management fee that includes an asset-based and a performance-based component.

While the details of the net return calculations are not required to be disclosed, it would be helpful to disclose whether performance fees are reflected in the net return when they are accrued, when they are due and payable (i.e., crystallized), or when they are paid.

Presence, Use, and Extent of Leverage, Derivatives, and Short Positions, if Material If the composite strategy includes a material use of leverage, derivatives, or short positions, the firm must disclose information about the use of these tools. The firm must describe how frequently leverage, derivatives, and short positions are utilized, as well as characteristics of each of these instruments or practices. The intent of the disclosure is to present enough information for the prospective client to understand that they are exposed to additional risks by the use of these tools. Note that this disclosure does not necessarily have to be a separate disclosure. If the composite description (a general overview of the composite strategy) is robust, and includes sufficient details about the composite strategy, the composite description may already include sufficient information to meet this disclosure requirement.

Significant Events   A firm must disclose all significant events that would enable a prospective client to better understand and interpret the information that is presented in a compliant presentation. There is no definition of what qualifies as a significant event, so it is left to each firm to decide for themselves what additional information should be disclosed. Examples of items that might qualify as a significant event include the following:

- Change in ownership of the firm.
- Departure of key investment personnel.
- Major transactions or modifications that occur within portfolios in the composite.

None of these items automatically qualify as a significant event requiring disclosure. The facts and circumstances of each case must be individually considered. For example, suppose a portfolio manager leaves the firm. If the firm's marketing materials put the spotlight on key portfolio managers, the departure of a star portfolio manager would most probably qualify as a significant event that must be disclosed. If the firm focuses on team management, and its marketing efforts emphasize the team approach to managing portfolios, the departure of a single portfolio manager may not qualify as a significant event that would require disclosure. However, when determining whether or not to disclose something as a significant event, if there is any doubt as to whether an event should be disclosed, a firm should default to disclosing the item.

For Any Performance Presented Prior to January 1, 2000, Any Periods of Noncompliance   If the compliant presentation includes performance that is not compliant, the firm must disclose the periods of noncompliance. Prior to the 2010 edition of the GIPS standards, a firm also had to disclose why the presentation was not in compliance. Thankfully this disclosure was deleted, as many firms struggled to explain why a presentation was not in compliance.
   Note that this disclosure only applies to non-compliant periods presented in the compliant presentation. If the firm has not complied with the GIPS standards for its entire history, it does not need to disclose this fact. For example, assume a firm has been in existence since 1985. The firm complies with the GIPS standards beginning January 1, 2000, and it presents history back to 2000 in its compliant presentations. The firm is not required to disclose that the firm was not in compliance prior to January 1, 2000.

Firm Redefinition   If the firm has been redefined, the firm must disclose the date of, description of, and reason for the redefinition. Firm redefinitions often occur when two divisions within one firm, previously defined as separate firms for GIPS-compliance purposes, merge and become one firm. For example:

> *Prior to January 1, 2006, the firm included only the institutional division. On January 1, 2006, the firm was redefined to include the wrap-fee division on a prospective basis.*

Composite Redefinition   If a composite is redefined, the firm must disclose the date of, description of, and reason for the redefinition. A composite definition is the set of detailed rules that determine the assignment of portfolios to composites. Any change to these detailed rules is considered a composite redefinition, and must be disclosed. Typical composite redefinition language would be:

> *On January 1, 2006, the Core Fixed Income Composite was redefined to exclude those portfolios that do not allow the use of futures. Beginning on that date, the Core Fixed Income strategy was modified with the intention to primarily use futures for duration management.*

A second example is:

> *On February 1, 2008, the Core Equity Composite was redefined to include mutual funds and other pooled vehicles as the firm determined that the legal structure of the different portfolio types no longer significantly impacted the management of the pooled vehicles. Previously all pooled vehicles were excluded from the Composite and were included in separate composites.*

Composite Name Change   Composite name changes must be disclosed. At times a firm may slightly modify their composite names, and minor changes may not necessarily be considered a name change that would require disclosure. Assume a firm has a composite named the Smallcap Value Composite. Renaming the composite the Small Capitalization Value Composite is not the kind of name change contemplated by this requirement and would not require disclosure. But renaming the Small Cap Value Composite to the Special Opportunities Composite is a change in name that must be disclosed. Note that a Q&A issued in January 2008 explains that this disclosure may be removed from the compliant presentation after one year if the firm determines that the disclosure is no longer relevant or meaningful.

Composite Minimum   A firm may establish a minimum size for a composite, whereby portfolios that are below the minimum size are not included in the composite as these portfolios are too small to be representative of the composite's strategy. If a composite has a minimum size for inclusion, the composite minimum must be disclosed. A firm must also disclose any changes to the composite minimum that have occurred during the period that is presented in the compliant presentation. For example:

> *The Core Fixed Income Composite includes only those portfolios that have a minimum size of $10 million. Prior to January 1, 2008 the minimum size for composite inclusion was $8 million.*

The firm's marketing minimum is not being disclosed here. While a firm may disclose the marketing minimum, it is not required to do so.

Treatment of Withholding Taxes   A firm must disclose how withholding taxes are reflected in the return calculations, that is, whether returns are gross or net of withholding taxes. This disclosure must be made only if withholding taxes are material. This is a change from the requirement in the 2005 edition of the GIPS standards, which did not have a materiality threshold. Whether returns are calculated gross or net of withholding taxes depends on how the firm records the transaction.

Assume a U.S. client's portfolio earns a $100 dividend on a foreign stock and is subject to a 15% withholding tax. The portfolio receives $85. If the firm wishes to record the dividend gross of withholding tax, it would record $100 of income, and an offsetting cash flow (outflow) of $15. If the firm wishes to record the dividend net of withholding tax, it would record $85 of income.

The firm must also disclose if benchmark returns are net of withholding taxes. This disclosure must be made only if this information is available. If a firm is not able to determine whether benchmark returns are net or gross of withholding taxes because this information is not provided by the benchmark source, no disclosure is required.

Previously, in the 2005 edition of the GIPS standards, if a firm used a benchmark calculated net of withholding taxes, the firm was required to disclose the tax basis of the benchmark. While this disclosure was deleted from the 2010 edition of the GIPS standards, it would make sense for a firm to continue to disclose the withholding tax basis of the benchmark if there is more than one version of the benchmark available, each with different assumed withholding tax rates.

Material Differences in Exchange Rates or Valuation Sources A firm may include portfolios valued using different valuation sources and/or exchange rates in one composite. If the firm determines that these differences are material, the firm must disclose that such differences exist between portfolios in the composite. The same is true if different valuation sources and/or exchange rates are used between the portfolios in the composite and the benchmark. For example, a U.S. mutual fund included in the International Equity Composite is valued in accordance with regulatory fair value requirements to prevent market timing. The same investments held by other portfolios in the composite are valued using closing prices in local markets. The benchmark is valued at the London close. While these differences are not expected to be material, at any given point in time the different sources could result in materially different returns.

If a firm determines that such differences will always be material, the firm should decide whether including portfolios with different valuation sources in the same composite is appropriate.

Conformity with Laws and Regulations That Conflict with the GIPS Standards Provision 0.A.2 requires firms to comply with all applicable laws and regulations regarding the calculation and presentation of performance. If a firm is subject to any laws or regulations that cause the firm to calculate a return or present performance information that is not in accordance with the requirements of the GIPS standards, the firm would be required to disclose this fact, as well as explain how the laws or regulations conflict with the GIPS standards. We've never seen a firm need to make this disclosure.

Method Used to Allocate Cash to Carve-Outs Until December 31, 2009, a firm could include in a composite portfolios that were carve-outs of broader portfolios, and for which cash was allocated. If a composite included carve-out portfolios with allocated cash, the firm must disclose the policy that was used to allocate cash to the carve-out. For example:

> *Prior to December 31, 2009, the Core Equity Composite included equity segments of balanced portfolios that were managed in the core equity strategy. Cash was allocated to the equity segment monthly based on the beginning of month value of equity assets relative to the total portfolio.*

Types of Fees That Are Included in Bundled Fees A *bundled fee* is a fee that combines multiple fees into one aggregate fee. Bundled fees can include any combination of investment management fees, trading expenses, custody fees, and/or administrative fees. Two examples of bundled fees are wrap fees and all-in fees.

In the United States this disclosure typically applies to two types of portfolios: fee-in-lieu portfolios and wrap-fee/Separately Managed Account (SMA) portfolios. Sample disclosures for each are as follows:

> *The majority of portfolios in this composite pay a fee in lieu of commissions to their broker and/or custodian. In addition to trading expenses, this brokerage fee generally includes advisory and custodian fees.*

Or,

> *The wrap fee includes charges for trading costs, portfolio management, custody, and other administrative and sponsor-related fees.*

Use of a Subadvisor Provision 0.A.14 requires a firm to include in total firm assets those assets that are managed by a subadvisor, if the firm has the ability to hire and fire the subadvisor. A *subadvisor* is a third-party investment manager hired by the firm to manage some or all of the assets for which a firm has investment management responsibility.

If a composite includes assets that are subadvised, the firm must disclose that a subadvisor is used, and for which periods the subadvisor is used. The firm does not have to name the subadvisor. This disclosure is required only for periods beginning on or after January 1, 2006. If a subadvisor was used for periods prior to this date, the firm is recommended to disclose the use of a subadvisor, but is not required to do so. For example:

> *As of August 1, 2008, the emerging market segment of global equity portfolios is managed by a subadvisor. Previously this segment was managed by an internal team.*

No disclosure is required if the firm itself acts as a subadvisor. Sub-advised portfolios are treated just like any other portfolio managed by the firm.

Portfolios Not Valued at Calendar Month End For periods beginning on or after January 1, 2010, portfolios must be valued as of calendar month end (or the last business day of the month.) Prior to this date, portfolios were not required to be valued as of calendar month end. If a firm did not value portfolios as of calendar month end for periods prior to January 1, 2010, the firm must disclose this fact. For example:

> *Prior to June 1998 portfolios that were custodied at [Brokerage Firm] were valued as of the last Friday of the month.*

Use of Subjective, Unobservable Inputs to Value Investments   Beginning on January 1, 2011, firms are required to value investments in accordance with the GIPS definition of fair value. The GIPS standards include a recommended valuation hierarchy for determining fair value. The last tier of the recommended valuation hierarchy includes investments that are valued based on "subjective unobservable inputs for the investment where markets are not active at the measurement date. Unobservable inputs should only be used to measure fair value to the extent that observable inputs and prices are not available or appropriate. Unobservable inputs reflect the firm's own assumptions about the assumptions that market participants would use in pricing the investment and should be developed based on the best information available under the circumstances."[2]

If investments valued using the last tier of the recommended hierarchy, or the equivalent in the firm's own hierarchy, are material to the composite, the firm must disclose this fact. Note that this disclosure is not a specific calculation as of a certain date. Instead the firm should approach this issue from the perspective of the prospective client: Would the prospect find it helpful to know that a significant proportion of portfolio assets are valued based on subjective, non-market-based criteria? For example:

> *The Distressed Debt strategy may invest up to 20% of assets in private or unlisted securities for which no market prices are available. Such investments are valued using subjective, unobservable inputs and are based on the firm's best estimate of the value of the investments.*

If the Firm's Valuation Hierarchy Materially Differs from the GIPS-Recommended Hierarchy   The GIPS standards include a recommended valuation hierarchy. This valuation hierarchy was not created in isolation. Any firm that complies with accounting standards will find the valuation hierarchy to be very familiar. While the firm's valuation hierarchy may be unique, most firms will create a hierarchy that is substantially the same as the GIPS valuation hierarchy. A firm creating a hierarchy that is not aligned with the recommended hierarchy is difficult to imagine.

---

[2]CFA Institute, "Global Investment Performance Standards (GIPS®): As Adopted by the GIPS Executive Committee on 29 January 2010" [2010 edition] (Charlottesville, VA: 2010), 27.

Why No Benchmark Is Presented   A firm may determine that no appropriate benchmark for the composite exists. This is the only reason a compliant presentation can exclude a benchmark return. Firms may not choose to exclude a benchmark just because they do not want to include benchmark returns. In rare cases where a firm determines that no benchmark is appropriate, the firm must disclose why no benchmark is presented. For example:

> No benchmark is presented as our Pure Alpha Strategy Composite opportunistically invests in a wide variety of investments. The strategy may invest in domestic and international markets, and may utilize derivative instruments. We do not believe that any benchmark is a proper point of reference for our strategy.

Benchmark Change   If the benchmark for a composite is changed, the firm must disclose the date of, description of, and reason for the change. There are two types of benchmark changes that can be made. A *spliced benchmark* occurs when the benchmark is changed on a prospective basis only. The benchmark history represents two (or more) benchmarks that are linked over time. For example:

> Effective January 1, 2000, the benchmark was changed to the J.P. Morgan Emerging Markets Bond Index Global from the J.P. Morgan Emerging Markets Bond Index Plus. The change was made as the J.P. Morgan Emerging Markets Bond Index Global is a better representation of this composite's strategy.

A firm may also determine that changing a benchmark retroactively is appropriate, and replaces the entire benchmark history with a new benchmark. A firm must not change the benchmark historically if the only reason for doing so is to make composite performance look better relative to the new benchmark. A legitimate reason for changing a benchmark retroactively occurs when a new benchmark that is better suited to the composite's strategy is created. Unless there is a compelling reason for retroactively changing a composite's benchmark, a firm may have difficulty convincing prospects that a benchmark change was warranted.

Custom Benchmark   A firm may choose to present a custom benchmark. There are many types of custom benchmarks. The most common is a benchmark calculated by blending market indexes. This is typically done for a balanced composite, where a blend of an equity index and a fixed income index is used to create the blended custom benchmark. If a custom benchmark is presented, the firm must disclose the benchmark components, weights, and rebalancing process. For example:

> *The Custom Balanced benchmark is a custom blend calculated monthly by weighting the returns of the S&P 500 Index and Barclays Capital U.S. Aggregate Bond Index in a 65/35 combination.*

A custom benchmark may also be created using the benchmarks of the individual portfolios in the composite. This is a common practice for fixed income composites where portfolios share a strategy but are managed to a different benchmark. For example:

> *The Core Custom Benchmark is a market weighted custom benchmark that is calculated using the benchmarks of portfolios in the composite. As of December 31, 2009, the breakdown of the benchmark was 82.6% Barclays Capital U.S. Aggregate Bond Index, 14.5% Citigroup Broad Index, and 2.9% Barclays Capital U.S. Government/Credit A+ Index. The benchmark is rebalanced monthly based on the composite's portfolio population and portfolio market values.*

If a firm uses a custom benchmark that is created using the benchmarks of the underlying portfolios within the composite, the nature of this type of custom benchmark is that it will change every month. This is not the type of change that will trigger the requirement to disclose benchmark changes. But if the composite's benchmark changed from a custom blend of the underlying portfolio benchmarks to a market index, this change would need to be disclosed and explained.

Significant Cash Flow Policy   As described in Chapter 2, a firm may adopt a policy whereby portfolios that experience an external cash flow above a certain size are temporarily removed from the composite. The rationale for this policy is that the size of the cash flow causes the portfolio to be temporarily considered nondiscretionary. The policy may be adopted on a composite-specific basis. If a composite has a significant cash flow policy, the firm must disclose how significant cash flow has been defined for that composite, and for which periods. For example:

> *Beginning January 1, 2005, portfolios are temporarily removed from the composite if they experience a cash flow greater than 25% of the portfolio's beginning of period market value. Prior to this date, portfolios were temporarily removed from the composite*

if they experienced a cash flow greater than 20% of the portfolio's beginning of period market value.

Why the Three-Year Annualized Ex-Post Standard Deviation Is Not Presented Provision 5.A.2 requires a firm to present the three-year annualized ex-post standard deviation of the composite and the benchmark as of each annual period end, for annual periods ended after January 1, 2011. The calculation must be done using monthly returns. However, the GIPS standards have required composites to be calculated monthly only as of January 1, 2010. A firm may have been calculating composite returns quarterly for periods prior to January 1, 2010. If so, then the firm may not have monthly composite returns available for the ex-post standard deviation calculation. In such a case the firm must explain why the ex-post standard deviation is not presented. For example:

> *A firm is required to present the three-year annualized ex-post standard deviation of the composite and the benchmark for annual periods ended after 2010. Monthly returns must be used in this calculation. Prior to January 2010 composite returns were calculated quarterly, therefore monthly returns for the 36-month period ended December 31, 2011 are not available and the standard deviation of the composite and benchmark are not presented.*

This specific disclosure could be used at most through November 30, 2012. As of December 31, 2012, all firms that comply with the GIPS standards must have 36 monthly returns available for all composites that have at least 36 months of history as of that date. If a firm is presenting a composite with less than 36 months of history, it would not have available 36 monthly returns. For example:

> *No three-year annualized ex-post standard deviation is presented as the composite does not yet have a 36-month history.*

Firms may choose a benchmark for which monthly returns are not available. For example:

> *The XYZ Benchmark returns are obtained from a published source that provides only quarterly returns. As monthly benchmark returns are not available, no ex-post standard deviation of the benchmark is presented.*

Why the Three-Year Annualized Ex-Post Standard Deviation Is Not Relevant or Appropriate　Provision 5.A.2 requires a firm to present the three-year annualized ex-post standard deviation of the composite and the benchmark for annual periods ended after January 1, 2011. If a firm determines that the ex-post standard deviation is not a relevant or appropriate measure of risk for the composite, it must present another ex-post measure of risk in addition to the standard deviation. The firm must disclose why it believes that standard deviation is not relevant or appropriate. For example:

> *Standard deviation is not a relevant measure of risk for the composite as the strategy is highly concentrated, which is expected to result in much higher volatility than the benchmark.*

Additional Risk Measure Presented　If a firm determines that the ex-post standard deviation required by provision 5.A.2 is not a relevant or appropriate measure of risk for the composite, it must present another ex-post measure of risk in addition to the standard deviation. The firm must describe the additional risk measure that is presented, and why it was selected. For example:

> *The Information Ratio is presented as an additional measure of risk, as we believe it is the most appropriate risk measure for the composite's strategy. The Information Ratio is a measure relating the benchmark relative return achieved to benchmark relative risk taken.*

Performance Is from a Past Firm　Provision 5.A.8 contains tests that must be met if history from a prior firm must be, or may be, linked to performance of a new or acquiring firm. If history from a prior firm is presented and linked to performance at the new firm, the firm must disclose that its performance is linked to performance from a prior firm. For example:

> *Performance shown prior to May 2009 represents performance achieved by the Small Cap team while at Former Asset Management.*

Correction of a Material Error　A firm that has a material error in a compliant presentation must correct the error and must disclose the change. This disclosure must be included in the compliant presentation for at least one year after the correction is made. This requirement is not in the GIPS provisions but instead is included in the *Guidance Statement on Error Correction*. Chapter 8 discusses establishing an error correction policy.

LENGTH OF TIME FOR DISCLOSURES

The GIPS standards do not have any time period associated with required disclosures. Theoretically all required disclosures must be included in a compliant presentation forever. (There are two exceptions: disclosures for a composite name change or for a material error correction can be removed after one year.) However, it is acknowledged that some disclosures lose relevance over time. When the 2010 edition of the GIPS standards was issued for public comment, feedback was requested on this topic. A wide variety of responses was received, but there was no consensus on which disclosures might qualify for removal after a certain length of time, as well as what the appropriate length of time might be for any specific disclosure. As a result, no change was made to the 2010 edition of the GIPS standards. While there is no allowance within the GIPS standards for a firm to remove disclosures after a certain length of time, some firms do remove disclosures if they believe that the disclosure is no longer relevant.

Assume Firm F manages a municipal bond strategy, which invests in securities issued within any state, and has a three-year target average duration. Firm F began managing the strategy in 2004. At that time the closest benchmark to the strategy was a National 0–5 Year Muni Bond Index, and that was the benchmark the firm used in the compliant presentation. Firm F included a disclosure about the differences between the composite and the benchmark in the compliant presentation. In 2007, a new 0–3 Year benchmark was created that is a subset of the 0–5 Year benchmark, and the benchmark was created retroactively. Firm F changed to report performance against this benchmark, for all periods, and disclosed the benchmark change as required. In 2011, is it relevant to a reader of the presentation that over five years ago the firm previously used the 0–5 Year benchmark? Firm F thinks not, and decides to remove this disclosure. It would be hard to argue that removing this disclosure would not be proper.

PRESENTATION AND DISCLOSURE RECOMMENDATIONS

The GIPS standards include several recommendations regarding composite presentations and disclosures. As with all recommended provisions, they should be viewed as best practice. Firms should not feel compelled to comply with any recommended disclosures. A firm should review each of the recommendations and determine which ones make sense for them to include in compliant presentations. The following is guidance on selected presentation and disclosure recommendations.

Present Gross-of-Fees Returns

The GIPS standards recommend presentation of gross-of-fees returns since gross returns allow for better comparability between firms. A firm may present gross-only returns, net-only returns, or both gross and net returns. All three options satisfy the GIPS standards. But the inclusion of both gross and net returns in compliant presentations is common. This is because the disclosure of only gross returns may not satisfy applicable regulatory requirements.

Present Quarterly and/or Monthly Returns

A compliant presentation must include annual returns. Compliant presentations may include returns for shorter time periods, but that is optional. Most compliant presentations, particularly for larger firms, include only annual returns. Larger firms typically include only the minimum required information in a compliant presentation to minimize the amount of effort needed to produce compliant presentations, as well as minimize the risk of errors occurring.

Update Compliant Presentations Quarterly

Because a compliant presentation is required to include annual returns at a minimum, compliant presentations must be updated at least annually. However, the GIPS standards recommend updating compliant presentations more frequently and including recent returns. Anecdotal evidence again supports the view that the larger the firm, the less likely it is to update compliant presentations more often than annually. Of course, other marketing materials are updated more frequently, but not the compliant presentations themselves.

Disclose Inclusion of Proprietary Assets

If a composite includes proprietary assets, firms are recommended to disclose this fact. Proprietary assets are investments owned by the firm, the firm's management, and/or the firm's parent company that are managed by the firm. The draft of the 2010 GIPS standards that was distributed for public comment included this disclosure as a requirement, which generated significant feedback. Many firms questioned exactly how a firm would be able to identify such assets, particularly in a large firm that has complex corporate relationships. Some comment letters also questioned the usefulness of this information, and stated the funding source of a portfolio should not matter, while others thought the information would be very helpful. This resulting GIPS recommendation is a compromise of the opposing views on this topic.

SUPPLEMENTAL INFORMATION

A firm is not limited to including in a compliant presentation only information that is required or recommended by the GIPS standards. The *Guidance Statement on the Use of Supplemental Information* states that firms are encouraged to present all relevant information needed to fully explain their performance, and describes how such information can be incorporated into a compliant presentation. This document differentiates additional information and supplemental information. *Additional information* is information included in a compliant presentation that is required or recommended by the GIPS standards. Additional information is information directly derived from composite data. Common examples of additional information include composite year-to-date returns, cumulative returns, annualized returns, and any other information calculated using the composite performance. Additional information does not need to be labeled in any special way.

On the other hand, *supplemental information* is not derived directly from a composite. Supplemental information is any performance-related information included as part of a compliant presentation that supplements or enhances the information that is required and/or recommended by the GIPS standards. Supplemental information needs to be clearly labeled and identified as supplemental to a specific compliant presentation. Common examples of supplemental information include segment (ex-cash) returns, ex-ante risk measures, and attribution information calculated using the composite's representative account.

Note that the definition of supplemental information clarifies that to be supplemental information the performance-related information must be *part of a compliant presentation.* If the performance-related information is not part of the compliant presentation itself, then it is not considered supplemental information.

This can get quite confusing once you start considering marketing materials that include the compliant presentation. For example, assume Firm G has a standard pitch book that is used when meeting with prospective clients. Included in every pitch book is the appropriate compliant presentation for the strategy under discussion. The compliant presentation is included as Appendix 1. Does the fact that the compliant presentation's inclusion as an appendix in the pitch book mean the first 50 pages of the pitch book are considered "part of the compliant presentation" and must therefore potentially be considered supplemental information? Some firms do take this approach, while others limit the potential for information to be considered supplemental only to those items that are included directly on the same page(s) of the compliant presentation itself (in this example, as part of Appendix 1).

The GIPS standards will likely be enhanced in the future to clarify the status of supplemental information. Until then, firms should seek guidance on this matter from their verification firm.

GIPS ADVERTISING GUIDELINES

In the same way that financial services firms communicate their capabilities to individual investors via advertising, institutional money managers also advertise their brands, products, and special capabilities to potential investors. Firms that comply with the GIPS standards are under no obligation to mention the GIPS standards in their advertisements. But the firm may choose to mention the fact that the firm is GIPS-compliant, especially if the advertisement includes performance information. If a firm wishes to mention the GIPS standards in an advertisement, it must meet the requirements discussed in this section.

The first step is to clarify what is meant by "advertising." The *GIPS Advertising Guidelines* include a definition of advertisement: "For the purposes of these guidelines, an advertisement includes any materials that are distributed to or designed for use in newspapers, magazines, firm brochures, letters, media, websites, or any other written or electronic material addressed to more than one prospective client. Any written material, other than one-on-one presentations and individual client reporting, distributed to maintain existing clients or solicit new clients for a firm is considered an advertisement."[3]

The next step is to determine whether or not the firm will refer to the fact that the firm claims compliance with the GIPS standards in the advertisement. A compliant firm has three options when preparing an advertisement:

1. Make no reference to the GIPS standards.
2. Include in the advertisement a compliant presentation.
3. Prepare an advertisement in compliance with the requirements of the GIPS Advertising Guidelines.

---

[3]2010 edition of the GIPS standards, 29.

Because each advertising piece may have specific goals, a firm can decide the appropriate option on a piece-by-piece basis. Regardless of the option selected, a firm still has an obligation under Provision 0.A.9 to make every reasonable effort to provide a compliant presentation to all prospective clients.

We will now examine each of the three options in turn.

Make No Reference to the GIPS Standards

A firm may choose to not refer to the GIPS standards at all when preparing an advertisement. This option is often chosen when there is limited space available in the advertisement or when the advertisement does not target institutional investors.

Include in the Advertisement a Compliant Presentation

A firm could choose to include a compliant presentation in an advertisement. The one type of advertisement where this is common practice is on a firm's web site because space is not an issue. As compliant presentations include the claim of compliance with the GIPS standards, a firm would be informing the web site reader that the firm claims compliance with the GIPS standards. However, posting compliant presentations on the firm's web site does not absolve the firm from the requirement to make every reasonable effort to provide a compliant presentation to all prospective clients. A firm still needs to ensure this requirement is met, even for prospective clients making an initial connection to a firm via the firm's web site.

Follow the GIPS Advertising Guidelines

The third option is to make mention of the GIPS standards, but not include a compliant presentation. To do this, the firm must follow the *GIPS Advertising Guidelines*. This option allows a firm to state that it claims compliance with the GIPS standards, but to do so in a more abbreviated format than is required by the GIPS standards in a compliant presentation.

The information that a firm must include in an advertisement that is prepared following the GIPS Advertising Guidelines depends on whether the advertisement includes performance.

Required Information in All Advertisements   These three disclosures must be included in all advertisements that comply with the GIPS Advertising Guidelines, whether historical performance figures are included or not.

1. *Firm definition.* This is the same disclosure that is required in a compliant presentation. The firm must disclose how it is defined for the purpose of complying with the GIPS standards.
2. *How to obtain a compliant presentation and/or list of composite descriptions.* The firm must inform the reader how to obtain these items. Common practice is to provide a phone number or e-mail address for the person at the firm who can provide the requested information. Directing a reader to the firm's web site will not suffice unless there is a specific location where this information can be obtained.
3. *Advertising Guidelines claim of compliance.* A much shorter claim of compliance is required for an advertisement versus the one required for a compliant presentation. If the reader of an advertisement qualifies as a prospective client, he or she will eventually receive a compliant presentation, which includes the full claim of compliance and discloses the firm's verification status. The Advertising Guidelines claim of compliance is: "[Insert firm name] claims compliance with the Global Investment Performance Standards (GIPS®)."

Additional Required Information in Advertisements That Include Performance If performance is included in the advertisement, the following text outlines the requirements that also apply:

4. *Composite performance in accordance with one of three options.* There are three options for presenting composite returns:
   a. One-, three-, and five-year annualized composite returns through the most recent period.
   b. Period-to-date composite returns, and the one-, three-, and five-year annualized returns through the same time period as presented in the corresponding compliant presentation.
   c. Period-to-date composite returns, and annual returns for the past five years for the same annual periods as presented in the corresponding compliant presentation.

   In all cases the period end date must be clearly identified. If the composite has less than five years of history, the firm must present performance from inception through the period end, as required by the option selected.

   The GIPS Advertising Guidelines are silent as to whether gross or net returns must be presented in the advertisement. Common practice in the United States is to include either net returns only, or gross and net returns, in order to satisfy SEC advertising requirements.

5. *Benchmark returns for the same periods as presented for the composite.* Whichever option is selected, the corresponding benchmark returns must also be presented. The benchmark presented in the advertisement must be the same benchmark as presented in the corresponding compliant presentation.

For example, assume Firm H prepares an advertisement following the GIPS Advertising Guidelines for its Aggressive Equity Composite as of March 31, 2011. The composite's inception date is October 1, 2008, and Firm H includes calendar year returns in compliant presentations. Table 6.3 is an excerpt from the compliant presentation for the Aggressive Equity Composite as of December 31, 2011.

Assume returns for Q1 2012 are:
- Composite gross-of-fees: −8.88%
- Composite net-of-fees: −9.03%
- Benchmark: −8.70%

The three options for presenting the composite's returns are illustrated in Table 6.4.

The following additional disclosures are required when returns are included in the advertisement:

6. *Composite description.* This is the same disclosure that is required in a compliant presentation. The composite description must include general information about the strategy. It does not need to be extremely detailed. However, all key features of the strategy must be included in the description.
7. *Whether returns are presented gross-of-fees or net-of-fees.* This requirement can be met by labeling the returns as gross or net. A firm could also choose to explain which returns are presented through a disclosure, but labeling the returns directly in the table is easiest.
8. *Benchmark description.* This is the same disclosure required for a compliant presentation. A firm must describe the investment, structure, and/or characteristics of the benchmark. If the benchmark is a widely known market index, peer group, or other reference point such as the 3 Month LIBOR rate, simply stating the name of the benchmark is sufficient.
9. *Why no benchmark is presented, if applicable.* In the rare case where a firm determines that no benchmark is appropriate for a composite, the firm must disclose why no benchmark is presented.
10. *Currency used to express performance.* This disclosure can be met through a short disclosure such as "Returns are expressed in U.S. dollars."

TABLE 6.3 Sample Compliant Presentation Excerpt: The Aggressive Equity Composite of Firm H from October 1, 2008 through December 31, 2011

Year	Gross Return (%)	Net Return (%)	Benchmark Return (%)	Internal Dispersion (%)	Number of Portfolios	As of December 31		
						Composite Assets ($ millions)	Total Firm Assets ($ millions)	
2011	17.61	16.85	17.57	1.2	38	744	4,028	
2010	7.96	7.26	8.11	1.5	39	702	3,780	
2009	14.18	13.44	13.93	0.8	16	350	2,941	
2008[a]	11.78	11.60	10.22	n/a	8	125	2,893	

[a] Returns are for the period from October 1, 2008 (inception) through December 31, 2008.

TABLE 6.4 GIPS Advertising Guidelines Sample Composite and Benchmark Returns

Option 1: One-, three-, and five-year (or since inception if sooner) annualized composite returns through the most recent period.

Annualized Returns as of March 31, 2012	Composite (gross)	Composite (net)	Benchmark
1-Year	1.62%	0.96%	1.82%
3-Year	10.48%	9.77%	10.52%
Since inception	11.78%	11.06%	11.36%

Option 2: Period-to-date composite returns, and the one-, three-, and five-year annualized returns through the same time period as presented in the corresponding compliant presentation.

YTD Returns through March 31, 2012	Composite (gross)	Composite (net)	Benchmark
	−8.88%	−9.03%	−8.70%

Annualized returns as of December 31, 2011	Composite (gross)	Composite (net)	Benchmark
1-Year	17.61%	16.85%	17.57%
3-Year	13.18%	12.45%	13.14%
Since inception	16.01%	15.26%	15.47%

Option 3: Period-to-date composite returns, and annual returns for the past five years, for the same annual periods as presented in the corresponding compliant presentation.

YTD Returns through March 31, 2012	Composite (gross)	Composite (net)	Benchmark
	−8.88%	−9.03%	−8.70%

Annual returns	Composite (gross)	Composite (net)	Benchmark
2011	17.61%	16.85%	17.57%
2010	7.96%	7.26%	8.11%
2009	14.18%	13.44%	13.93%
10/1/08–12/31/08	11.78%	11.60%	10.22%

11. *Presence, use, and extent of leverage, derivatives, and short positions.* If the composite strategy includes a material use of leverage, derivatives, or short positions, the firm must disclose the presence, use, and extent of these instruments or practices. The firm must describe how frequently these tools are used, as well as characteristics of these tools. Enough information must be provided so the reader understands the additional risks inherent in these instruments or practices. Note that this disclosure does not necessarily have to be made in a separate distinct statement. If the composite description (a general overview of the composite strategy) is robust, and includes sufficient details about the composite strategy, the composite description should already include sufficient information to meet this disclosure requirement.

12. *Any periods of noncompliant performance.* If the advertisement includes any performance for periods prior to January 1, 2000 that is not compliant, the firm must disclose the period of noncompliance. Note that the previous requirement to disclose the reason why the performance was noncompliant (included in the 2005 edition of the GIPS standards, but removed in the 2010 edition) is no longer a requirement.

13. *If the advertisement conforms with laws or regulations that conflict with the GIPS Advertising Guidelines or the GIPS standards.* If a firm is required to follow a law or regulation that causes the firm to prepare the advertisement so that it does not comply with a requirement of either the GIPS standards or the GIPS Advertising Guidelines, the firm must disclose how the law or regulation conflicts with the GIPS standards or the GIPS Advertising Guidelines.

An advertisement may also include information that goes beyond what is required as described above. Additional information may be included in the advertisement as long as it meets two tests:

1. The information must be shown with equal or lesser prominence relative to the information required by the GIPS Advertising Guidelines.
2. The information does not conflict with the requirements of the GIPS standards or the GIPS Advertising Guidelines.

SUMMARY

When preparing compliant presentations, a firm should always keep in mind that the goal is not to produce the shortest, most concise presentation possible. In addition to including all required disclosures and other information, a firm should also include any other information that would help a reader of the compliant presentation understand and interpret the historical performance of the composite and any other information that is included in the compliant presentation. When questions arise as to what information should be presented to a prospective client, the firm should be guided by the ethical principles underlying the GIPS standards: fair representation and full disclosure of historical performance.

CHAPTER 7

Wrap-Fee/SMA, Private Equity, and Real Estate

The main body of the GIPS standards (Sections 0–5) applies to all investment management firms that wish to comply with the GIPS standards. These provisions were originally written to address what are typically considered traditional asset classes and portfolio types. However, the GIPS standards recognize that some asset classes and portfolio types do not fit neatly into the main provisions and are distinctive enough to warrant a separate section within the GIPS standards with customized provisions. These asset classes and portfolios include:

- Wrap-fee/Separately Managed Accounts (SMA)
- Private equity
- Real estate

This chapter reviews the most significant points about the customized provisions that apply to each of these types of investments. First, it is important to understand the following considerations, which apply to all three:

- Unless it is explicitly stated that a provision within the main body of the GIPS standards does not apply to an asset class, firms must comply with the main body (Sections 0–5) of the GIPS standards, *as well as* the requirements specific to the asset class or portfolio type.
- Chapter 2 discussed the significance of the *minimum effective date*. The minimum effective date for the GIPS standards reviewed thus far is January 1, 2000. The minimum effective compliance date for all of the customized provisions is January 1, 2006. This date is later because guidance for wrap-fee/SMA, private equity, and real estate portfolios was not included in the original version of the GIPS standards issued in 1999. This guidance was first included in the 2005 edition of the GIPS

standards, and so the effective date equals the 2005 GIPS standards' effective date. Compliant presentations for composites prepared following the wrap-fee/SMA, private equity, or real estate provisions must disclose if any noncompliant performance for periods prior to January 1, 2006 is presented.

WRAP-FEE/SEPARATELY MANAGED ACCOUNTS

Wrap-fee portfolios go by several names. They are sometimes called *wrap*, *wrap-fee*, or *separately managed accounts*. Because wrap-fee portfolios are most commonly referred to either as separately managed accounts or SMA portfolios, we use the term SMA to refer to wrap-fee portfolios.

The target SMA client is an individual investor, as opposed to an institution. Most SMA portfolios do not meet the minimum portfolio size warranting the attention of an institutional money manager. However, through an SMA program, individual investors can gain access to institutional money managers.

Wrap-fee programs are offered by sponsors. The *sponsor* can be a brokerage firm or other financial services organization. An employee of the sponsor, or a financial advisor associated with the sponsor, helps the client set his goals and objectives and determine an appropriate allocation of assets. Then the sponsor and client select investment managers from a pool that has been chosen by the sponsor to manage a portion or all of the client's assets. These investment managers are firms that claim compliance with the GIPS standards and are our main concern when we consider wrap-fee/SMA provisions of the GIPS standards.

After the client's assets are allocated to the selected investment managers, the sponsor continues to manage the relationship with the client and typically holds regular account and performance reviews. While the investment managers are responsible for managing the client's account, these firms do not have a direct relationship with the end client. The investment manager typically communicates only with the sponsor. The sponsor informs the investment manager of any new clients, terminating clients, or other changes with existing client accounts.

From the investment manager's point of view, once the account is established and ready to be traded, the firm is responsible for managing the account. The next step is the unique and key point driving the GIPS standards for SMA portfolios: While the firm *determines* the appropriate trades according to their strategy the same way it would for an institutional client, the firm that manages an SMA portfolio does not *execute* the trades, as it would for an institutional portfolio. Most wrap-fee/SMA contracts between sponsors and investment managers require the investment manager to conduct all trades, with some allowed exceptions, through the sponsor. The investment manager instructs the sponsor's organization to make the trades, and no commissions are charged on the trades.

No commissions are charged on the trades due to the typical compensation arrangement for wrap-fee/SMA portfolios. The individual client pays the sponsor an asset-based fee that combines, or "wraps," a variety of fees into a single fee. The wrap fee includes all of the expenses and costs incurred, including the sponsor's fee, the investment manager's fee, custodial expenses, and trading expenses. The total wrap fee is paid to the sponsor, and the sponsor shares a portion of the wrap fee with the investment manager.

Why do SMA portfolios require dedicated GIPS guidance? First, because there are normally three parties in the client relationship (the client, a sponsor, and the investment manager) the firm acting as the investment manager may have no access to or interaction with the SMA client. Second, the wrap-fee structure creates performance calculation issues, as SMA portfolios typically do not pay commissions on trades. (In some cases, however, the investment manager may place trades outside the normal arrangement with the sponsor, and commissions on these trades would be charged.) Because transaction costs are included in the total wrap fee, portfolio returns that are calculated following the normal process for generating gross returns will not reflect the deduction of trading expenses, as is required by the GIPS standards. A return that does not reflect the deduction of trading expenses or any other expenses is referred to as a *pure gross return*. Pure gross returns are not proper returns for GIPS purposes. They may be presented to prospects, but only as supplemental information.

The GIPS Wrap-Fee/SMA provisions and the related Guidance Statement address the issues faced by managers of SMA portfolios. While a firm may combine SMA portfolios and non-SMA portfolios in the same composite, firms rarely do so, as most sponsors wish to see the performance of only SMA portfolios. We assume that SMA composites include only SMA portfolios unless stated otherwise. The rest of this section describes the key concepts in the wrap-fee/SMA provisions and related guidance.

Prospective Clients

As described in Chapter 1, firms are required to make every reasonable effort to provide a compliant presentation to all prospective clients. A manager of SMA portfolios has two types of prospective clients: prospective new sponsors and prospective individual end clients. Even though the firm may have no direct contact with the end prospect, the firm is still obliged to make every reasonable effort to deliver a compliant presentation to every prospect. Many SMA managers attempt to meet this obligation by:

- Providing compliant presentations to sponsors and asking the sponsor to provide the compliant presentation to individual prospective clients.
- In cases where the firm does have contact with the individual prospective client, such as when the firm is responsible for providing a welcome package to new clients, including a compliant presentation with this correspondence.
- Posting compliant presentations on the firm's web site.

Even if a firm does all of these things, the end prospects may still never see a GIPS-compliant performance presentation. However, if a firm does take these, or similar, steps it would be hard to argue that the firm has not made every reasonable effort to provide a compliant presentation to all prospective clients.

Style-Defined Composites

All firms are required to create composites that are defined according to investment mandate, objective, or strategy. All portfolios meeting that definition must be included in that composite. The same is true for SMA portfolios and composites. Once a firm manages SMA portfolios, the firm must create SMA composites that include all portfolios that meet that composite's definition, regardless of sponsor. This is referred to as a *style-defined composite* and is a term that is unique to the wrap-fee/SMA provisions. For example, if a firm manages a large cap strategy for five sponsors, all large cap portfolios managed for the five sponsors must be included in the style-defined, large cap composite. This is the composite that must be presented to new, prospective wrap fee sponsors.

Sponsor-Specific Composites

Sponsors may ask firms to prepare a compliant presentation that includes only the portfolios that are managed for that sponsor. Firms are allowed to create sponsor-specific "subcomposites." Sponsor-specific composites can be used by the sponsor in two ways: for internal use only or when meeting with new individual prospective SMA clients. All sponsor-specific compliant presentations prepared by the firm must incorporate the name of the sponsor. If the sponsor-specific composite's compliant presentation will be provided to new individual prospective SMA clients, returns that are net of the total wrap fee must be included in the presentation. If the sponsor-specific compliant presentation does not include these net returns, the firm must include a prominent disclosure that the sponsor-specific compliant presentation is only for the internal use of the named sponsor.

Net Return Calculations

Performance presented to SMA prospective clients must be net of the total wrap fee. Even though the sponsor determines the total wrap fee, and the firm earns only a portion of the total wrap fee, the firm must calculate returns that reflect the deduction of the total wrap fee. This can be a challenge for some firms as they may not know the total wrap fees that are charged to the individual clients, and may not be able to obtain that information. Because determining actual total wrap fees charged to individual SMA portfolios is so difficult, using a model wrap fee is common. If a firm uses a model fee, the firm must determine the highest wrap fee that was charged to SMA clients, or would be charged to SMA clients for a new SMA composite. However, once again determining the highest fee may not be possible for a firm. If the firm is unable to definitively identify the highest fee charged to SMA clients, common practice is to default to an assumed annual 3% total wrap fee.

Borrowing History from a Non-SMA Composite

A firm may wish to market a strategy to SMA sponsors before the firm has any SMA portfolios managed according to the strategy. A firm may create a proxy SMA composite history using the performance from another composite within the firm if the other composite is representative of the strategy that the SMA client will receive. Assume Firm A manages a growth equity strategy for institutional clients, maintains a Growth Equity Institutional Composite, and wishes to market its growth equity capabilities to SMA sponsors. Firm A may create a Growth Equity SMA Composite using the history of the Growth Equity Institutional Composite as long as the composite is included within the defined firm. Firm A must deduct a model total wrap fee from the institutional composite's gross returns. Because most wrap fees are assessed quarterly, common practice is to deduct one-quarter of the assumed annual wrap fee from the institutional composite's quarterly gross return.

Once a firm begins managing SMA portfolios, the performance presented to prospective SMA clients for a specific strategy must include the performance of all SMA portfolios managed in that strategy. Continuing with Firm A, assume Firm A successfully markets the Growth Equity strategy and begins managing SMA growth equity portfolios as of August 1,

2011. At that point Firm A must include the growth equity SMA portfolios in a composite. Firm A has three options for doing this:

1. Continue the Growth Equity SMA Composite, using the history from the institutional composite, and redefine the composite to include only SMA portfolios prospectively.
2. Continue the Growth Equity SMA Composite, using the history from the institutional composite, and include both institutional and SMA portfolios prospectively.
3. Create a new SMA-only Growth Equity Composite, with an inception date of August 1, 2011. This composite would have no history.

In all cases, if the firm has borrowed performance from a non-SMA composite, the firm must disclose, for each period presented, that the composite does not contain any SMA portfolios. Common practice is to include in the compliant presentation a column for the percentage of the composite that is represented by SMA portfolios. Until the composite includes any SMA portfolios, this will be 0%. Adding this column will also allow the firm to meet the requirement to disclose, as of each period end, the percentage of the composite that is represented by portfolios that pay bundled fees. (A wrap fee is a type of bundled fee.) Once the composite includes wrap-fee/SMA portfolios, the firm must disclose the types of fees that are included in the wrap fee.

Recordkeeping Considerations

One of the biggest challenges faced by firms managing SMA portfolios is ensuring the firm meets the GIPS recordkeeping requirements for those portfolios. As discussed in Chapter 1, Provision 1.A.1 requires a firm to have records that support all information that is included in compliant presentations. Firms usually meet the requirement for maintaining records to support composite returns and underlying portfolio-level returns via the records available on the firm's accounting and performance systems. Many firms maintain SMA portfolios on in-house systems and treat them as they would any other portfolios managed by the firm, thereby eliminating any recordkeeping problems.

However, given the nature of a typical SMA arrangement, along with the high volume of SMA portfolios that firms sometimes manage, some firms choose to not maintain SMA portfolios on their accounting or performance systems. Instead, because the SMA sponsors calculate returns on behalf of their clients, a firm could choose to view the sponsor as a third party that is responsible for calculating performance, and place reliance on the sponsor's performance information. If a firm chooses to rely on performance information from the sponsor, the firm must ensure that placing reliance on the sponsor is proper. Also, relying on the sponsor's performance information does not absolve the firm from its recordkeeping responsibilities. The firm must be able to obtain records to support the sponsor-calculated returns, and must also be satisfied that the returns provided by the sponsor meet the requirements of the GIPS standards.

Discretionary Status of Each Program

When the guidance for wrap-fee/SMA portfolios was originally created under the AIMR-PPS standards, the wrap-fee/SMA program concept was implemented in a more standard manner across the industry than is done today. SMA program structures are continually evolving. The introduction of new types of SMA programs requires a careful analysis in order to determine how the assets managed in these programs should be treated for GIPS compliance purposes.

When performing this analysis, the key consideration is discretion. In a traditional SMA structure, the firm that has been hired by the client, via the sponsor, has full discretion to manage an SMA client's assets in accordance with the selected mandate. Typically, the investment manager maintains a model portfolio for each SMA strategy. When changes are made in the model portfolio, all SMA portfolios managed to that strategy are rebalanced to align with the new model portfolio. SMA portfolios are also rebalanced to the model portfolio as they experience cash flow activity.

Some SMA programs work in a different way. Instead of the firm managing individual client portfolios, the firm provides the SMA model portfolio and any subsequent changes in the model to the sponsor. The sponsor then implements the transactions required to manage the client portfolios in keeping with this SMA model. The firm has no involvement in the management of the individual portfolios. For a model-only program, the firm is typically compensated by the sponsor based on a percentage of assets managed by the sponsor following the firm's model portfolio. In this scenario, the firm must *not* include model-only program assets in GIPS firm assets. If assets are not included in GIPS firm assets, then the firm cannot include them in a GIPS-compliant composite.

Analyzing programs that fall somewhere between a fully discretionary, more traditional SMA program and a nondiscretionary, model-only program can be challenging. In a hybrid program, discretion is shared between the firm and the sponsor. A Unified Managed Account (UMA) program is an example of a shared discretion program. A typical hybrid arrangement works like this:

- The firm provides the model portfolio to the sponsor.
- For new SMA clients, the sponsor invests the new client's assets according to the current model portfolio, and then informs the firm that the portfolio has been initially invested and is ready to trade.
- The firm then assumes responsibility for managing the new SMA client's portfolio, along with all other similar SMA portfolios, and rebalances the portfolio whenever the firm makes changes to the model portfolio.
- When the SMA client contributes or withdraws cash, the sponsor makes the required portfolio trades.

While the details of each program are different, many share the characteristics of this typical arrangement. The implication of the arrangement is that the firm does not possess sole discretion to manage the individual wrap-fee portfolios.

If a firm manages SMA assets in a hybrid program with shared discretion, the firm must first decide whether to include these assets in GIPS firm assets and then whether or not to include these assets in a composite. In the United States, an SEC-registered firm must also decide whether or not to include these assets in assets under management (AUM) for Form ADV reporting. Even for the same program, there is no consistency in how such programs are treated by different firms. Some firms will include SMA portfolios managed in hybrid programs in SEC AUM, GIPS firm assets, and in a composite. Other firms will exclude such assets from all three. Most commonly, in an arrangement where there is shared discretion, a firm will take the following three actions:

1. Include these assets in SEC AUM as nondiscretionary assets.
2. Include them in GIPS firm assets.
3. Not include them in a composite, as they are not considered discretionary for GIPS compliance purposes.

A firm should document its rationale for how it has decided to treat portfolios managed in all SMA programs, for both the firm assets calculation and composite assignment purposes.

Defining Discretion for Wrap-Fee Portfolios

A firm is often required to define discretion differently for SMA portfolios than it does for institutional portfolios. This is primarily due to the quantity—often in the thousands or tens of thousands—of SMA portfolios that a firm typically manages. Some SMA portfolios will have a restriction against buying one or more individual securities. Analyzing the impact, or potential impact, of security restrictions for thousands of portfolios requires significant resources. Therefore, common practice is to establish a simple rule for defining discretion. For example:

> *All SMA portfolios with any client-specific restrictions are considered nondiscretionary and are excluded from all composites.*

Firms taking this approach should take care to differentiate between client-specific restrictions and sponsor-level restrictions. Many sponsors are affiliated with a publicly traded company, so all portfolios for that sponsor will have a restriction against buying shares of the sponsor. If a firm were to consider as nondiscretionary SMA portfolios that have any restriction, including sponsor-level restrictions, the firm would probably not end up with any discretionary SMA portfolios to put into composites. Given that a sponsor-level restriction is known by the firm in advance, and the restriction applies to all portfolios of the sponsor, firms should be able to work around such a restriction.

Because SMA portfolios are managed on behalf of individual investors, tax considerations often come into play. For example, clients may instruct the firm, via the sponsor, to alter the trading strategy toward year end due to tax considerations. Two such instructions are the harvesting of tax losses and requests not to trade whenever a taxable realized gain would result. Firms need to determine how temporary client instructions such as these impact a portfolio's discretionary status and related composite assignment. Some firms will automatically remove such portfolios from composites for the periods for which the restrictions are in place. Other firms will leave these portfolios in composites and try to work around the restrictions as best as they can. And firms may have a policy combining both approaches. For example:

> *Portfolios with temporary client-imposed tax restrictions will remain in the composite if the time period impacted is less than five business days. If the time period is more than five days then portfolios will be removed from the composite.*

Firms must determine for each SMA composite whether temporary trading restrictions impact the management of the portfolios within the composite.

Given the large number of portfolios typically managed by firms in SMA programs, applying the GIPS standards to SMA portfolios can be a formidable task. Firms that successfully maintain SMA composites do so by establishing very objective composite inclusion policies, and then they apply the selected policies consistently. This is one area where a firm should establish the minimum procedures necessary to maintain composites and be prepared to accept a wider dispersion of portfolio returns than would normally be considered acceptable in the institutional world.

Consider significant cash flows. A firm may choose to adopt a policy for a composite to temporarily exclude a portfolio that experiences a client-directed cash flow above a previously specified amount, as the cash flow is big enough to cause the portfolio to be temporarily classified as nondiscretionary. If the portfolio is one out of 3,000 SMA portfolios in a composite, there is a low probability that the impacted portfolio's return would distort the composite return. Where an individual portfolio might have minimal impact on the composite return, monitoring thousands of portfolios for cash flows could be more effort than it is worth. To ensure the proper and efficient maintenance of SMA composites, we recommend establishing very simple rules for the inclusion and exclusion of portfolios in these composites.

PRIVATE EQUITY

Institutional investors diversify their assets across a range of asset classes. Nontraditional asset classes include real estate, hedge funds, commodities, and investments in private companies. A common type of *private equity* investment is *venture capital* funds, where a firm pools contributions from multiple institutional investors in order to make investments in start-up companies. Private equity strategies go beyond venture capital; for example, there are private equity investment strategies that focus on taking mature public companies private. Because most portfolios invested in private equity are organized as pooled funds, we will use the term fund versus portfolio when discussing private equity.

The private equity provisions are very different from the provisions included in the main body of the GIPS standards. Private equity requires a different approach for the following three reasons:

1. Private equity investments are valued infrequently.
2. Unlike typical marketable securities portfolios, the private equity manager often *does* control the timing and amount of cash flows into and out of the fund.
3. Private equity funds are usually structured differently than traditional investment portfolios.

Because of these reasons, returns reported for private equity composites are money weighted returns as opposed to time weighted returns. The industry standard is to use a *since inception internal rate of return* to measure private equity fund performance.

Because of this significant difference, the first step is to determine which assets managed by the firm are covered by the private equity provisions. The private equity provisions do not apply to all investments that firms might classify as private equity. Just because a portfolio is invested in private equity investments does not automatically mean that the private equity provisions apply to that portfolio. Instead, a firm must consider each portfolio's investments, whether these investments are made directly or indirectly through other funds, and the structure of the portfolio.

For purposes of applying the GIPS standards, private equity investments include those investments that meet the traditional definition of private equity: direct investments in companies that are not publicly traded. Private investment in public equity (PIPE) investments, distressed debt investments, and venture factoring are also considered private equity investments.

The next consideration is determining the manner in which each fund makes investments in assets that are considered private equity investments. A fund that makes investments directly into privately held companies—that is, *direct investments*—is referred to as a *primary fund*. A fund that does not make direct investments but instead makes investments in funds that are in turn invested in private equity investments is referred to as a *fund of funds*.

A *secondary fund* is a fund that buys interests in existing funds. If a secondary fund takes over an investor's interest in a primary fund, the secondary fund is considered a primary fund for GIPS compliance purposes. If the secondary fund takes over an interest from an investor in a fund of funds, the secondary fund must follow the fund of funds guidance.

While the GIPS standards are not very specific as to which types of investments qualify as private equity, they are more specific as to the actual structure of the fund vehicle. A firm must categorize each private equity fund as either closed-end or open-end. A *closed-end fund* is a type of pooled fund that has a fixed number of investors who have committed a specific amount of money to the fund. In the United States, most private equity closed-end funds are organized as limited partnerships. The investors in the fund are *limited partners*, and the firm that manages the fund takes a position as the *general partner*. The manager of the fund determines when investors must provide the capital that they have committed to the fund, and the firm also determines when earnings of the fund will be distributed to fund investors. An investor in a closed-end fund is not able to withdraw or redeem an investment in a closed-end fund. An *open-end fund*, on the other hand, allows for new investors in the fund, and also allows fund investors to redeem their investment in the fund.

For the private equity provisions to apply, a primary fund invested in private equity investments must be a closed-end fund. An open-end primary fund that is invested in private equity investments must follow the main body of the GIPS standards (Sections 0–5), and not the private equity provisions. However, a fund of funds that is invested in private equity funds can always be considered private equity. It does not matter whether the fund of funds is open-end or closed-end.

To recap, the private equity provisions apply to three types of funds that invest in private equity investments:

1. Closed-end primary funds.
2. Closed-end funds of funds.
3. Open-end funds of funds.

While many of the private equity provisions apply to both primary funds and funds of funds, there are some differences between the two. The rest of this section describes the key concepts that private equity managers should consider.

Vintage Year

Vintage year is a critical concept in private equity performance measurement. *Vintage year* determines the start date for calculating performance and is the inception year of a fund. Private equity funds are compared with peers based on their vintage year. This allows investors to evaluate manager performance by comparing the performance of funds that share the same set of investment opportunities available to them, and then experience the same shifting market conditions for their investments. Vintage year can be defined one of two ways:

1. Based on the date when the first capital commitment to the fund from the fund's investors becomes legally binding (also referred to as the *initial subscription date*).
2. Based on the date the fund's manager first calls capital from the fund's investors (also known as the *first drawdown*).

Firms must disclose the vintage year of the composite, which is often accomplished by including the vintage year in the name of the composite. Because there are two methods for determining vintage year, the firm must disclose the method used for each specific composite. Eventually the firm must disclose the composite's final liquidation (or termination) date, which is when the fund's capital is fully distributed to the investors.

Composite Definition

Primary funds must be included in a composite that is defined by both vintage year *and* strategy. Given this requirement, as well as the way private equity funds are typically organized and capital is raised, in most cases primary fund composites will include only one fund. For example, assume Firm B specializes in venture capital direct investments, and the firm typically raises money for one fund each year. Firm B would have a series of composites that include only one fund, as the firm would have only one fund for each vintage year and strategy (e.g., 2009 Venture Capital Composite, 2010 Venture Capital Composite). If Firm B started a second venture capital fund with a vintage year of 2010, and the funds shared the same strategy, then the 2010 Venture Capital Composite would include both venture capital funds with a 2010 vintage year.

The requirement is different for funds of funds. Funds of funds must be included in composites that are defined by vintage year *and/or* strategy. Assume Firm C specializes in venture capital, but instead of making direct investments as is done by Firm B, the firm makes investments in other venture capital funds. Firm C could have the same composites described for Firm B, which are composites based on vintage year and strategy. Alternatively, as a fund of funds manager, Firm C could instead create a Venture Capital Composite that includes all venture capital funds, regardless of vintage year.

However the firm decides to define its composites, the composite definitions must remain consistent throughout the life of the composite. For example, a venture capital composite will remain a venture capital composite for the life of the composite, even if the investments held within the fund have moved out of the venture capital stage and have gone public.

Valuation

As of January 1, 2011, all investments, including private equity investments, must be valued in accordance with the GIPS standards' definition of fair value. For periods prior to January 1, 2011, private equity investments must be valued either in accordance with this definition of fair value or in accordance with the GIPS Private Equity Valuation Principles published in the 2005 edition of the GIPS standards. Although this makes it sound like there are two different sets of rules to follow, they all effectively say the same thing: Private equity investments must be fair valued.

TABLE 7.1 Quarterly Valuation Roll Forward

ABC Opportunity Fund IV

September 30	Valuation	$12,294,600
October 15	Management fee paid	($37,500)
October 31	Called capital	$1,500,000
December 31	Valuation	$13,757,100

For a fund of funds, determining portfolio valuations is not completely under the control of the fund of funds manager. Typically the fund of funds manager will receive a quarterly or semiannual valuation report from the general partner of the underlying funds. However, these reports are often received well after the valuation date. Because of this delay, a fund of funds manager will commonly value investments on what is effectively a quarter lag and adjust for any capital activity since the last valuation. For example, assume Firm D is valuing the portfolio of a fund of funds, which includes positions in several underlying funds. The valuation is being performed in January, as of December 31. Table 7.1 provides an example of what the valuation reconciliation for each underlying fund would look like.

Calculating the roll forward valuations seen in this table is the first step. The fund of funds manager will start with these calculated valuations, and will follow their policies to determine whether these values represent the fair value of the underlying funds.

All private equity investments must be valued annually for GIPS purposes. Because private equity valuations involve subjectivity, firms must disclose the methods used to determine the private equity valuations for the most recent period presented in the compliant presentation. Additionally, if the firm has changed the composite's valuation policies or methodologies, and the changes are material, the firm must disclose these changes if these changes occurred after January 1, 2011. Finally, if the firm values private equity investments in accordance with other industry valuation guidelines, such as the International Private Equity and Venture Capital Valuation Guidelines, the firm must disclose this fact.

Money Weighted Returns

Most private equity funds are closed-end funds, and the manager is responsible for selecting the private equity investments as well as determining the timing of capital calls and distributions. Money weighted returns are used to calculate returns that reflect both the return on investments as well as the timing of the cash flows. Therefore, the GIPS standards require internal rate of return (IRR) calculations. The IRR is calculated from inception of the fund through each annual period end. This is the reason why private equity investments must be valued annually.

Assume that Firm E's 2008 Buyout Strategy Composite has an inception date of June 1, 2008, and that Firm E is updating the composite's compliant presentation in 2012, to include performance through December 31, 2011. The compliant presentation must include a since inception annualized IRR (SI-IRR) for each of the following periods:

- June 1, 2008 through December 31, 2008.
- June 1, 2008 through December 31, 2009.
- June 1, 2008 through December 31, 2010.
- June 1, 2008 through December 31, 2011.

Many firms use the Excel XIRR() function to calculate annualized SI-IRRs. However, firms must be careful when using this function for a period that is less than one year, as all returns in the XIRR() function are annualized. In the example above, if the cash flows from June 1, 2008 through December 31, 2008 are entered into Excel, with the ending value as of December 31, 2008, the XIRR() function would calculate an annualized return for 2008. Annualized returns for periods of less than one year are not permitted by the GIPS standards, so the annualized return for 2008 must be "de-annualized."

Gross- and Net-of-Fees Since Inception IRRs

The general provisions of the GIPS standards allow a firm to present gross returns only, net returns only, or both. The private equity provisions do not allow a firm to choose. Instead, a private equity composite presentation must include both gross and net returns.

All private equity returns must reflect the deduction of transaction expenses. These are the costs incurred as a result of buying, selling, or maintaining private equity investments. These costs include the legal and investment banking fees associated with private equity transactions.

Gross returns must reflect the deduction of actual transaction expenses. Net returns must reflect the deduction of actual transaction expenses and actual investment management fees. (Investment management fees must include both asset-based fees as well as any performance-based fees.) Unlike the general provisions of the GIPS standards, where a firm may choose to use either actual or model investment management fees to calculate net returns, only actual investment management fees may be used for private equity funds.

Just like any other pooled fund, private equity funds will typically incur a variety of other operating fees and expenses, such as accounting fees and audit fees. A firm is not required to reflect the deduction of these fees, or any other administrative fees, when calculating gross or net returns. If the firm chooses to reflect the deduction of any administrative fees, the firm must disclose the specific fees over and above transaction expenses and investment management fees (for net returns) that are reflected in returns. For example, a firm may choose to present a return that reflects the deduction of all of the fees and expenses an investor in the fund would pay, which is commonly referred to as a "net-net" return. The firm would then describe which additional fees and expenses were deducted in order to arrive at the net-net return.

Fund of Funds Returns Net of All Underlying Fund Fees and Expenses

A fund of funds has a portfolio that consists of investments in other private equity funds. These underlying funds have their own fees and expenses, including investment management fees. Any expenses incurred by the underlying funds must be reflected in all fund of funds returns, whether paid by the underlying funds themselves or charged separately to the fund of funds. A fund of funds may not gross up returns for any of the expenses incurred by the underlying funds. The same is true for a portfolio that is invested in a portfolio of publicly traded mutual funds. In this case, the firm would never decompose the returns of the underlying mutual funds and decide which expenses of the mutual funds would be reflected in returns and which would not. The fees and expenses of the underlying mutual funds or private equity funds are a cost of investing in those funds, and so grossing up returns for any of those expenses would not be appropriate.

Cash Flows

Private equity SI-IRRs are calculated using two inputs: cash flows and the end of period valuation. Cash flows for periods through December 31, 2010 must be recorded on a daily or monthly basis, and must be on a daily basis as of January 1, 2011. When a firm changes from using monthly cash flows to daily cash flows the change is made on a prospective basis only. There is no need to recalculate historical returns using daily cash flows.

To recap, when bringing a historical track record into compliance, an SI-IRR calculation must reflect cash flows using the following frequency for the respective periods:

- For periods through December 31, 2010: Monthly or more frequently.
- As of January 1, 2011: Daily.

Firms must disclose the frequency of the cash flows that are used to calculate the SI-IRR if anything other than daily cash flows are used for periods prior to January 1, 2011. The IRR calculation is demonstrated in Chapter 3.

Recallable Distributions

Private equity funds sometimes maintain the right to recall distributions that have been made to fund investors. If a fund recalls a distribution, the recalled distribution must be treated as an increase to paid-in capital. However, a recalled distribution has no impact on the fund's total committed capital.

Benchmarks

A firm must present the SI-IRR for a benchmark for the same periods that are presented for the composite. The benchmark must reflect the composite's strategy, and must also have the same vintage year as the composite. Common practice in private equity is to use peer group comparisons as a performance benchmark. Cambridge Associates and Thomson Reuters Venture Economics are two organizations that maintain private equity peer universes.

As an alternative to using a peer group as a benchmark, a firm could instead use a customized market index to provide a measure of the value added by the firm. A *public market equivalent* (PME) allows a firm to compare its returns to those that would have been earned if the fund invested its assets in a market index, such as the S&P 500. To create a PME, a synthetic portfolio is created that invests in the index using the same pattern of cash flows as those of the fund.

Whichever benchmark is presented, the firm must disclose how the returns of the benchmark are calculated. If a PME is used as the benchmark, the firm must disclose the underlying index that the firm used to calculate the returns of the PME.

Additional Statistical Measures

A compliant presentation for a private equity composite looks quite different from a compliant presentation that is prepared for a composite that follows the general provisions of the GIPS standards. While some items are very similar (composite returns, benchmark returns, composite assets, etc.), all private equity composites must present the seven additional statistical measures listed in Table 7.2 as of each annual period end.

An eighth statistical measure is required for periods ending on or after January 1, 2011. If a primary fund composite has investments in other funds in addition to direct investments, the firm must present the percentage of composite assets that is invested in fund investments as of each annual period end. A similar requirement applies to fund of funds composites. If a fund of funds composite has made any direct investments, as opposed to investments in other funds, the firm must present the percentage of composite assets that

TABLE 7.2 Private Equity Statistical Disclosures

Statistic	Definition
Committed Capital	Total amount of money that is committed to the fund by the fund's participants.
Paid-in Capital	Amount of committed capital that has been called or drawn down from fund participants.
Cumulative Distributions	Amount of cash and stock that has been returned to fund participants.
PIC Multiple	Ratio of paid-in capital to total committed capital. This ratio measures how much of the total committed capital has been drawn down. A ratio of 1 indicates that all of the committed capital has been drawn down.
Investment or TVPI Multiple	Ratio of total fund's value (residual value plus distributions) to paid-in capital. This ratio measures the fund's total value relative to its invested capital.
Realization or DVPI Multiple	Ratio of cumulative fund distributions to paid-in capital. This ratio measures how much money has been returned to fund participants relative to the amount of money that has been called from fund participants. From the perspective of fund participants, a realization multiple of 1 or greater indicates that the fund participants have received distributions from the fund that equal or exceed the amount of money that has been invested in the fund to date.
RVPI Multiple	Ratio of the fund's residual value at period end to total paid-in capital. Also known as the unrealized multiple, this ratio indicates how much of the fund's SI-IRR is based on gains that have not yet been realized.

is invested in direct investments as of each annual period end. In both cases these items must be disclosed for periods ending after January 1, 2011, and the disclosure must be made only if it is applicable. If the percentage that would be disclosed is 0%, then no disclosure is required.

Composite and Firm Assets

When preparing compliant presentations, firms should be careful to ensure that the proper amounts are presented for composite and firm assets. Common practice in private equity is to disclose the amount of assets that are committed to both the firm as a whole and to a particular fund/composite. A firm must ensure that the committed assets totals are not used in error when calculating total composite assets or firm assets. A firm is required to disclose committed assets for a composite, but committed assets is a different concept than composite assets. A firm may choose to disclose total assets committed to the firm, but this information must be clearly identified as supplemental information in the compliant presentation.

Disclosures

The disclosures that must accompany the numerical information are substantially the same as those that are required for any other composites. But there are numerous disclosures included in the general provisions that are not applicable to private equity composites, or are superseded by private equity–specific requirements. The inapplicable general provisions are listed in the private equity provisions of the GIPS standards.

Additional Fund of Funds Presentation Requirement

A fund of funds composite may be defined by vintage year and strategy, or only based on strategy. If a fund of funds composite is defined only by strategy, the firm must calculate and present additional information based on the vintage year of the underlying fund of funds investments. This information must be presented only as of the most recent annual period end. Assume Firm F has a Venture Capital Fund of Funds Composite that is invested in 15 underlying funds. The underlying funds have vintage years ranging from 2008 to 2010. Firm F must create what are effectively subportfolios for each vintage year, and include in the subportfolios the underlying funds with the same vintage year. In this case the firm would create subportfolios for 2008, 2009, and 2010. For each vintage year subportfolio, as of the most recent annual period end, the firm must calculate the gross-of-fees SI-IRR and the seven additional statistical measures described above, as required by provision 7.A.23.

Effective Date Difference

As described earlier, the minimum effective date for the private equity provisions is January 1, 2006. Only compliant performance may be presented for periods ended after January 1, 2006. But how does a firm determine a period of compliance when the time period reflected in the since inception internal rate of return calculation extends over several years, and policies have changed over that time period? The key factor is the end date of the SI-IRR calculation. Assume a firm prepares private equity compliant presentations that include SI-IRRs through December 31. All SI-IRRs ended as of December 31, 2006 and thereafter must be prepared in compliance with the GIPS standards.

In addition, when considering other provisions from Sections 0–5 that are also applicable to private equity, any provision that includes the words "for periods beginning" should be read as "for periods ending" for private equity. For example, Provision 1.A.7 requires composites to have consistent beginning and ending annual valuation dates for periods beginning on or after January 1, 2006. A private equity composite must meet this requirement for periods ending on or after January 1, 2006.

REAL ESTATE

Similar to private equity, many institutional investors diversify their portfolios via investments in real estate. Real estate portfolios are managed both by external investment advisors specializing in the asset class and managers of real estate–based strategies as part of a broader lineup. There are many different classes of investable property, ranging from timberland to hotels, apartments, and offices. Real estate managers offer investors both separate accounts and commingled vehicles. These portfolios get exposure to real estate returns via direct property purchases and indirect investments. Examples of indirect investments are portfolios that purchase mortgage-backed securities or invest via commingled property funds such as real estate investment trusts (REITs).

The main reason that these portfolios have special requirements is because real estate is an illiquid asset class and thus performing valuations as frequently as can be done for liquid securities is not possible. Portfolios invested in the following types of indirect real estate investments are not subject to this constraint, therefore the real estate provisions *do not* apply to portfolios invested in:

- REITs and any other publicly traded real estate securities.
- Mortgage-backed securities, whether backed by residential or commercial properties.
- Commercial and residential loans where the expected return is solely related to contractual interest rates without any participation in the economic performance of the underlying real estate.

In general these assets are all valued frequently, and so portfolios invested in these instruments follow the same provisions as marketable securities portfolios in Sections 0–5 of the GIPS standards.

Given the nature of these assets, the real estate provisions in Section 6 do apply to portfolios invested in:

- Properties, whether complete or under development.
- Land, whether developed or not.
- Unlisted private placement securities issued by REITs or real estate operating companies (REOCs).
- Private interest in a property where some portion of the return is related to the performance of the underlying real estate.

The following sections outline the key concepts for complying with the real estate provisions. These concepts apply to all portfolios invested in real estate, and the last section describes additional requirements applicable only to closed-end real estate portfolios.

Definition of Discretion

As discussed in Chapter 2, each firm has to decide how it defines discretion for each strategy. Defining discretion for real estate portfolios can be a challenge, particularly because it is not uncommon for institutional clients to retain some degree of decision making. For example, a client could maintain the right of refusal on all or selected proposed transactions. In the context of real estate investment management, a portfolio where the client has retained some decision making authority is often still considered discretionary if the firm has been granted enough decision making authority to manage the portfolio to the intended strategy. The firm must document its real estate–specific definition of discretion, and in compliant presentations disclose how discretion has been defined for the composite.

Portfolio Valuation Frequency

Special valuation rules apply to real estate investments since they cannot be valued as easily or frequently as securities trading in liquid markets. Real estate investments must be valued at least once every 12 months until December 31, 2007, and at least quarterly after that. There are two types of real estate portfolio valuations: internal valuations and external valuations. *Internal valuations* are conducted by the firm itself. *External valuations* must be performed by an independent, professionally designated appraiser, such as a Member of the Appraisal Institute (MAI). The quarterly valuations can be either external or internal valuations.

External Valuation Frequency

Real estate investments must be externally valued with the following frequency for the respective periods:

- Prior to January 1, 2012, at least once every 36 months.
- After January 1, 2012, at least once every 12 months, with one exception: If the client's agreement specifies a valuation frequency that is greater than 12 months, then external valuations must be conducted at least once every 36 months or in accordance with the client agreement if the client agreement requires more frequent external valuations.

This exception acknowledges that, due to the expense of a real estate appraisal, some clients specify a minimum period between external valuations. In some cases, clients will even prohibit external valuations once a portfolio has gone into liquidation. But no matter the reason, the maximum time period allowed to elapse between external independent valuations is 36 months.

Firms must disclose the external valuation frequency for the composite's investments. Also, there may be cases where a firm obtains an external property valuation for a real estate investment but decides not to use this valuation in the return calculation for the associated portfolio. The firm must disclose any situation where there is a material difference between the external valuation and the valuation used to calculate returns. In addition, the firm needs to disclose the rationale for overriding the external valuation.

Valuation Date

Beginning January 1, 2010, real estate valuations must be as of quarter end or the last day of the business quarter. Previously, the GIPS standards did not specify a preferred real estate valuation date. This requirement should not be of concern to the real estate manager because real estate valuations do not typically change from one day to the next.

Quarterly Portfolio and Composite Return Frequency

As of January 1, 2001, the general provisions of the GIPS standards require portfolio returns to be calculated at least monthly. However, because of the illiquidity of real estate investments, real estate portfolio returns must be calculated at least quarterly. But consider that until January 1, 2008 real estate investments must be valued only annually. Quarterly valuations are not required until January 1, 2008. So how does a firm that values real estate portfolios annually calculate a quarterly return? Each quarter end, the firm could carry forward the most recent annual valuation and make adjustments to the valuation for cash flows and any income and expenses accrued. This is similar to the method for rolling forward private equity valuations illustrated in Table 7.1. Real estate composite returns must be calculated at least quarterly using the asset weighted quarterly portfolio returns. Chapter 4 demonstrates the options for asset weighting portfolio returns to calculate composite returns.

Deduction of Transaction Expenses

Consistent with the GIPS requirements for calculating the returns on all other investments, real estate returns must reflect the deduction of the expenses that are incurred to buy, sell, finance, or develop real estate investments. However, determining which specific fees should be considered transaction expenses is not always easy. Some of these expenses may be borne by the firm managing the portfolio and not by the portfolio. These expenses are funded by the investment management fees paid by the portfolio to the firm.

For firms that maintain the expertise required to perform all of the functions associated with buying and selling properties internally, transaction costs may not be as easily identifiable as the explicit costs incurred by similar managers using third parties to perform transaction services. If this is the case, while not explicitly recommended by the GIPS standards, the firm should disclose in the compliant presentation the transaction-related services that the firm has opted to perform in-house.

Income and Capital Component Returns

In addition to calculating portfolio-level total returns, a real estate manager must also calculate returns for the income component and the capital component. The *income component return* reflects the income earned on all real estate investments less any property taxes or interest expense on debt. The income component return also includes income on cash or cash equivalents held in the portfolio. The *capital component return* reflects all other components of the total return that are not reflected in the income component return.

In the past, it was not unusual for a real estate manager to calculate the total return and one of the component returns and then derive the other, making the assumption that the two component returns sum to the portfolio's total return. For example, the firm would calculate the total return and the income return and deduct the income return from the total return to calculate the capital return. This method is allowed for periods ended prior to January 1, 2011. Thereafter, component returns cannot be derived, but instead must be calculated independently. The real estate firm must disclose how component returns are calculated, for all periods presented.

Internal Dispersion Measure

All composites, except private equity composites, must disclose a measure of the internal dispersion of annual portfolio returns using only the returns of those portfolios included in the composite for the full year. This requirement also applies to real estate composites. However, unlike other composites, the real estate firm does not choose the measure of internal dispersion that it would like to present to prospects. Instead, the firm must present the highest and lowest annual returns of those portfolios included in the composite for the full year. This information is not required for any year for which the composite includes less than six portfolios for the full year.

Closed-End Real Estate Funds

If a firm manages real estate portfolios, and any of those real estate portfolios are closed-end funds, the firm has additional requirements. The closed-end fund requirements are new to the 2010 edition of the GIPS standards. Even though these are new requirements, the firm must apply them retroactively. These requirements are in addition to all of the requirements previously discussed for all real estate portfolios.

Generally speaking, the firm must apply all of the *private equity provisions applicable to primary funds* to all closed-end real estate portfolios.

There are two significant differences between the private equity provisions and the real estate provisions for closed-end real estate portfolios. Both exceptions relate to the calculation of the since inception internal rate of return (SI-IRR):

1. Unlike private equity composites that *must* calculate both gross-of-fees and net-of-fees SI-IRRs, only net-of-fee SI-IRRs are required for closed-end real estate composites. The firm *can* choose to calculate and present the gross-of-fees SI-IRRs as well. If it does so, the gross- and net-of-fees SI-IRRs must be presented for the same periods.
2. The second difference relates to the frequency of the cash flows used in the calculation of SI-IRR. When calculating the SI-IRRs for closed-end real estate portfolios, cash flows must be recorded at least quarterly. Unlike in private equity, there is no requirement to transition to the use of daily cash flows.

When preparing the compliant presentation for a closed-end real estate composite, the firm must include both time weighted and SI-IRRs for the composite, along with all of the disclosures and multiples required for private equity composites.

SUMMARY

This chapter described the requirements for and provided advice on presenting performance for wrap-fee/SMA, private equity, and real estate portfolios. While the current GIPS standards give specific guidance for these portfolios, the dynamic nature of the investments industry means that there will never be specific guidance tailored to the requirements of every nontraditional asset class and investment vehicle. Even within the private equity industry alone, there are many special situations. For example, a hedge fund could be invested primarily in liquid assets, but also have a series of side pockets segregating certain securities that became illiquid. How does a firm that manages portfolios like this, or others that also have no specific rules, determine which GIPS provisions apply and how to apply them?

First, the firm should always keep up-to-date with any new guidance statements or Q&As. Second, the firm could help drive the ongoing GIPS standards development process by submitting a question to the CFA Institute GIPS Help Desk. And finally, firms should apply the GIPS standards as best as they can to their unique situation by preparing presentations in light of the underlying goals of the GIPS standards: the fair representation and full disclosure of historical performance.

CHAPTER 8

Maintaining Compliance with the GIPS Standards

We've seen that a series of decisions needs to be made for a firm to achieve GIPS compliance. Once the firm has achieved compliance, it must then implement new processes in order to maintain ongoing compliance. In most firms, the task of maintaining GIPS compliance falls to the Performance Department. But the Performance Department alone cannot ensure that the firm maintains compliance with the GIPS standards. Almost every department within the firm must play a role. This chapter summarizes best practices for keeping the firm in compliance with the GIPS standards.

ORGANIZATION AND OVERSIGHT

Maintaining compliance with the GIPS standards requires an ongoing commitment of resources from all areas of a firm. While the Performance Department plays a lead role, it cannot do it alone. The Performance Department depends on input and support from all areas of the firm. Compliance personnel must provide input to ensure the firm complies with regulatory requirements that go beyond GIPS requirements. Operations analysts must know when to flag transactions that impact GIPS-required calculations. Client relationship managers must relay information about client guidelines changes or temporary trading restrictions. Sales personnel meeting with prospective clients must know what GIPS-related information must be delivered to prospects, and when. This section provides recommendations to help a firm create a solid infrastructure that supports the GIPS compliance process.

Establish a GIPS Oversight Committee

Previous chapters presented the set of decisions that need to be made on an ongoing basis to ensure that the firm's performance presentations are up-to-date. But who makes these decisions? Given the nature of GIPS compliance, decisions usually need to be evaluated from multiple points of view. Almost every department within a firm is a key stakeholder in the GIPS compliance process. Maintenance of successful compliance requires buy-in and support from most, if not all, departments within a firm, not just the Performance Department. The larger and more complex the firm, the more the firm needs to collaborate across disciplines to maintain compliance.

In order to achieve this, firms should create a *GIPS Oversight Committee* that meets on a regular basis to discuss and provide firmwide governance over GIPS-related matters. The committee should include representatives from each of the departments that plays a role in the firm's GIPS compliance process. These departments typically include compliance, portfolio management, operations, marketing, sales, and client service. The mission of the GIPS Oversight Committee is to help a firm maintain its compliance with the GIPS standards by:

- Establishing and ensuring the firm is following its GIPS policies and procedures.
- Providing interpretation of the GIPS standards where necessary, such as when the GIPS standards don't address a specific issue.

The topics for review and discussion during these meetings vary based on the needs of the individual firm. Ideally, the GIPS Oversight Committee would address all GIPS-related matters where interdepartmental input benefits compliance efforts. Examples include composite creation, composite redefinitions, review and approval of changes to GIPS policies and procedures, review and approval of standard marketing materials, review of composite membership changes and other composite maintenance activities (e.g., decisions to exclude portfolios from composites), review of error corrections, and any other topics that may arise related to the GIPS standards. Note that one of the key findings from the SEC performance sweep exam discussed in Chapter 1 was that the firms found to have fewer deficiencies had established composite committees that met at least quarterly to review accounts to ensure proper composite assignment.

Create a Detailed GIPS Manual

As discussed in Chapter 1, a firm that claims compliance with the GIPS standards is required to document the policies and procedures used to establish and maintain compliance in a *GIPS Manual*. Although the actual format of the GIPS manual is left to the discretion of the firm, it should be as detailed and thorough as possible. Making sure that the policies and procedures in the GIPS manual are clearly articulated simplifies the process of claiming compliance and, importantly, minimizes errors—both of which are vital in maintaining the firm's compliance over time. For example, assume a firm has selected a policy whereby portfolios that terminate are included in composite(s) through the last full month for which the firm has discretion, and then are subsequently removed. To ensure this policy is followed, the firm's personnel responsible for composite maintenance must be informed of the date the firm no longer has discretion to manage the portfolio. To ensure portfolios are removed from composites at the correct time, the firm should establish procedures to ensure the details behind portfolio terminations are provided to the Performance Department. This procedure will help prevent composite return errors caused by keeping terminated portfolios in composites past the date when discretion ended.

Once the GIPS Manual is created, the firm must determine how it will handle updates or changes to policies or procedures. Some firms review and update the GIPS Manual periodically, such as once a year, and create a new version and retire the current version. At any point in time the firm will therefore have a GIPS Manual reflecting current policies and procedures. The downside to this approach is that it can be a challenge to determine which policies were in place at particular times. We instead suggest that the GIPS Manual be maintained as a continuously updated document including both current and historical policies and procedures. The manual should reflect all changes to policies and procedures over all periods for which the firm claims compliance with the GIPS standards. The firm should also date stamp the changes. Table 8.1 shows an example of policies that have changed over time.

Finally, a firm should periodically review the GIPS Manual with a fresh eye to ensure it is complete, accurate, and up-to-date. This review is often performed annually in conjunction with preparation for the firm's annual verification.

TABLE 8.1 Sample GIPS Manual Policy Change Record: New Portfolio Inclusion Policy

Applicable Time Period	Policy
1/00–12/03	First full quarter under management.
1/04–6/05	If funded within first 15 days of the month, the first full month under management.
	If funded after the 15th of the month, after the first full month under management.
7/05–current	After the first full month under management.

Define Prospective Client

The GIPS standards require firms to make every reasonable effort to provide a compliant presentation to all prospective clients. This seems like a simple requirement, yet it is sometimes harder to meet this requirement than it appears. Policies and procedures intended to ensure that the firm meets this requirement often require collaboration across several departments. Let's examine these procedures by first considering the definition of a prospective client.

Not everyone a firm meets with or interacts with as part of sales and marketing efforts is automatically considered a prospective client. The GIPS standards state that two qualities combine to define the prospective client. A *prospect* becomes a *prospective client* when:

1. The prospect has expressed interest in one of the firm's composite strategies.
2. The prospect qualifies to invest in the composite.

Until the firm determines that a prospect meets both of these tests, the firm does not have to provide the prospect with a compliant presentation. Practically speaking, this means that the sales staff charged with introducing the firm to prospects does not always have to be armed with a stack of compliant presentations. It also means that broadly distributed marketing materials such as mail or e-mail newsletters that discuss the firm's strategies do not need to include compliant presentations.

A firm must establish policies documenting when the firm believes a prospect becomes a prospective client. For many firms that manage institutional assets, this transition in status occurs when a client meeting is held to discuss a specific product. At that point the firm knows which products are of specific interest to the prospective client, and will include the appropriate compliant presentation(s) in the *pitch book*, or overall presentation to the client.

When marketing to institutional investors, the sales process can take many months (or years), over which the firm may meet with the prospective client periodically. In a follow-up meeting with a prospective client who has previously received a compliant presentation, the firm is not always required to provide another compliant presentation. As long as the firm has provided a compliant presentation to the prospective client within the past 12 months, the firm may choose whether or not to provide another compliant presentation.

Investment consultants and other third parties that represent prospective clients may fall under the definition of prospective client. Most firms also provide performance information to several databases every month or quarter. Best practice is to assume that each of these third-party entities qualifies as a prospective client. Common practice is to provide a compliant presentation for a specific composite the first time that the composite's performance is reported to that third party. Then, the firm distributes to all third parties compliant presentations annually for each of the strategies reported to that third party during the year. Alternatively, because it could be time consuming to track who has received performance information for which specific composites, some firms will compile and deliver a CD containing all compliant presentations for all strategies marketed or reported during the year to all third parties that the firm deals with. This is normally done after all compliant presentations are updated for the most recent annual period.

Periodically Sign Off on Composite Populations

The Performance Department maintains composites on an ongoing basis using the information known to them. Unfortunately, no matter how strong the firm's procedures are, key facts about portfolios do not always get communicated to the Performance Department. For example, changes to investment mandates or temporarily imposed client restrictions may not be communicated. To check for this, the firm should require the portfolio managers to review and sign off at least quarterly on each of the composites and the portfolios they manage. The information provided for their review and approval should include the portfolios in the composite, and portfolio-level and composite-level returns, along with a list of those portfolios that are excluded from the composite due to restrictions or other reasons. While focusing composite reviews on only marketed composites on a quarterly basis may be operationally necessary, the GIPS standards do not differentiate between marketed and nonmarketed strategies and all composites, regardless of marketing status, should be treated consistently. Therefore, the firm should require that the portfolio managers sign off at least annually on the membership and information presented for all composites that they oversee.

Establish an AUM Reconciliation Process

As a best practice, firms should perform an *assets under management* (AUM) reconciliation. The total firm assets reported in the GIPS-compliant presentation should be reconciled to the total firm assets calculated for corporate and/or regulatory reporting purposes (e.g., assets under management reported in Form ADV). A regular reconciliation to a data source independent of the composite system database will help ensure that all portfolios managed by the defined firm have been considered for composite member-ship and that GIPS firm assets are correctly reported.

As discussed in Chapter 1, the firm as defined for GIPS purposes is not necessarily the same as the definition used for corporate or regulatory reporting purposes. For example, a GIPS-defined firm may include only institutional assets, but both the institutional and retail businesses are in-cluded in total firm assets for regulatory reporting purposes. The AUM reconciliation should identify assets that are included in AUM calculated for regulatory purposes but excluded from GIPS total assets due to differences between the GIPS firm definition and the definition used in corporate or regulatory reporting. The reconciliation should also ensure that total firm assets reported in the GIPS-compliant presentation equals the market value of all discretionary and nondiscretionary (as defined for GIPS compliance purposes) portfolios, including fee-paying portfolios, non-fee-paying port-folios, and portfolios that have been assigned to a subadvisor where the firm has discretion over the selection of the subadvisor.

Common issues that may create AUM reconciling items include port-folios that are included in more than one composite, different naming or coding conventions across the firm's systems, and double-counted assets. Double counting can occur in situations such as when an institutional port-folio invests a portion of its assets into one of the firm's pooled funds. The firm must ensure there is no double counting of assets when reporting total firm assets. The reconciliation should be performed as often as the GIPS-compliant presentations are updated, or at least annually.

Stay Current with the GIPS Standards

Firms must comply with all requirements of the GIPS standards, as well as any updates or clarifications to the GIPS standards. This additional guidance typically comes in the form of Guidance Statements or Questions & An-swers (Q&As). Therefore, firms must establish policies for keeping current with the GIPS standards, which includes identifying any new guidance that is issued.

All Q&As and Guidance Statements are available on the GIPS standards web site (www.gipsstandards.org). CFA Institute sends e-mail alerts about new developments and publishes the periodic *GIPS Standards Newsletter* covering the latest news and interpretations. The newsletter is available on the GIPS web site, where you can also subscribe to the e-mail updates or an RSS feed.

CFA Institute sponsors an annual GIPS conference in North Amer-ica, and periodically sponsors similar conferences in other locations. These two-day conferences cover a wide range of topics relating to performance measurement and the GIPS standards and always include a session on updates or upcoming changes to the GIPS standards.

Usually there is a one-day workshop preceding these annual conferences that includes a discussion on upcoming changes, as well as a full review of the major topics in the GIPS standards. These one-day workshops are also held several times each year in additional cities.

Finally, many verifiers provide their clients with newsletters and other tools, such as disclosure checklists, to inform their clients about new guidance, and to help them maintain compliance with the GIPS standards.

RETURN CALCULATION

The GIPS standards include requirements for calculating portfolio-level and composite-level returns, but much is left to the judgment of the firm. This section includes several recommendations that, if adopted, can help a firm more effectively and efficiently comply with the calculation requirements of the GIPS standards. The section also includes recommendations for simplifying the process and minimizing the risk of errors.

Periodically Test the Adequacy of Supporting Records

The GIPS standards require firms to maintain books and records to support all calculations and other information included in compliant presentations. Firms must be able to produce supporting documentation to validate and recreate all information in their compliant presentations. There is no specific list of required documents, so firms must determine for themselves which records must be kept in order to meet this requirement. Firms should document policies in their GIPS Manual regarding which records are kept, the format of the records (electronic or hard copy), where the records are maintained (on-site or off-site), the length of time the records are retained, and the departments responsible for obtaining and maintaining the documentation. Where applicable, the GIPS Manual should also contain procedures for purging documents.

Document retention policies should include information about both the firm's clients and the accounting records for their portfolios. Client document retention policies should address records related to account start-up, maintenance, and termination. These include the management agreement, investment guidelines, and all client correspondence (e.g., memos and e-mails), and other documentation supporting composite inclusion and exclusion. Policies regarding accounting records should address both internal and custodian information that supports security positions, market values, income accruals, management fees, and cash and security transactions.

Firms should establish and document policies for reconciling portfolio-level information to custodian records. Policies should specify the types of reconciliations that are performed, the team responsible for performing the reconciliations, and the frequency with which the reconciliations are performed. While not explicitly required by the GIPS standards, the focus on custodian reconciliations will help firms meet the requirement to prove the existence of client assets and help ensure the integrity of the input data used in performance calculations.

The firm's compliance with the GIPS recordkeeping requirements relies on the fact that the actual supporting records can be obtained. Firms often store records off-site, or may have contracted with third parties to maintain supporting records. Firm should conduct periodic tests to ensure that all of the records that the firm needs to support its claim of GIPS compliance continue to be available.

Analyze Net Returns Calculated Using Actual Fees

When calculating composite net returns, firms have a choice between using model fees or actual fees. When using actual fees, ensuring that the correct fees are being applied to each portfolio is important. This can be harder than it appears. Some clients may have their fees deducted from their portfolio, while others may pay their fees using assets outside of the portfolio. Or fees may be calculated by combining related portfolios and the fee may be paid out of one portfolio on behalf of all. Assuming a quarterly payment schedule and a methodology where fees impact the net return on a when-paid basis, we should normally observe four fee payments a year. A simple test can be performed quarterly to compare portfolio-level quarterly gross and net returns. If the numbers are the same, the firm likely missed the application of a quarterly management fee.

Even if a firm is confident it can apply the proper fees to each portfolio, other decisions must be made. Should the firm reflect fees on an accrual or a when-paid basis? If accrued, are the fees accrued and recognized at quarter end, or are they estimated and applied monthly? Firms that charge their client performance-based fees must not only create and apply what are sometimes very complex calculation tools, but must also determine when performance-based fees will be reflected in net returns. Will performance-based fees be accrued throughout the year or will they be reflected only when the performance-based fees are due and payable (i.e., crystallized)?

Because of the difficulty in capturing all actual fees, as well as all the complexities associated with the calculations themselves, many firms choose to not use actual fees in the calculation of composite returns. Generally, the larger the firm, the more likely it is that the firm will not use actual fees when calculating net returns and will instead use model fees. But if actual fees are used, the firm must establish policies and procedures that ensure the proper fees are captured for the correct periods.

Consider Using Model Fees

To simplify the process for calculating net returns, many firms will use a model fee. Firms choose to use model fees for the following reasons:

- Calculating net returns using model fees can be easier and less time consuming than using actual fees.
- Model net returns can be calculated as soon as gross composite returns are finalized. There is no need to wait for all management fees to be calculated and finalized.
- From a purely recordkeeping perspective, less documentation is needed to support model fee net returns versus actual fee net returns.
- Because there are fewer moving parts when using model fees, there is less risk of error.

If the firm uses a model fee, the GIPS Manual should describe the process for determining the applicable fee to be used in the composite net return calculation. Changes to the model fee over time also need to be tracked.

Review Composites for Outlier Returns

Firms should have a review policy in place to compare the portfolio-level returns within a composite. The comparison will help to identify potential return calculation issues or composite assignment errors. This process should be conducted monthly, or as frequently as composites are updated. A firm should also review the high and low portfolio returns within a composite. If the same portfolio consistently produces an outlier return from month to month, this may indicate that the portfolio is being managed differently than the other portfolios in the composite. Many problems with composite assignment can be identified by performing an outlier review.

Care should be taken when using the composite return to identify outliers. Because the composite return is impacted by the outlier returns, it may not clearly expose portfolio-level return problems. For example, if the largest portfolio in the composite has the most extreme return of all portfolios in the composite, then the composite return is heavily impacted by the outlier. To deal with this, a firm should also compare portfolio returns to the composite equal weighted return and the return of the representative account for the strategy.

Ensure All Non-Wrap-Fee Portfolios Pay Commissions

For GIPS purposes, all returns must reflect the deduction of trading expenses, which are the actual costs of buying or selling investments. The one type of portfolio that normally does not pay trading expenses is a wrap-fee portfolio. Here, the trading expenses are included in the total wrap fee. A firm can typically easily identify wrap-fee portfolios and ensure the wrap-fee-specific requirements are met.

However, there are other portfolios that may not pay commissions or other trading expenses. These portfolios often have a special arrangement with a broker or other entity whereby commissions are paid in some other way than with the actual portfolio trades. For example, the portfolio may have entered into a directed brokerage arrangement that waives transaction expenses. Many firms have not paid much attention to this issue because they have assumed that all non-wrap-fee portfolios are paying transaction-based commissions. A firm should consider taking the following five steps:

1. Run a commissions report across all portfolios within the firm. For equity portfolios that pay explicit commissions, this is the quickest way to prove that commissions are being paid. For fixed income portfolios that do not pay explicit commissions, the firm could instead look for the use of multiple brokers. If multiple brokers are used, the likelihood that bid-offer spreads are not reflected in security trades is lessened. If only one broker is used, or a majority of trades are placed using one broker, it may indicate that the portfolio is not paying trading expenses and the firm should do additional checking to determine whether or not the portfolio is paying trading expenses.
2. Talk to the firm's traders. Ask them about any portfolios that do not pay commissions, or that have special trading arrangements, including directed brokerage arrangements. Establish a procedure for traders to inform the Performance Department about any trading changes on behalf of existing portfolios.
3. Include the Compliance Department in discussions with the traders. Compliance is typically aware of special trading arrangements (if the firm allows them at all).
4. Include information about trading expenses on the new account documentation that is provided to the Performance Department.

5. Periodically conduct tests of all portfolios to ensure the commission paying status has not changed, and that the procedures established to identify all portfolios that are not paying commission are working as intended.

ERROR CORRECTION

Performance measurement is at the end of a "food chain," consuming data created in client instructions, trading, accounting, market data, valuation, and other functions. An error that occurs within these functions or in the portfolio return and composite presentation preparation process could create a situation where the information previously presented to the firm's prospects is found to be incorrect. This section discusses requirements related to establishing an error correction policy, and provides a suggested approach for establishing this policy.

Establish a GIPS-Focused Error Correction Policy

Firms are required to make every reasonable effort to provide a compliant presentation to all prospective clients. Inherent in this requirement is the assumption that compliant presentations are accurate and that they do, in fact, include all the elements that are required to be included in a compliant presentation. However, no matter how strong a firm's system of checks and balances, mistakes will occur. Therefore, firms are required to establish policies and procedures for handing errors discovered in compliant presentations. These policies and procedures must be in accordance with the *Guidance Statement on Error Correction.*

These error correction policies address only errors that appear in compliant presentations, or other materials directly related to compliant presentations. These other materials include the list of composite descriptions and the firm's policies for calculating performance, valuing portfolios, and preparing compliant presentations. (A firm must disclose in compliant presentations the availability of these items, which is why they are subject to the firm's error correction policies.) These error correction policies will probably supplement procedures the firm has already established for dealing with performance errors that appear in other materials, such as fact sheets or newsletters.

An error results when any item that is included, or should be included, in a compliant presentation is discovered to be missing or inaccurate. Errors are not limited to mistakes in composite returns. There could be errors in benchmark returns, errors in required disclosures, and errors in statistics such as the number of portfolios in a composite, dispersion measures, and the total firm assets.

A firm must differentiate between material and immaterial errors. If the firm determines that an error in a compliant presentation is a material error, the firm must take the following steps:

1. Correct the compliant presentation and include disclosure of the change. This disclosure must remain in the compliant presentation for at least one year after the correction is made.
2. Make every reasonable effort to provide the revised compliant presentation to all parties that received the incorrect presentation, with one exception: The firm is not required to provide a corrected presentation to a former prospective client who is no longer considered a prospective client.

After correcting the material error, the firm may create a second version of the compliant presentation that reflects the correction of the material error but does not include the disclosure of the change. This second version can be the version of the compliant presentation that is delivered to new prospective clients who have never received the incorrect presentation.

A firm has no specific obligations to correct or communicate errors that are not material, with one exception: If the firm determines that a required disclosure is missing from the compliant presentation, the presentation must be corrected to include the disclosure, regardless of the materiality or significance of the disclosure.

A firm needs to establish policies for how it will determine whether an error is material or not. The definition of materiality is left to the firm. As in the auditing profession, there is no specific definition of materiality, even though materiality is a consideration in all judgments made during an audit. When considering how to define materiality, a firm should ask themselves this question: Which errors are large enough, or significant enough, to make a reader of the compliant presentation change their judgment about the composite or the firm? This is the level at which the firm should define materiality.

Firms need to take a different approach for determining materiality for an error in a composite return versus, for example, an error resulting from an incorrect disclosure about the method for calculating net returns. For the purposes of drafting an error correction policy and establishing a framework for using it, the firm should consider using the following categories for classifying presentation errors:

- *Assets error.* An assets error would include, but is not limited to, an incorrect, incomplete, or missing statement of total firm assets, composite assets, number of portfolios in a composite, or percentage of non-fee-paying portfolios included in a composite.

- *Performance error.* A performance-related error would include, but is not limited to, an incorrect, incomplete, or missing composite return, benchmark return, excess return, or measure of dispersion.
- *Disclosure error.* Any omission or misstatement of a required GIPS disclosure.

Some considerations for materiality may include the quantitative impact of the error, the asset type affected (e.g., equities, fixed income, emerging market equities), reporting periods (e.g., monthly, quarterly, or annual returns), and relative time periods (e.g., prior to a specific date, more than five years ago). The sample policy in Table 8.2 may serve as a reference for determining the minimum appropriate action for the firm to take when an error is discovered. Note the assumption that only annual returns are included in compliant presentations. If other returns are included, such as quarterly or multi-year annualized returns, the firm would need to define materiality for each of those returns as well. The policies are provided as a suggestion to help a firm that does not yet have an established error correction policy formulate the policy appropriate for their firm. Under all circumstances the error, cause of the error, and course of action should be documented internally, reviewed, and approved by the appropriate level of management (e.g., Performance Manager, Chief Compliance Officer).

Sample Error Correction Policy

For our purposes, the word "material" is used in a broader context than in the Error Correction Guidance Statement. Only Level 5 errors, as described in the Table 8.2 sample error correction levels, would be equivalent to a material error as described in the Guidance Statement.

The firm has developed the following categories for actions to be taken once an error has been identified and materiality has been determined. In order to establish a framework for the consistent application of an error correction policy for different types of potential errors, the following categories and thresholds for materiality have been created. For errors that occur that are unanticipated and are not covered by the policies and procedures the firm has currently defined, the GIPS Oversight Committee will review the individual incident and determine materiality and the proper course of action to take. Any such findings and determinations will be added to the error correction policy to ensure consistent application going forward.

In order to establish a framework for the consistent application of an error correction policy for different types of potential errors, the following

TABLE 8.2 Sample Error Correction Levels

Error Level	Corrective Actions
Level 1	Take no action.
Level 2	Correct the data error in the performance system but take no further action.
Level 3	Correct the data error in the performance system, if appropriate. Correct the compliant presentation. Do not disclose the change.
Level 4	Correct the data error in the performance system, if appropriate. Correct the compliant presentation. Disclose the change. Do not distribute the corrected presentation.
Level 5	Correct the data error in the performance system, if appropriate. Correct the compliant presentation. Disclose the change. Make every reasonable effort to provide a corrected presentation to all prospective clients and other parties that received the incorrect presentation.

categories and thresholds for materiality have been created. For errors that occur that are unanticipated and are not covered by the policies and procedures the firm has currently defined, the GIPS Oversight Committee will review the individual incident and determine materiality and the proper course of action to take. Any such findings and determinations will be added to the error correction policy to ensure consistent application going forward.

The definition of materiality for the three categories of potential errors is as follows:

1. *Assets errors.* The materiality threshold provides a guide to the minimum action required when these types of errors are found.

Error	Materiality	Minimum Action
Total firm assets	$\geq \pm 5\%$	Level 3
Composite assets	$\geq \pm 5\%$	Level 3
Number of portfolios	$\geq \pm 5\%$	Level 3
% of non-fee-paying portfolios	$\geq \pm 15\%$	Level 3

2. *Performance errors.* The materiality provides a guide to the minimum action required when these types of errors are found.

Error	Composite Type	Materiality	Minimum Action
Annual composite return	Equity	≥ +/− 10 bps	Level 3
	Fixed Income	≥ +/− 5 bps	Level 3
	Emerging Market	≥ +/− 10 bps	Level 3
	Private Equity	≥ +/− 15 bps	Level 3
	Any	≥ +/− 50 bps	Level 5
Annual benchmark return	Equity	≥ +/− 25 bps	Level 3
	Fixed Income	≥ +/− 10 bps	Level 3
	Emerging Market	≥ +/− 25 bps	Level 3
	Private Equity	≥ +/− 20 bps	Level 3
	Any	≥ +/− 50 bps	Level 5
Dispersion	Any	≥ +/− 50 bps	Level 3

   a. Any error deemed material will require a more comprehensive review to determine the appropriate course of action. For those errors found below the threshold, action Level 1 or 2 will be taken. Should an error be identified in excess of 50 bps in any performance category, Level 5 action will be followed.

   b. Any error in composite returns that exceeds the materiality threshold and has a relative impact (based on the originally reported composite return) of more than 5% will be escalated to action Level 5.

   c. Any error in composite returns that causes the corrected composite to change from outperforming the benchmark to underperforming the benchmark will be escalated to action Level 5.

3. *Disclosure errors.* The omission or misstatement of a required GIPS disclosure requires action in all circumstances. At a minimum, the compliant presentation will be corrected immediately, the corrected version will be posted to the web site in a timely fashion, and the error will be documented internally. Each error will then be thoroughly evaluated on a case by case basis by the Performance Manager and Compliance Manager to determine whether any additional corrective action is necessary. Any error in disclosures that is deemed to have potentially impacted a prospective client's decision to invest will be escalated to an action Level 5.

Disclosure of an error (action Level 4 or 5) must be included in the compliant presentation for a minimum of 12 months following the correction of the presentation. The redistribution of compliant presentations will be handled collectively by the Performance, Client Service, Marketing, and Compliance Departments. Corrected presentations will be distributed via e-mail using the ABC database. All clients that received the incorrect presentation will receive a copy of the corrected presentation. All reasonable efforts will be taken to ensure that prospective clients associated with the composite strategy will also receive a corrected presentation. Copies of the corrected presentation will also be e-mailed to sponsors, investment consultants, and other known third parties associated with the sale of the composite strategy. A copy of the corrected presentation will be placed on the web site.

Create a GIPS Error Form

To manage the error correction process, firms should create a *GIPS Error Form* and then assign responsibility for maintaining these forms to a specific person or department. The GIPS Oversight Committee should have responsibility for approving the steps taken to address errors. The form should include, at a minimum, the following information about the error:

- The composite(s) affected by the error.
- The portfolio(s) affected by the error.
- Impacted periods, if applicable.
- When and how the error was discovered.
- Description of the error.
- Materiality calculation, if applicable.
- Action level taken.
- Steps to be taken to prevent error from recurring.
- Changes needed to the current error correction policies, if any.

MANAGING COMPOSITES AND PRESENTATIONS

Over and above the calculation of returns, the preparation of compliant composite presentations is at the heart of ongoing GIPS compliance. This section provides tips for developing an efficient process for maintaining composites and their related compliant presentations.

Ensure the List of Composite Descriptions Is Complete

A composite description is brief information about the composite strategy, and is a required disclosure in the compliant presentation. Additionally, a firm must maintain a list of composite descriptions that includes all composites within the firm, and the firm must disclose in all compliant presentations that this list is available upon request. A firm should ensure that all composites, both marketed and nonmarketed, are on the list. The list must also include all composites that terminated within the past five years. Finally, a firm should ensure that all composite descriptions are detailed enough so the reader would understand each strategy, and also be able to understand the differences between composites managed using similar strategies.

Prepare a Final Compliant Presentation for Terminated Composites

A firm must be able to prepare a compliant presentation for all composites included on the list of composite descriptions. This list must include all composites currently managed by the firm, as well as any composite that terminated within the past five years. When a composite terminates, the firm should note the date of termination on the list of composite descriptions so the firm knows when the composite can be removed from this list. Also, the firm should take the time to prepare the final compliant presentation for the terminated composite at that time. Doing so will prevent difficulty when a verifier or regulator asks for the terminated composite's compliant presentation in the future. Also remember that if the composite terminates after January 1, 2011, the final partial year of performance must be included in the presentation. For example, if the firm prepares compliant presentations as of December 31 and the composite terminates August 5, the firm must include performance from January through the last full period during the year (usually through July).

Include Only Required Information in Compliant Presentations

Along with updating compliant presentations annually, a firm should also consider including only the minimum required information in the compliant presentation. Taking this approach will also help minimize the risk of an error occurring. A firm may provide all sorts of other information that would qualify as either additional or supplemental information, but this should be done separate and apart from the compliant presentation itself.

A firm should also consider standardizing disclosures as much as possible to, once again, mitigate the risk of error. Numbering disclosures in the compliant presentation can help personnel responsible for preparing or reviewing compliant presentations ensure all required disclosures are included. For example, if standard disclosure #6 includes the benchmark description and other information about the benchmark, it would be quite obvious if this disclosure was missing from a specific presentation. It also facilitates the comparison of presentations, as the reviewer can justify any differences between presentations.

Reconsider the Use of Composite Minimums

A firm is allowed to establish a minimum size for inclusion in the composite. For example, "the Growth Equity Composite includes portfolios that are greater than $5 million." This composite minimum is supposed to represent the amount of money needed to implement the strategy. Portfolios below the minimum size are considered nondiscretionary as they cannot be managed according to the composite's strategy and thus are excluded from the composite. In many firms it has become common practice to establish a minimum size for all composites. Unfortunately, this is often done without consideration for how much money is actually required to allow the firm to manage the portfolio using the intended strategy. The use of composite minimums should not allow a firm to drastically reduce the number of portfolios included in composites merely to simplify the composite maintenance process. Firms should consider the GIPS recommendation that prospective clients not be presented with composites whose minimum is greater than the prospect's ability to invest.

For many firms, the tracking and monitoring of portfolios for proper inclusion or exclusion from composites based solely on composite minimums creates a lot of work, and it often leads to errors. We encourage firms to take a step back and ensure they can rationalize their composite minimums. Continuing with the example above of the Growth Equity Composite with a $5 million minimum, the firm that has established this policy should ask itself the following question: Do we manage a Growth Equity portfolio that has a $5.1 million value differently from the way we manage a Growth Equity portfolio with a $4.9 million value? If the answer is no, then the firm should eliminate the composite minimum or determine if the composite minimum should be lower. Firms should also keep in mind that smaller portfolios carry less weight in the composite calculation, so any minor differences due to a portfolio's smaller size may not even have an impact on the composite return.

Ensure Composite Definitions Are Complete

A composite definition is the set of detailed rules a firm follows for assigning portfolios to composites. The logical place to maintain composite definitions is in the GIPS Manual. A composite definition begins with the composite description, and also includes all the additional criteria for determining which portfolios go in a specific composite. Significant cash flow policies, large cash flow policies, composite minimums, new portfolio inclusion policies, and detailed discretion considerations are examples of criteria that are included in a composite definition. Only the composite description must be disclosed in a compliant presentation, and not the composite definition. However, the firm must provide the composite definition if requested to do so. While the firm does not have to disclose that composite definitions are available upon request, the firm must be able to provide this information.

The components of a composite definition can usually be pieced together by integrating information found in different parts of the GIPS Manual. Often the GIPS Manual includes policies and procedures that apply to all composites. For example, the firm may document the new portfolio inclusion composite policies for all composites within a firm. To determine which new portfolio inclusion policy applies to a specific composite, the firm must go to this section of the GIPS Manual and identify which new portfolio inclusion policy applies to the composite. This same approach can be used for all policies in the GIPS Manual. Therefore if the information is not organized by composite, pulling together all of the details that comprise a specific composite's definition can be difficult. A firm should consider creating a composite definition for each composite that includes all of the detailed rules for maintaining the composite. Preparing composite definitions for all composites could be a large project but, once completed, the ongoing process of keeping the definitions updated will be more efficient. The following is a list of the information that should appear in a composite definition:

- Composite name.
- Composite strategy description.
- Composite benchmark.
- Details of benchmark changes.
- Types of portfolios included in composite (e.g., taxable, tax-exempt, institutional, pooled funds).
- Definition of discretion at the composite level.
- Inclusion of non-fee-paying portfolios.
- Inclusion of carve-outs.
- Minimum size for composite inclusion.
- Significant cash flow policy level and applicable periods.

- New portfolio inclusion policy.
- Closed portfolio exclusion policy.
- Description of composite redefinitions.
- Composite name changes.
- Composite inception date.
- Composite creation date.
- Period for which the composite is examined.

Maintain a List of Excluded Portfolios

While a firm must include all actual, fee-paying, discretionary portfolios in at least one composite, at any point in time most firms will have a number of portfolios that are not included in a composite. Some portfolios may be permanently excluded from composites, such as portfolios that are not considered discretionary for GIPS purposes or non-fee-paying portfolios if the firm has decided to exclude such portfolios from composites. Some portfolios may be temporarily excluded from composites, such as new portfolios that are in the process of opening, portfolios that fall below the composite minimum size, or portfolios that are temporarily nondiscretionary due to a no-trading restriction for tax purposes.

Firms should ensure that they can identify all such portfolios and provide support for the decision to permanently or temporarily exclude them from composites. Some firms create administrative composites to help manage excluded portfolios. For example, a firm might maintain a restricted version of each composite that includes portfolios with a restriction that prevents them from being included in the respective composite. While these administrative groupings may be maintained on the firm's composite system, these are not composites for GIPS purposes and must not be included on the firm's list of composite descriptions. A firm should also periodically review each portfolio on the excluded portfolio list and ensure the reason for exclusion is still valid. Maintaining an ongoing process to track excluded portfolios will help to ensure no portfolio is inadvertently excluded from its correct composite.

Ensure All Multi-asset Portfolios Are Included in a Multi-asset Composite

As we discussed in Chapter 2, all actual, fee-paying, discretionary portfolios that are included in total firm assets must be included in at least one composite. But what does this mean for a portfolio that has assets invested in more than one asset class? Consider a balanced portfolio that has equity and fixed income subportfolios. Each subportfolio is managed as a stand-alone portfolio and is included in the respective asset class composite. Because all assets of the balanced portfolio are included in a composite, has the requirement to include all actual, fee-paying, discretionary portfolios in at least one composite been met? The answer is that it depends. If the firm has been hired to manage two subportfolios, and the firm does not have discretion at the total balanced portfolio level, including the two subportfolios in the respective composites meets the requirement. However, if the firm has discretion at the total balanced portfolio level, and has responsibility for asset allocation decisions, then the total portfolio must be included in a balanced composite. The firm may include the subportfolios in composites as well, but this is not required. Firms should establish policies to ensure that all multi-asset portfolios for which the firm has discretion at the total portfolio level are included in a multi-asset composite.

Update Compliant Presentations Annually

A firm must update compliant presentations at least annually, but may do so more often. However, each time a firm changes the information that is included in the compliant presentation, it risks making an error. While updating compliant presentations more frequently may be a simple process for smaller firms, this may not be the case for larger firms that manage thousands of portfolios and maintain many composites. Each time a compliant presentation is changed it creates the risk that an error will occur. As we discussed previously, a firm that has an error in a compliant presentation will potentially be required to distribute a corrected compliant presentation to anyone who received the incorrect presentation—a process that can be time-consuming and may send a bad message to prospective clients.

The firm also has to keep track of who received which version of the compliant presentation. This process becomes more complicated if the firm updates compliant presentations frequently. For example, assume a firm updates compliant presentations quarterly. When providing a compliant presentation to a prospective client on July 20, did the firm provide the presentation that included year-to-date results through March 31 or June 30? If there was an error in the March 31 presentation but not the June 30 presentation, the firm would need to know which presentation was provided. Remember that just because the compliant presentation was updated only as of the most recent annual period end does not mean the firm is restricted from providing more recent performance information. Performance results through the most recent quarter, or month, or yesterday can be provided to the prospective client, but this information would be provided outside of the context of a GIPS-compliant presentation. An error in other marketing materials does not subject the firm to its GIPS error correction policies.

SUMMARY

This chapter provided guidance for organizing firmwide governance and oversight to maintain compliance with the GIPS standards, as well as tips for managing the process. Once the firm has the process up and running, it may wish to have an independent third party test its policies and procedures for maintaining compliance. This third party test is called verification and is the subject of the next chapter.

CHAPTER 9

Verification

Any firm can make the claim that it complies with the GIPS standards. There is always some chance that an investment manager is falsely claiming compliance, or worse, promoting a fraudulent performance record. Therefore, to add credibility to a firm's claim of compliance, the GIPS standards recommend that GIPS-compliant firms be independently verified. A verification, which must be performed by an independent third party, is intended to provide additional confidence to a firm, the firm's clients, and prospective clients that the firm actually does comply with the GIPS standards. The GIPS standards describe two types of testing:

1. *Verification*, which is concerned with the firm as a whole.
2. *Performance Examination* (or *performance audit*), which is performed at the composite level.

Performance examinations must be conducted in conjunction with or after the firmwide verification. Firms may not have a GIPS performance examination performed on composites if the firm has not yet been verified.

In the United States, as well as some other countries, institutional investors and their investment consultants typically require that firms interested in managing their assets comply with the GIPS standards. Many also require verification, or at least inquire as to the firm's verification status. Additionally, some institutional investors and their investment consultants may also require a performance examination of the composite representing the strategy in which they are considering investing.

Common practice for U.S. institutional money managers is to engage an independent third party to conduct a firmwide verification and performance examinations for the composites representing the key strategies that they are currently promoting to investors.

VERIFICATION

Independent verification provides assurance as to:

1. Whether the firm has complied with all the composite construction requirements of the GIPS standards on a firmwide basis.
2. Whether the firm's policies and procedures are designed to calculate and present performance in compliance with the GIPS standards.

The first assertion is essentially a test of whether the firm has included the correct portfolios in the correct composites for the correct time periods. The second assertion is a test of a firm's *policies and procedures* to determine if portfolio-level returns and composite-level returns meet the calculation requirements of the GIPS standards, and whether the firm has adequate policies and procedures in place to properly assemble all of the required components of a compliant presentation.

The verification must be conducted on a firmwide basis. A verification report is issued to a firm—that is, Firm A is verified as a whole, not specific composites of Firm A. All portfolios and composites of the firm, whether marketed or not, are subjected to testing by the verifier. However, verification does not provide assurance on the results of any specific composite. If a firm wishes to obtain an opinion that provides this specific assurance, it may engage a verifier to conduct a performance examination on a specific composite.

This is an important point, so it is worth looking at from the prospect's point of view. Prospective investors need to understand that an independent verification validates whether the firm has the proper policies and procedures in place to calculate and present composite returns, but it does not validate whether the firm has actually followed those policies. A composite-specific performance examination is required to validate a specific composite's returns and accompanying disclosures as summarized in the composite's compliant presentation.

During the time period when the draft version of the 2010 edition of the GIPS standards was out for public comment, several firms that claimed compliance with the GIPS standards and had been verified (or claimed to be verified) were unfortunately revealed to be either Ponzi schemes or fraudulently reporting assets under management. This resulted in a substantial overhaul of the required verification procedures. In addition, a great deal of misunderstanding about the level of assurance provided by a verification report persisted. This led to a revised *claim of compliance*. The new claim of compliance, which is a required disclosure in compliant presentations, was rewritten to require a firm to disclose its verification status. Additionally, if the firm is verified, the claim of compliance now includes language that clearly states what verification is, as well as what verification is not. The newly required claim of compliance for a verified firm is as follows:

> *[Insert name of firm] claims compliance with the Global Investment Performance Standards (GIPS®) and has prepared and presented this report in compliance with the GIPS standards. [Insert name of firm] has been independently verified for the periods [insert dates]. A copy of the verification report(s) is/are available upon request."*
>
> *Verification assesses whether (1) the firm has complied with all the composite construction requirements of the GIPS standards on a firmwide basis, and (2) the firm's policies and procedures are designed to calculate and present performance in compliance with the GIPS standards. Verification does not ensure the accuracy of any specific composite presentation.*

The two paragraphs of the claim of compliance may be combined into one paragraph, but must not be separated in order to ensure that a reader of the compliant presentation understands what it means for a firm to be independently verified.

The claim of compliance for a firm that has not been verified is as follows:

> *[Insert name of firm] claims compliance with the Global Investment Performance Standards (GIPS®) and has prepared and presented this report in compliance with the GIPS standards. [Insert name of firm] has not been independently verified.*

A third claim of compliance is available for a composite of a verified firm that has undergone a performance examination.

PERFORMANCE EXAMINATIONS

As stated above, a verification does not provide assurance on the results of a specific composite. If a firm wishes to receive this assurance, it may do so by engaging a verifier to conduct a performance examination on that composite. As with verifications, performance examinations must be performed by an independent third party. The same verification firm that conducts the verification typically conducts the performance examinations as well, and performs the two engagements at the same time.

For a composite that has been examined, the claim of compliance is modified to reflect the fact that the firm has received assurance as to the accuracy of the composite's presentation. The claim of compliance for an examined composite is as follows:

> *[Insert name of firm] claims compliance with the Global Investment Performance Standards (GIPS®) and has prepared and presented this report in compliance with the GIPS standards. [Name of firm] has been independently verified for the periods [insert dates].*
>
> *Verification assesses whether (1) the firm has complied with all the composite construction requirements of the GIPS standards on a firmwide basis and (2) the firm's policies and procedures are designed to calculate and present performance in compliance with the GIPS standards. The [insert name of composite] has been examined for the periods [insert dates]. The verification and performance examination report(s) are available upon request.*

An additional claim of compliance option is used for an examined composite if the end date of the performance examination period is more than 24 months from the end date that is included in the composite's compliant presentation. This option was discussed in Chapter 6.

Because a verification must be conducted either before or along with any performance examination, our discussion focuses primarily on the verification process.

VERIFICATION CONSIDERATIONS

Once a firm decides that it wishes to be verified, the firm must then determine for which period it wishes to be verified, how frequently subsequent verifications will be performed, and which verification firm it will engage.

Verification Period

The minimum period that must be covered by a verification is one year, or since the firm's inception if the firm has been in existence for less than one year. For example, assume Firm B had an inception date of April 15, 2010, and immediately began managing a seed money portfolio provided by the firm's owners according to the firm's only investment strategy. Firm B reports performance of the strategy beginning May 1. Firm B has chosen

December 31 as the end date by which annual performance will be presented in compliant presentations. In January 2011, Firm B decided to undertake the verification process. The firm could obtain a verification covering the period from May 1, 2010 through December 31, 2010. The firm did not have to wait until it had a one-year history in order to be verified.

As long as at least a one-year period (or the period since inception) is covered by the verification, the firm may determine the period over which it is verified. Firms that are being verified for the first time will often choose to have the initial verification cover the period since firm inception or the most recent 5- or 10-year period. While a firm could choose to be verified only over the minimum one-year period, or indeed over any longer period, prospective clients may well wonder why the initial verification does not extend further back in time, or why it covers what appears to be an arbitrary period.

While the cost of the verification is certainly an important factor when determining which period will be covered, a five-year verification should be less than five times the cost of a one-year verification. Assuming there have been no significant changes in a firm's operations over the past five years, conducting a verification for a five-year period is typically not five times more work than doing a verification for a one-year period.

The period of the firmwide verification also determines the maximum period for which a composite can be examined. Assume Firm C has been verified for the period from January 1, 2006 through December 31, 2010. Firm C intends to actively market the Core Equity Composite, so it wishes to have the Core Equity Composite examined. The Core Equity Composite has an inception date of June 1, 2004. The maximum period the Core Equity Composite could be examined is the same as the firm's verification period: January 1, 2006 through December 31, 2010. The GIPS performance examination cannot cover any period prior to January 1, 2006 as the firm was not verified prior to this date.

Verification Frequency

How often should the firm be verified? The GIPS standards do not state a preference for the verification frequency. Instead, through the claim of compliance that is included in compliant presentations, a firm will inform prospective clients for which period and how recently the firm has been verified. Most, but not all, firms choose to be verified annually. Some verifiers encourage quarterly verification. Typically, smaller firms are more willing to undertake this process quarterly. However, larger firms often feel that a quarterly verification is more work than an annual verification without much added benefit. Ultimately, this decision is up to the firm. Verifiers will accommodate the firm's preference.

Verification Cost

The price for verification is usually based primarily on the verifier's estimate of how much time and effort will be required to perform the engagement. The cost can vary widely depending on several factors, including:

- The time period covered by the verification.
- The number of composites (if any) that will be examined.
- If composites are to be examined, the period of time that will be covered by the performance examination.
- The number of portfolios within the firm.
- The number of composites within the firm.
- Assets under management.
- The types of portfolios managed.
- The types of strategies managed.
- The turnover of portfolios during the verification period.
- The capabilities of the systems used to calculate portfolio-level and composite-level returns.
- The firm's internal control structure.

The verifier may also consider other factors, such as whether the firm has been previously verified or not, as well as any recent changes within the firm that could impact the GIPS compliance process.

Verifier Independence and Qualifications

The GIPS standards require that a verification must be performed by a qualified, independent third party. The *Guidance Statement on Verification* provides some additional guidance as to what would qualify a person or firm to provide verification services. Verifiers must be knowledgeable about all requirements and recommendations included in the GIPS standards, as well as all other guidance for complying with the GIPS standards, including Guidance Statements and GIPS Questions & Answers. Verifiers must also have knowledge of any laws or regulations pertaining to the calculation and presentation of the firm's performance.

There is no specific examination or professional certification granting someone the formal role of GIPS Verifier. The guidance alone cannot prevent unqualified individuals or firms from stating that they have the expertise needed to provide verification services.

There is also a lack of clear-cut guidance describing exactly what it means for verifiers to be independent of the firms that they are reviewing. The *Guidance Statement on Verifier Independence* explicitly states that defining independence is not a simple process, and attempts to recognize that practices differ across countries. The Guidance Statement does, however, state that verifiers must perform their work in an unbiased manner and that they cannot verify their own work.

What does it mean for a verifier to not verify their own work? A verifier should not be providing services that are properly the function of firm management and it should not take on decision making roles with respect to the implementation of and compliance with the GIPS standards. For example, the verifier should not be responsible for calculating portfolio or composite returns.

A verifier must also not have any other kind of business or financial relationship with the verification client that might prevent an unbiased review. How does the firm decide whether or not a verifier is truly independent? Although this assessment is the joint responsibility of both the firm and its prospective verifier, the final decision is the responsibility of the firm.

Selecting a Verifier

Since any firm or person can claim to be qualified to perform a verification, firms should conduct thorough due diligence in order to select a qualified, experienced, reputable, and independent verifier.

To assist firms with conducting this search, several years ago the (then named) Investment Performance Council (IPC) Verification Subcommittee issued a document titled "Suggested Questions to Ask Prospective Verification Firms." This document is available on the GIPS standards web site, and provides a list of questions that firms should ask potential verifiers in order to understand their experience.[1]

A critical consideration should be the verifier's reputation within the industry. In the process of due diligence, firms should request that the prospective verifier provide several client references. The references should be for asset management firms similar in size, complexity, and types of assets managed.

Beyond experience and reputation, firms may want to look for a verifier that focuses on client service. A client-focused verifier will emphasize timely communication throughout the year by providing ongoing support and advice. Firms may find that their verifier can provide support for unforeseen issues or new situations that the firm has not dealt with before.

---

[1]Investment Performance Council (IPC) Verification Subcommittee, "Suggested Questions to Ask Prospective Verification Firms," www.gipsstandards.org/standards/guidance/develop/pdf/questions_verification_firms.pdf.

These could include mergers and acquisitions, new product offerings, and the implementation of new complex instruments.

The Becoming Compliant tab on the GIPS standards web site also includes a link to a list of software vendors and verifiers who support money managers with their GIPS compliance needs.[2] Please be aware that firms on this list are neither endorsed nor approved by CFA Institute.

REQUIRED VERIFICATION PROCEDURES

The GIPS standards establish minimum procedures that a verifier must perform when conducting a verification. The procedures are written broadly to encompass all types of firms. Depending on the nature of the engagement, verifiers will use their professional judgment to decide if any additional testing not addressed by the GIPS standards will be performed.

The *Guidance Statement on Performance Examinations* includes guidance as to the tests that must be performed when conducting a performance examination of a composite. Performance examination guidance is substantially the same as the firmwide verification guidance, with additional requirements to ensure that all of the required procedures are conducted on the composite being examined. Because the procedures for verification and examination are the same, only the verification procedures are discussed below. When a composite is being examined, the same procedures apply; they are just applied to a specific composite.

Pre-verification Procedures

The pre-verification procedures can be thought of as the body of knowledge verifiers are required to obtain prior to performing the actual verification. This section summarizes the preparatory knowledge to be gained.

Knowledge of the GIPS Standards The verifier must have expertise in the GIPS standards themselves and all related interpretive guidance. Beyond knowing each provision in the GIPS standards and how to apply it, a verifier must also have a thorough knowledge of all Guidance Statements, interpretations, Q&As, and all other related guidance issued by CFA Institute or the GIPS Executive Committee.

---

[2]CFA Institute, "GIPS Service Providers," www.gipsstandards.org/compliance/providers/index.html.

Knowledge of Regulations   The verifier must have knowledge of laws and regulations applicable to the firm with respect to the calculation and presentation of performance. For example, when conducting a verification of an SEC registered firm, the verifier should be familiar with applicable SEC rules and regulations as well as numerous no-action letters related to performance and advertising. For example, even though the GIPS standards do not require a disclosure reflecting the impact of fees on performance, the SEC may, and the knowledgeable verifier will have an understanding of when this disclosure must be included in a compliant presentation.

Knowledge of the Firm   Because a verification is conducted on a firmwide basis, the verifier must acquire a thorough understanding of the firm and how the firm is defined for the purpose of complying with the GIPS standards. Understanding the firm could be a very straightforward exercise if the firm is independent and held out to the public as a stand-alone entity. At the other extreme, understanding the definition of a firm that is composed of several business units of a large, complex financial services company can take some effort. Since this definition determines the assets included in firm assets that are subject to firmwide testing, obtaining a clear understanding of the firm definition is critical for the verifier.

Knowledge of the Firm's Policies and Procedures   Provision 0.A.5 requires a firm to document in its GIPS Manual the policies and procedures used to establish and maintain compliance with the GIPS standards. The verifier must obtain these policies and procedures from the firm and determine which policies the firm has adopted. The verifier must review the GIPS Manual to ensure it is complete, and that all applicable policies and procedures have been included. In addition to determining if the GIPS Manual is complete, the verifier will also determine whether the adopted policies meet the requirements set forth in the GIPS standards. For example, if a firm has adopted a policy of recording income on fixed income securities on a cash basis, even though the firm has documented this policy in the GIPS Manual, this policy does not meet the requirements of the GIPS standards. (Interest income must be recognized on an accrual, not cash, basis).

The verifier must also determine if policies and procedures are adequately documented. For example, when documenting policies for calculating portfolio-level returns, simply stating that portfolio returns are calculated using a time-weighted return does not suffice. The firm should include enough information so the verifier can determine exactly how portfolio-level returns are calculated. Knowing that the manager calculates portfolio-level returns daily using an end-of-day cash flow assumption, the verifier will test portfolio returns to ensure these returns are calculated in accordance with the stated firm policy.

Knowledge of Valuation Basis and Performance Calculations   As the GIPS standards have requirements related to valuations and performance calculations, the GIPS Manual should include policies and procedures that cover these items. Verifiers have an explicit requirement to understand policies, procedures, and methodologies related to both portfolio valuation and performance measurement.

Verification Procedures

After completing the pre-verification procedures, the verifier will be ready to begin the actual verification testing. The GIPS standards include a series of steps that must be performed as part of the verification. These tests are written very broadly, so the actual tests could take many forms. Much is left to the verifier's discretion. While testing procedures may differ between verification firms, most verifiers would be expected to perform testing similar to the procedures described in this section.

Firm Definition   The way in which a firm defines itself for GIPS compliance purposes determines the population of portfolios to which the GIPS standards apply. Verifiers are required to determine if the firm has been appropriately defined. To determine whether the firm definition for GIPS purposes is reasonable and appropriate, the verifier will typically review the firm's marketing materials, web site, and regulatory filings (e.g., Form ADV). These materials help the verifier understand how the firm is organized and how it holds itself out to the public. If the definition of the firm is not clear-cut, then the verifier will consider the relationship of the firm to other entities. These entities could be sister business units within a larger corporate entity and those covered by joint marketing arrangements.

Verifiers must also test to determine if the firm has properly calculated its total firm assets and presented the correct amounts in compliant presentations. One of the more challenging tests for a verifier is to determine whether all the portfolios that should be incorporated into firm assets are appropriately included. While the firm is required to provide to the verifier a list of all portfolios within the defined firm, the verifier must perform testing to determine that this list is complete. This testing will be very firm-specific. It may include testing relative to regulatory filings, such as the firm's Form ADV, or to client billing records or other independent sources of information about assets under management.

Composite Construction   As part of the verification report, the verifier must provide an opinion stating that the firm has complied with all of the composite construction requirements of the GIPS standards on a firmwide basis. In order to reach this conclusion, the verifier will test to determine that the firm has:

- Defined composites according to reasonable guidelines.
- Included all actual, fee-paying, discretionary portfolios in at least one composite.
- Established composite membership rules for inclusion and exclusion that are reasonable and consistently applied.
- Selected composite benchmarks that are consistent with the composite definition.

The firm is required to provide to the verifier information about the population of portfolios that are included in composites. The firm must provide lists of all new, existing, and closed portfolios for every composite within the firm. These lists must cover the entire period that is being verified. Note that there is no specifically required format for these lists. The verifier will work together with the firm to determine which reports will best provide the information the verifier needs.

From this composite population information, the verifier will select portfolios to test. Most verifications are conducted using sample-based testing and the verifier will draw conclusions based on the results of those tests. While the entire firm must be subjected to testing, this does not mean that the verifier must test each and every portfolio within a firm. This means that the verifier must consider the entire population of portfolios and composites within the firm when conducting the verification. The GIPS standards recognize that verifiers will not test all portfolios and all composites and will perform testing using a sampling methodology. However, the GIPS standards do not provide a specific number of portfolios or percentage of the firm's portfolios or composites that must be tested. Rather, the GIPS standards simply state that the verifier may use samples, and include a list of criteria the verifier must consider when selecting samples, such as the firm's total number of portfolios and composites. This list of criteria represents only the minimum criteria that must be considered by the verifier. To help determine the size of the sample to test, verifiers will also consider other factors such as the firm's internal control structure, the verifier's risk analysis of the firm, and materiality considerations.

New Portfolios   A portfolio that entered a composite during the verification period will be tested to determine if it met the criteria for inclusion in the composite, and that the timing of inclusion in the composite was correct. The verifier will review the investment management agreement, including guidelines and restrictions, to determine if the portfolio is discretionary and that the portfolio's strategy is consistent with the composite's strategy. The verifier may also review portfolio holdings to ensure that these holdings are consistent with the composite strategy. The verifier will review custodian statements and transaction reports to determine the date the portfolio was funded. If the composite has any other criteria for inclusion, such as a minimum size requirement, the verifier will ask for supporting documentation proving that the portfolio meets all composite criteria. Knowing the funding date, as well as the composite's definition, the verifier will conclude whether the portfolio was included in the proper composite at the proper time.

Closed Portfolios   A portfolio that exited a composite during the verification period will be tested to determine if it was properly removed from the composite, and that the timing of removal was correct. If a portfolio was removed from the composite because its owner terminated the relationship with the firm, the verifier will review pertinent correspondence from the client. The verifier might also review transaction reports to see when trading stopped or when the portfolio was liquidated. A portfolio may also be removed from a composite because it no longer qualifies for inclusion in the composite. The type of supporting records to prove proper and timely removal from the composite will depend on the reason the portfolio was removed. For example, a client might instruct the firm to stop trading for a 10-day period to allow for the transfer of assets to a new custodian bank. In this instance the verifier would ask to see the instruction from the client directing the firm to stop trading, as well as the transaction report to see that trading was in fact stopped for the instructed time period. Knowing the reason for removal from the composite, as well as the firm's policies for removing portfolios from composites, the verifier will conclude whether the portfolio was removed from the composite for a proper reason and at the proper time.

Existing Portfolios   *Existing portfolios* are portfolios that are included in the composite at the beginning of the verification period. For example, if a verification covers the period from January 1, 2005 through December 31, 2010, and a portfolio has been in the composite since 2003, this would be considered an existing portfolio. The verifier will review investment management agreements, including investment guidelines and restrictions, as well as any other documents necessary to prove that the portfolio was properly included in the composite for the proper time period.

Switched Portfolios   The verifier will test portfolios that were moved from one composite to another during the verification period to ensure proper removal from the old composite and proper inclusion in the new composite. The verifier will ask for documentation, such as the old and new investment guidelines, to prove that the portfolio changed its strategy based on client direction. The verifier will also ask for support to prove the timing of the change, such as a transaction report showing the security trades required to implement the strategy change. Considering the former and new composite definitions, the verifier will conclude whether the portfolio was properly moved between composites and at the proper time.

Excluded Portfolios   The verifier will test portfolios that are excluded from composites for proper exclusion, and will ask for support to prove proper exclusion. The documents required to prove proper exclusion will depend on the reason for exclusion from composites. For example, if a portfolio is excluded from composites because it has restrictions that prevent the firm from managing the portfolio according to the selected strategy, the verifier will review the investment management agreement, guidelines, and restrictions, as well as the respective composite definition(s), to determine if the portfolio was properly excluded from all composites. If a portfolio was temporarily removed from a composite due to a significant cash flow, the verifier will perform testing to ensure the removal was in accordance with the composite-specific significant cash flow policy. Considering the firm's exclusion policies, the verifier will conclude whether the portfolio was properly excluded from composites, for the proper time period.

Full-Inclusion Testing   Each of the tests above determines whether the portfolios that the firm has included in a composite or has excluded from composites are properly assigned. Testing only the portfolios that are already included in a composite or classified as excluded from composites is not enough. The verifier must also perform testing to determine that all portfolios that should be in a composite are included in the composite. This testing will be very firm-specific and will depend on the firm's policies and procedures. This testing is often done in conjunction with testing of total firm assets.

Portfolio-Level Returns   The verifier must determine that the methodology used to calculate portfolio-level returns meets the GIPS standards' input data and calculation requirements. For example, interest income on bonds is accrued and is not recorded on a cash basis. The verifier will then test to ensure the data inputs to the portfolio-level returns are proper, based on supporting internal records and external custodian statements. The mechanics of this testing will be tailored to the specific methodology and software tools used by the firm to calculate portfolio-level returns. The verifier will ask for a variety of supporting records, such as portfolio-level performance reports, holdings reports, accrued income reports, cash flow/transaction reports, custodian statements and reconciliations, and so forth.

Composite-Level Returns   The verifier must determine that the formula used to calculate composite-level returns meets the technical requirements of the GIPS standards. For example, portfolio-level returns must be weighted based on the portfolio's beginning value, or a method that reflects both beginning value and external cash flows. The verifier will then test to ensure the data inputs to the composite-level returns are proper, based on supporting portfolio-level records.

Compliant Presentations   The verifier will test to ensure compliant presentations are accurate and complete. A compliant presentation will typically have two components: a table of returns and other numerical information for the composite and its benchmark, and a series of disclosures. For the data table, the verifier will test that the monthly composite returns correctly geometrically compound (link) to derive the annual composite returns. The verifier will test the calculation of and supporting records for the firm's selected measure of internal dispersion (e.g., equal weighted standard deviation). The verifier will also test to ensure the number of portfolios in the composite and the related composite market values as of year end are correct.

The verifier will test any other numerical information included in the compliant presentation, such as the benchmark returns, total firm assets, the percentage of the composite that is composed of non-fee-paying portfolios, the three-year annualized ex-post standard deviation of the composite and the benchmark, and so forth. Section 5 of the GIPS standards has a complete list of all of the numerical information that is required to be included in a compliant presentation.

A compliant presentation must also include a series of disclosures. Section 4 of the GIPS standards contains a complete list of all of the disclosures that are required in a compliant presentation. The verifier will test to ensure that all the required disclosures are included and are accurate. For example, a compliant presentation must include the composite description. The verifier will test to ensure the composite description is proper and consistent with the description included in the firm's list of composite descriptions.

The verification procedures described here provide a brief overview of the minimum procedures firms should expect a verifier to perform during the verification. The testing will be tailored to the firm, and will reflect the verifier's own unique approach to testing. Firms should not be surprised if the verifier's testing includes tests extending beyond those described here. For example, if the firm manages a series of mutual funds or private equity funds, the testing for those portfolios could be very different from the testing described here.

THE VERIFIER'S REPORT

Based on the results of the verification testing, the verifier will decide whether to issue a verification report. If the verifier is not satisfied with the results of the testing, the verifier may decline to issue a report. In such a case, the verifier must provide the client with a statement as to why a verification report was not issued. If, on the other hand, the verifier is satisfied with the results of the testing, the verifier will issue a verification report. The verifier will also determine whether issuing any performance examination reports is appropriate. Before any report can be issued, the verifier is required to obtain a *management representation letter* from the firm. This letter includes confirmation that the firm has complied with the GIPS standards for the verification period, as well as any other specific representations made to the verifier during the verification. This letter is typically signed by several members of the verification client's management, including the person who is ultimately responsible for the firm's claim of compliance.

After the verification and any examination reports are issued, the verifier can choose to provide the firm with a list of recommendations that the verifier believes would allow the firm to more effectively and efficiently maintain compliance with the GIPS standards.

PREPARING FOR VERIFICATION

How should the firm prepare for the verification? It is important to remember that each verifier may have a unique approach for conducting a verification engagement. There will, however, be certain key elements consistent for all verification engagements. Firms will save time, effort, and money if they proactively prepare for the verification and ensure the proper information requested is provided to the verifier. At least a portion, if not all, of the verification fee is normally dependent on the amount of time incurred to conduct the engagement. The preparation we recommend in this section will:

- Help the firm identify and address issues before the verification team finds them.
- Ensure that the verification runs as efficiently as possible.

- Help the firm minimize the risk of errors being found, which could cause the verifier to expand the quantity of items that are tested, or, in a worst-case scenario, cause the verifier to terminate the verification and conclude that the firm is not in compliance.

Ensure the GIPS Manual Is Complete

As part of the verifier's pre-verification procedures, the verifier is required to obtain the firm's GIPS Manual. The GIPS Manual will be a reference point for all of the verifier's testing. The firm should review the manual to ensure that it has clearly written policies and procedures addressing all of the applicable requirements of the GIPS standards. A detailed and thorough GIPS Manual will allow the verifier to plan the engagement appropriately and conduct their testing efficiently.

Ensure the List of Composite Descriptions Is Complete

While conducting composite population testing, the verifier will rely heavily on the list of composite descriptions. This list should be reviewed to ensure it includes all active composites, both marketed and nonmarketed, as well as all composites that have been terminated within the past five years. The firm should ensure that all composite descriptions include enough information so that the verifier (and other readers) can understand each composite's strategy. For example, simply restating the name of the composite as the composite strategy (such as, "the Core Equity Composite includes all portfolios invested in the core equity strategy") is insufficient. The firm should also ensure that enough information is included in composite descriptions to allow the verifier to differentiate composites representing similar strategies.

Ensure Compliant Presentations Can Be Produced for Every Composite

During the course of the verification, the verifier will request a sample of compliant presentations to review. Typically this request includes the compliant presentations for all examined composites and a sample of composites that are not examined. While most firms have no trouble providing a compliant presentation for examined or even marketed composites that are not examined, the firm must be able to provide a compliant presentation for any composite listed on the firm's list of composite descriptions. This list will include any nonmarketed or terminated composites. While the firm does not have to prepare a compliant presentation for all composites in advance of the verification, it should ensure that, once requested, a compliant presentation can be provided for any composite in a timely manner. This is also a good opportunity for the firm to review a sample of the firm's compliant presentations to ensure that these presentations include all of the required numerical items and disclosures.

Ensure Marketing Materials Include Proper References to the GIPS Standards

The verifier will likely request a sample of the firm's advertising and marketing materials that were used during the period under review. To prepare for this request, the firm should select a sample of these materials and review them to ensure that where the GIPS standards are referenced, these references adhere to the GIPS standards. A firm may reference the GIPS standards in one of two ways: either by including the fully compliant presentation in a one-on-one presentation or via an advertisement prepared in accordance with the GIPS Advertising Guidelines. The firm should also review its web site to ensure that if the GIPS standards are mentioned, the reference is appropriate and accompanied by all of the required disclosures and data.

Reconcile GIPS Firm Assets to Total Firm Assets

The GIPS standards require that a firm include all actual, fee-paying, discretionary portfolios in at least one composite. A good way to ensure that all portfolios within the firm have been identified is to perform a reconciliation of composite assets and excluded portfolios to total firm assets under management (AUM). For example, many firms produce a monthly or quarterly AUM file for corporate reporting purposes and/or regulatory reporting (e.g., Form ADV for SEC registrants). The reconciliation of total firm assets included in GIPS-compliant presentations with the AUM computed for other purposes can be a valuable quasi-independent reconciliation. One reason for this is that the AUM for these purposes is typically computed by Corporate Finance or another department distinct from the Performance Measurement department responsible for GIPS compliance.

A firm that does not already compute AUM for other reasons could look to billing records as the source for total firm assets. Regardless of the source, to be most beneficial to the verifier, the date of the AUM reconciliation should be the same as the annual period end used in a compliant presentation. A detailed AUM reconciliation should give the firm confidence that all of the firm's portfolios have been identified and considered for inclusion in the firm's composites.

Ensure All Excluded Portfolios Can Be Identified

At any point in time a firm will probably have a number of portfolios that are excluded from composites because these portfolios do not qualify for inclusion in a composite. Whether portfolios are permanently or temporarily excluded from composites, the firm should ensure all such portfolios can be identified as of any given point in time. Also, once the AUM reconciliation described above is complete, this is a good opportunity to review the excluded portfolio population as of a selected point in time to ensure that each portfolio's exclusion is proper and that there is adequate support for why each portfolio is excluded from composites. For those portfolios that are permanently excluded from composites, the firm should ensure that nothing has changed since the last review and that the portfolio's nondiscretionary status is still proper. For portfolios that are temporarily excluded from composites, the firm should ensure that the reason for each portfolio's exclusion is valid.

Review Portfolio-Level Returns for Reasonableness

A firm should periodically analyze the returns for each portfolio in the composite and identify any outlier returns. There can be valid reasons for outliers, but outlier returns can also point to a problem with a portfolio return calculation or identify that a portfolio is assigned to the wrong composite. If the same portfolio consistently produces the outlier return, the firm should investigate to determine if something has changed with the portfolio and whether the portfolio still belongs in the composite.

If net returns are calculated using actual fees, the firm should also compare monthly gross and net portfolio-level returns, to confirm that the differences between the two are reasonable in relation to the method the firm uses to calculate net returns. The methodology used to determine the composite net-of-fee return can introduce the need to check the results for reasonableness. As a basic example, if fees are accrued quarterly, then the gross and net returns should only differ four months in a year. Firms should also ensure that the size of the difference is reasonable relative to the firm's fee schedules.

Carefully Review All Information Provided to the Verifier

Once the verifier provides the firm with a list of all of the documentation it will want to review during the engagement, the contact person responsible for overseeing the engagement should review the list to ensure that she understands what is being requested before passing the request to other departments within the firm. For example, if the verifier requests a termination letter for a specific portfolio, there is no need to provide the full client correspondence file. If there is any confusion as to what is being requested, or the firm knows that some documentation is not available or may take a long time to obtain, the firm should inform the verifier. The verifier may be able to accept alternative information if certain records cannot be located.

Finally, to ensure that the engagement proceeds as efficiently as possible, the requested documents should be ready and organized when the verification team arrives on-site to begin testing. Because the cost of verification is usually directly linked to the time it will take the verifier to perform the engagement, the firm can save money by ensuring that the verification team does not waste time waiting for requested information or spend their time sorting through stacks of documents or boxes. The same is true for any electronic documents that are provided to the verifier. The firm should ensure all information is clearly identified so the verifier is not forced to incur extra time trying to organize hundreds of electronic documents.

SUMMARY

Money managers and their clients both benefit from an independent verification. This chapter explained what verification means and what a verifier does. The specific procedures may vary depending on the situation, but the process outlined here gives the firm insight into how it should structure its internal process and recordkeeping to maintain and then demonstrate compliance with the GIPS standards.

Index

247